CHICKEN FOR THE CAT LOVER'S SOUL

Stories of Feline Affection, Mystery and Charm

Jack Canfield
Mark Victor Hansen
Marty Becker, D.V.M.
Carol Kline
Amy D. Shojai

Health Communications, Inc.
Deerfield Beach, Florida

www.hcibooks.com
www.chickensoup.com

We would like to acknowledge the following publishers and individuals for permission to reprint the following material. (Note: The stories that were penned anonymously, that are in the public domain, or that were written by Jack Canfield, Mark Victor Hansen, Marty Becker, Carol Kline or Amy D. Shojai are not included in this listing.)

Oscar, the Garbage-Can Kitty. Reprinted by permission of Audrey Kathleen Kennedy. ©1997 Audrey Kathleen Kennedy.

My Mother's Cat. Reprinted by permission of Renie Burghardt. ©2003 Renie Burghardt.

Music-Loving Tabby. Reprinted by permission of Beverly Faith Walker. ©2004 Beverly Faith Walker.

(Continued on page 397)

Library of Congress Cataloging-in-Publication Data

Chicken soup for the cat lover's soul : stories of feline affection, mystery, and charm / Jack Canfield . . . [et al.].
    p. cm.
ISBN-13: 978-0-7573-0332-6
ISBN-10: 0-7573-0332-3
    1. Cats—Anecdotes.   2. Cat owners—Anecdotes.   3. Human-animal relationships—Anecdotes.   I. Canfield, Jack, 1944–
SF445.5.C55 2005
636.8'088'7—dc22

2005051163

HCI, its logos and marks are trademarks of Health Communications, Inc.

Publisher: Health Communications, Inc.
            3201 S.W. 15th Street
            Deerfield Beach, FL 33442-8190

R-12-06

Cover photo ©2005 Best Friends/Troy Snow
Cover design by Andrea Perrine Brower
Inside formatting by Dawn Von Strolley Grove

This book is dedicated to the millions of people around the world who share their hearts and homes with cats, celebrating the limitless affection, "purr-fect" love, wacky charm and serene mystery of these unique creatures who so richly bless human lives.

We also dedicate this book to veterinarians and other pet-care professionals, whose compassion and expertise nurture and protect these furry wonders who have become such an intrinsic part of our health and well-being.

We dedicate this book as well to the responsible cat breeders and exhibitors who celebrate, sustain and strive to improve the physical and emotional health of their special kitties—whether lap-sitter or ankle-rubber, striped, spotted, pocket-size or purring armful, curly coated, satin-slick, profusely furred or peach-fuzz bald—preserving the unique legacy of the feline race in all its wondrous variations.

And to those heroic individuals and organizations everywhere, who dedicate themselves to helping homeless pets find loving homes, aiding sick, injured or misbehaving kitties, and who strive one pet at a time for that glorious day when all needy fur-kids have loving forever-homes.

And finally, to God, who chose to bless us so richly with cats—surely, they offer us a little taste of heaven on Earth, and for that, we are eternally grateful.

Contents

v

3. A FURRY R$_X$

4. CAT-EGORICALLY WONDERFUL

5. CATS AS TEACHERS

6. FAREWELL, MY LOVE

7. RESCUE ME!

8. ONE OF THE FAMILY

Acknowledgments

We wish to express our heartfelt gratitude to the following people who helped make this book possible:

Our families, who have been chicken soup for our souls!

Jack's family, Inga, Travis, Riley, Christopher, Oran and Kyle for all their love and support.

Mark's family, Patty, Elisabeth and Melanie, for once again sharing and lovingly supporting us in creating yet another book.

Marty's soul-mate, fellow pet lover and wife, Teresa, who inspires him with her inexhaustible love for, and attention to, all animals. And his beloved children, Mikkel and Lex, who bring so much joy into his hectic life and remind him to relax, tease, laugh and repot himself by taking time off. To Virginia Becker and the late Bob Becker, who taught farm-reared Marty to love all God's creatures, from spoiled family pets to soiled dairy cows. To Valdie and Rockey Burkholder, whose goodness and support have allowed Marty to thrive in the world's greatest oasis of beauty, goodness and serenity—magnificent Bonners Ferry, Idaho. And to all the pets—past, present and future—who, with their gifts of love, loyalty and laughter, have made his life so much richer and more meaningful.

To Carol's family—Lorin, McKenna, and especially her

dearly loved husband Larry—who make it possible for Carol to spend all her time writing and editing. To Carol's mother, Selma, brothers Jim and Burt, and sisters Barbara and Holly, and their families, for being her favorite people in the world.

To Amy's husband, Mahmoud, for his unflagging encouragement, love and support. And to her parents Phil and Mary Monteith, who inspired and fostered her love of pets from the beginning. To her wonderful brothers and their families, Laird, Gene, Jodi, Sherrie, Andrew, Colin, Erin and Kyle Monteith—and their assorted beloved pet members, past, present and future. And to Seren, who leaves her paw-marks deep in the hearts of her family.

Our warm thanks also to: Marci Shimoff, who, as always, is an inspiration, a support and, of course, the best friend ever.

Cindy Buck, whose excellent editing skills we rely on deeply, and whose friendship matters even more.

Christian Wolfbrandt, pet-sitter *extraordinaire*—and good friend. Your help was so appreciated!

Our publisher Peter Vegso, a cherished friend, both personally and professionally, and from whom we've learned so much about writing and successfully marketing a book and remaining doggedly loyal.

Patty Aubery and Russ Kamalski, for your brilliance, insight and continued support, as well as for being there on every step of the journey, with love, laughter and endless creativity.

Barbara Lomonaco, for nourishing us with truly wonderful stories and cartoons.

D'ette Corona—our very own angel—for being indispensable, cheerful, knowledgeable and as steady as the Rock of Gibraltar. We couldn't do it without you.

Patty Hansen, for her thorough and competent handling of the legal and licensing aspects of the *Chicken Soup for the Soul* books. You are magnificent at the challenge!

Laurie Hartman, for being a precious guardian of the *Chicken Soup* brand.

Veronica Romero, Teresa Esparza, Robin Yerian, Jesse Ianniello, Jamie Chicoine, Jody Emme, Debbie Lefever, Michelle Adams, Dee Dee Romanello, Shanna Vieyra, Lisa Williams, Gina Romanello, Brittany Shaw, Dena Jacobson, Tanya Jones and Mary McKay, who support Jack's and Mark's businesses with skill and love.

Lisa Drucker, for editing our final readers' manuscript. Thank you once again for being there whenever we need you.

Bret Witter, Elisabeth Rinaldi, Allison Janse and Kathy Grant, our editors at Health Communications, Inc., for their devotion to excellence.

Our great friend, Terry Burke, who takes a personal interest in all the books and who doggedly pursues sales so that, in this case, pets and people can benefit.

Lori Golden, Kelly Maragni, Sean Geary, Patricia McConnell, Ariana Daner, Kim Weiss, Paola Fernandez-Rana and Julie De La Cruz, the sales, marketing and PR departments at Health Communications, Inc., for doing such an incredible job supporting our books.

Tom Sand, Claude Choquette and Luc Jutras, who manage year after year to get our books translated into thirty-six languages around the world.

The art department at Health Communications, Inc., for their talent, creativity and unrelenting patience in producing book covers and inside designs that capture the essence of *Chicken Soup*: Larissa Hise Henoch, Lawna Patterson Oldfield, Andrea Perrine Brower, Anthony Clausi, Kevin Stawieray and Dawn Von Strolley Grove.

To Marty's colleague, producer, coauthor and friend, Dr. Janice Willard, who has made his life easier and richer, and allowed him to take on even more projects that help pets, people and the profession we love.

Special thanks to Frank Steele for the gift of a special friendship. Your support during the birthing of this book means so very much.

And a thousand thanks to the Cat Writers Association, OWFI, the "Colorado Gang" and the "Warpies," whose helping "paws" aided enormously in the success of this book.

Thanks also to all the *Chicken Soup for the Soul* coauthors, who make it such a joy to be part of this *Chicken Soup* family.

And to our glorious panel of readers, who helped us make the final selections and made invaluable suggestions on how to improve this book:

Jo Braley Birmingham, Kathy Bumgardner, Ina Bushon, Susan Catania, Marci DeLisle, Sharon DeNayer, Robin Downing, D.V.M., Susan Fucini, Wanda Rachel Glinert, Jean Greenwood, Diane Lopez, Cindy Lovern, D.V.M., Priscilla Maltbie (author of the children's picture book *Picasso and Minou,* based on the story of young Pablo Picasso and his cat, Minou), Angie McGee, Sandy Meyer, Patti Morelock, Kim Ossi, Jane Popham, Eliyahu Rooff, Diane Bolte Silverman, Jesse Gunn Stephens, Mary Summers, Sue Teumer, Susan Tripp and Tim Vande Giessen.

Most of all, thank you to everyone who submitted your heartfelt stories, poems, quotes and cartoons for possible inclusion in this book. While we were not able to use everything you sent in, we know that each word came from a heartfelt place and was meant to celebrate cats as the family they are.

Because of the size of this project, we may have left out the names of some people who contributed along the way. If so, we are sorry, but please know that we really do appreciate you very much.

We are truly grateful and love you all!

Introduction

The cat is a being like no other. From the cave drawings of prehistoric felines to today's fancy show-kitties, cats continue to fascinate people. Though a cat may choose to share her affection with a human or two, she will always retain that quixotic mix of unpredictability and individuality that challenges the understanding of the most patient among us. It is as if they know that when they first stepped into the human ring of firelight, they forever altered our history, influencing our religions, our literature, our art—our very lives.

Whether exalted as in ancient Egypt, or reviled and persecuted as they were during the Middle Ages, cats have struck an emotional chord deep in the human imagination. The cat is the envied Wild Sibling that cannot be tamed; the Gentle Companion that purrs a mantra to ease aching human souls; the Eternal Kitten that coaxes a smile from the stingiest of human hearts. We delight in our cats—and, we hope, they in us.

Devoted feline fans rejoice that the cat has finally been returned to the pedestal from which she was once so cruelly deposed. While in the past we may not have admitted these strong affections, today our love affair with cats has become a very public one.

After all, cats are good for what ails us. This positive "pet effect" has been documented in countless human health studies and promoted by organizations like the Delta Society. The mere presence of a loving cat helps relieve chronic pain, lifts our spirits, detects pending health crises, lowers our blood pressure, helps us recover from devastating illness, and even lowers our children's risk for adult allergies and asthma. This human-animal bond, or simply "The Bond," grows stronger year by year!

In fact, it is the strength and power of The Bond that inspired this book's creation. In response to our call for stories, we received thousands of submissions from cat-lovers around the globe who shared with us the myriad ways their cats have positively impacted their lives. *Chicken Soup for the Cat Lover's Soul* celebrates the enduring love humans and cats feel toward each other. The chapters in the book illustrate some of the wonderful ways cats benefit us: They love us, heal us, teach us, make us laugh and sometimes break our hearts with their passing.

Felines fill a very special niche in modern human lives. Day in and day out, cats meet us at the door with affectionate ankle-rubs, demand lap-snuggles, and dole out whisker-kisses and head-bonks when we need them most. Cats don't care what we look like, how much money we make, if we're famous or unknown—they love us no matter what, because we love them. Whatever our age or situation, people relish the interaction and unconditional love offered by cats.

Try as we might, it is impossible for us to remain indifferent to the cat—especially at 4 A.M. when the food bowl runs dry! So smile at their many "c'attitudes" and feed your feline passion by "purr-using" these pages. May the stories you find delight and amuse, surprise and educate, and, most of all, celebrate the mysteries and marvels of the wonderful cats that share our lives.

Share with Us

We would like to invite you to send us stories you would like to see published in future editions of *Chicken Soup for the Soul*.

We would also love to hear your reactions to the stories in this book. Please let us know what your favorite stories are and how they affected you.

Please send submissions to:

Chicken Soup for the Soul
P.O. Box 30880
Santa Barbara, CA 93130
fax: 805-563-2945

You can also visit the *Chicken Soup for the Soul* Web site at:

www.chickensoup.com

We hope you enjoy reading this book as much as we enjoyed compiling, editing and writing it.

$\overline{\underline{1}}$

ON LOVE

What greater gift than the love of a cat?

Charles Dickens

Stubbly Dooright

A meow massages the heart.

Stuart McMillan

For years, my wife Teresa taught physical education at the elementary school level. Traveling on a regular schedule to the six schools in her district, she had a chance to get to know most of the kids in the area and see them at their best—and their worst.

Childhood is tough enough, but gym class strips away all the veneers, exposing the unvarnished truth beneath. There's nothing like PE class to display your strengths or frailties, your bravado or timidity, your blue-ribbon-winning athletic skills or complete lack of coordination. Worst of all, with people choosing sides, there's no doubt where you stand in life's pecking order. Some of us have been, and all have suffered for, the person picked last.

At one of the schools, whose gray façade and asphalt playgrounds reflected the mood of the depressed downtown area in which it stood, Teresa noticed a third-grade child who was one of those always picked last. The girl, let's call her Meagan, was short and grossly overweight, with a closed and hopeless look on her face. Meagan always sat alone in class, played alone at recess and ate alone out of a recycled-paper sack at lunch. The teachers and staff were kind to Meagan, but the students were not.

The stories made your shoulders drop. Teresa heard that when the playground supervisors turned their backs, kids would run up and touch Meagan on a dare, then run off to "infect" others with her "cooties." Mockingly calling her "Meagan the Munchkin," they did far worse than iso-late her; they filled her school days and walks home with physical and emotional torment. Teachers who had met with Meagan's single mother, a hard-working woman who was trying her best to "make two ends that had never met each other meet," were told that weekends were spe-cial for Meagan—not because she had sleepovers and was invited to movies or parties, but because being away from the other kids, in the privacy of her room, meant the mis-ery would stop, at least until Monday and the long walk to school.

Meagan's situation disturbed my wife deeply. After talk-ing with the principal and other teachers, Teresa came up with an idea. She knew from talking to Meagan that the child had never had a pet. Teresa was sure a pet would be the perfect way to inject some high-powered love and acceptance into Meagan's life. Teresa told Meagan that she needed to talk with her mom about something important and asked her if she'd have her pick her up from school one day soon. Anxious that something was wrong, Meagan's dutiful and caring mother came the very next day.

Teresa recounted Meagan's school problems to her and, finally, broached the subject of a pet for Meagan. To my wife's surprise and delight, Meagan's mom said she thought it would be a great idea. She agreed to come down to the veterinary hospital where I practiced so she could look at the various strays and castoffs we'd accumulated, selecting from among them the perfect pet for Meagan.

The very next Saturday afternoon—after we had closed, but before we'd left for the day—Meagan and her mom walked in the back door as we had arranged. When the door buzzer sounded, the dogs engaged in a predictable and vigorous clinic-chorus of barking.

Getting down on one knee, I introduced myself to Meagan and welcomed her and her mother to my office. I noticed that Meagan, like any creature that has been abused, had a lot of hurt in her eyes—so much, in fact, that I had to look away momentarily to compose myself.

I escorted them to the back runs, where the homeless pets were kept. I fully expected Meagan to fall for one of the mixed-breed terrier puppies who had been dropped off in a box at our door earlier that week. The puppies had spiky hair, huge, liquid brown eyes and pink tongues that ran in and out like pink conveyor belts on overtime.

But, while Meagan really liked the puppies, she didn't love them. As we moved down the row to examine some more "used models," out sauntered the clinic mascot, a tiger-striped American shorthair cat that had lost one leg to a hay mower while he was out mousing in an alfalfa field at first cutting. With a stub for a right hind leg, he had been given the name Stubbly Dooright.

Stubbly had a peculiar habit of rubbing up against you, purring, and then biting you hard enough to get your attention but not enough to break the skin. It was love at first bite when Stubbly clamped onto Meagan's pinky finger, and she playfully lifted the cat almost off the ground. You could plainly hear Stubbly purring in his vertical position.

Meagan left the clinic that Saturday afternoon, glowing with happiness. Now she had a living, breathing friend who wanted to play with her, who loved to cuddle up next to her on the sofa and sleep next to her on the bed. Her mother later told us that when Meagan came home from school, Stubbly would rush to the door, Lassie-like, and follow her from room to room through the house. Like a feline boomerang, Stubbly would leave to do "cat things," but would always find his way back to her side.

Energized by Stubbly's unconditional love, limitless affection and loyalty, Meagan began to blossom. Though she still might never be Homecoming Queen, she did find fellow pet lovers who befriended her, and things began to improve for her—physically, emotionally and socially.

Ten years later, Teresa and I received an invitation to the high-school graduation ceremony from Meagan, whom we were thrilled to read was one of the co-valedictorians of her class.

On graduation day, we joined the throngs of family and friends seated in the auditorium watching the seniors get their diplomas. When Meagan strode to the podium, head high and beaming, I hardly recognized her. Now an attractive young woman of average height and athletic build, Meagan gave a speech on the importance of acceptance and friendship that kept the crowd riveted. She was going to be a communications major in college and clearly was gifted in this regard.

At the conclusion of the speech, she talked about the special friend she'd met in the third grade who had helped her climb the steep and treacherous slope of her childhood. The friend who had comforted her when there wasn't enough to eat in the house because her mother had been laid off from work, and who had stayed by her while she sobbed her heart out after a boy had asked her to a dance on a dare with no intention of taking her. The special friend who had been there to mop up her tears or to make her laugh when she needed it most.

With the gymnasium full of people in the palm of her

hand, Meagan said she'd now like to introduce this special friend, and she asked her friend to come to the stage to be recognized. Meagan looked to the right; no one was coming down the aisle. Meagan looked to the left; still no one approached the stage.

It was one of those moments when you ache for the speaker, and people started swiveling in their seats, craning their necks, buzzing with conversation. After what seemed like an eternity, but was actually less than a minute, Meagan suddenly said, "The reason my friend didn't come to the stage is because he's already here. Plus, he's only got three legs, and it's hard for him to walk sometimes."

What? There wasn't anybody new at the stage, and what kind of person has three legs?

With high drama, Meagan lifted her hands high—displaying a photograph of Stubbly Dooright. As she described her beloved cat, the crowd rose to their feet with cheers, laughter and long, thunderous applause.

Stubbly Dooright may not have been there in person, but he was definitely there in spirit—the same spirit that had made all the difference in the life of a very lonely child.

Marty Becker, D.V.M., with Teresa Becker

Oscar, the Garbage-Can Kitty

People who don't like cats haven't met the right one yet.

Deborah A. Edwards, D.V.M.

Oscar was named after the *Sesame Street* character who lives in a garbage can because that is where we first became acquainted. I was working at a pizza-delivery chain and had been assigned garbage duty. While tossing bags into a Dumpster, I heard a faint meow. I began digging through the trash, and several layers down I found a cat—bruised and thin. I wasn't sure if the cat had crawled into the Dumpster to scavenge for food or if he had been put there purposely. Our establishment sat directly behind an apartment complex, and unsupervised and abandoned pets were common.

Back on solid ground, it became evident that the cat had an injured leg. He couldn't put any weight on his right hindquarters. The situation created a dilemma for me. Finances were tight, and I was moving back home to my parents' house—with two cats already in tow. Dad barely tolerated the two established felines. His reaction to another injured stray was sure to be less than receptive.

I took the stray to the vet, hoping to patch him up. After shots and X-rays, the vet discovered the cat had a cracked pelvis. I posted notices, hoping someone would claim the cat or adopt him.

Meanwhile, the response at home was swift and firm: No more cats! Dad insisted I take the cat to the Humane Society immediately. I protested that the cat would be put to sleep. Luckily, my mother intervened. She agreed the injury would make the cat unadoptable, so we would keep him long enough for his hip to heal. Then he would have to go—no arguments.

Oscar must have somehow understood his situation. He seemed to study the other two cats and their inter-actions with my father. We suspect he bribed Tanner, our golden retriever, with table scraps in exchange for eti-quette lessons. When the other cats were aloof, Oscar was attentive. He came when his name was called, and he would roll over on his back to have his belly scratched. As his injury began to heal, he would jump on the ottoman by my father's favorite chair, and, eventually, into his lap. Initially, Dad pushed Oscar away, but persistence paid off. Soon, Oscar and a muttering Dad shared the chair.

At mealtimes, Oscar would come to sit with us. Positioned on the floor by my father's chair, every so often Oscar would reach up with one paw and tap Dad on the knee. At first, this provoked great irritation and colorful expletives expressed in harsh tones. Oscar, however, refused to be put off. Repetitive knee-taps soon led to semi-covert handouts of choice morsels.

Oscar greeted my father at the top of the stairs every morning and waited for him at the door every evening. My father sometimes ignored Oscar, and, at other times, stepped over him, complaining the whole time. Oscar mastered opening doors by sticking his paw underneath the door and rocking it back and forth until it opened. Soon, he was sleeping in the master bedroom at the foot of the bed. My father was completely disgusted, but couldn't stop the cat from sneaking onto the bed while they were sleeping. Eventually, Dad gave up.

Before long, Oscar, aspiring to his own place at the table during meals, began jumping up into my lap. He was allowed to stay as long as his head remained below table level. Of course, an occasional paw would appear as a reminder of his presence.

Three months passed, and the vet pronounced Oscar healthy and healed. I was heartbroken. How could I take this loving soul away from what had become his home, from the people he trusted? Sick at heart, I brought Oscar home and told my parents what should have been good news: Oscar was a healthy cat with a healed hip. "I'll take him to the Humane Society like I promised," I said dully.

As I turned to put Oscar in the carrier for the trip, my father spoke, uttering three magic words: "Not *my* cat!"

Oscar is home to stay. He now has his own chair at the table and sleeps—where else?—in the master bedroom between my mother and father. He is their official "grand-kitten" and living proof that deep within the most unlikely heart, there is a cat lover in all of us.

Kathleen Kennedy

My Mother's Cat

When my nineteen-year-old mother died two weeks after giving birth to me, I inherited her cat, Paprika. He was a gentle giant, with deep orange stripes and yellow eyes that gazed at me tolerantly as I dragged him around wherever I went. Paprika was ten years old when I came into this world. He had been held and loved by my mother for all ten years of his life, while I had never known her. So I considered him my link to her. Each time I hugged him tightly to my chest, I was warmed by the knowledge that she had done so, too.

"Did you love her a lot?" I would often ask Paprika, as we snuggled on my bed.

"Meow!" he would answer, rubbing my chin with his pink nose.

"Do you miss her?"

"Meow!" His large yellow eyes gazed at me with a sad expression.

"I miss her, too, even though I didn't know her. But Grandma says she is in heaven, and she is watching over us from there. Since we are both her orphans, I know it makes her happy that we have each other," I would always say, for it was a most comforting thought to me.

"Meow!" Paprika would respond, climbing on my chest and purring.

I held him close, tears welling in my eyes. "And it makes me so very happy that we have each other." Paprika's orange paw reached up and touched my face gently. I was convinced he understood me, and I knew I understood him.

At that time, we lived in the country of my birth, Hungary, and I was being raised by my maternal grandparents because World War II had taken my young father away, too. As I grew, the war intensified. Soon, we were forced to become wanderers in search of safer surroundings.

In the spring of 1944, when I was eight, Paprika and I snuggled in the back of a wooden wagon as we traveled around our country. During the numerous air raids of those terrible times, when we had to scramble to find safety in a cellar, closet or ditch, he was always in my arms—I absolutely refused to go without him. How could I, when one of the first stories I was ever told as a child was that of my dying mother begging her parents to take care of her cat as well as her baby?

After Christmas in 1944, when we were almost killed in a bombing of the city we were in, Grandfather decided that we would be safer in a rural area. Soon, we settled in a small house neighboring a cemetery. Here, Grandfather, with the help of some neighbors, built a bunker away from the house. In the early spring of 1945, we spent one entire night in the bunker. Paprika was with me, of course. Once again, I refused to go without him.

Warplanes buzzed, tanks rumbled, and bombs whistled and exploded over our heads all night while I held on to Paprika, and my grandmother held on to the both of us, praying the entire time. Paprika never panicked in that bunker. He just stayed in my arms, comforting me with his presence.

Finally, everything grew still, and Grandfather decided

it was safe to go back to the house. Cautiously, we crept out into the light of early dawn and headed toward the house. The brush crackled under our feet as we walked. I shivered, holding Paprika tightly. Suddenly, there was a rustle in the bushes just ahead. Two men jumped out and pointed machine guns directly at us.

"*Stoi!*" one of the men shouted. We knew the word meant, "Stop!"

"Russians!" Grandfather whispered. "Stand very still and keep quiet."

But Paprika had leapt out of my arms when the soldier shouted, so, instead of listening to Grandfather, I darted between the soldiers and scooped him up again.

The tall, dark-haired young soldier approached me. I cringed, holding Paprika against my chest. The soldier reached out and petted him gently. "I have a little girl about your age back in Russia, and she has a cat just like this one," he said, smiling at us. I looked up into a pair of kind brown eyes, and my fear vanished. My grandparents sighed with relief. We found out that morning that the Soviet occupation of our country was in progress.

In the trying weeks and months that followed, Paprika's love made things easier for me to bear, for he rarely left my side. He was my comfort, my best friend.

By the fall of 1945, Grandfather, who had spoken up about the atrocities taking place in our country, had gone into hiding to avoid being imprisoned as a dissident by the new communist government. Grandmother and I prepared for a solemn Christmas that turned into my worst nightmare when I awoke on Christmas morning to find Paprika curled up next to me as usual—but he was lifeless and cold. I picked up his limp body, and, holding it close to me, sobbed uncontrollably. He was nineteen years old, and I was nine.

"I will always love you, Paprika. I will never give my

heart to another cat," I vowed through my tears. "Never, ever!"

"Paprika's spirit is in heaven now, with your mama, sweetheart," my grandmother said, trying to comfort me. But my heart was broken on that terrible Christmas Day in 1945.

Grandfather stayed hidden until the fall of 1947, when we were finally able to escape our communist country by hiding among some ethnic Germans who were being deported to Austria. In Austria, we landed in a refugee camp where we lived for four years. These were difficult times for me, and I longed for Paprika often. I saw other people's cats and knew it would be so comforting to feel a warm, furry creature purring in my arms. But my loyalty to Paprika—mixed up in my mind with loyalty to my mother—never wavered. I had made a vow, and I would keep it.

A ray of hope pierced this darkness when, eventually, we were accepted for immigration to the United States. In September 1951, we boarded an old U.S. Navy ship. We were on our way to America.

That year, we spent our first Christmas in the United States. The horrors of war and the four years of hardship in a refugee camp were behind us now, and a life filled with fresh possibilities lay ahead. On that Christmas morning, I awoke to a tantalizing aroma wafting through the house. Grandmother was cooking her first American turkey. Grandfather, meanwhile, pointed to one of the presents under the Christmas tree. This gift seemed alive, for the box was hopping around to the tune of "Jingle Bells," which was playing on the radio. I rushed over, pulled off the orange bow and took the lid off the box.

"Meow!" cried the present, jumping straight into my lap and purring. It was a tiny orange tabby kitten, and, when I looked into its yellow eyes, the vow I had made in 1945 crumbled like dust and fell away. I was a new person in a new country. Holding the cat close, I let the sweetness of love fill my heart once again.

That Christmas day, I do believe my mother smiled down at us from heaven approvingly, while Paprika's spirit purred joyfully at her side.

Renie Burghardt

Music-Loving Tabby

In July 1999, our world changed forever when five little words were delivered to my husband during a telephone call that woke us in the wee hours of the morning: "Your son did not survive."

Our son, Don Jr., was living in North Carolina and working toward achieving his doctorate in classical guitar so that he could one day teach. He had already received his Master of Music Performance degree from Southern Methodist University in Texas. On July 17, he fell asleep at the wheel of his car and hit a bridge abutment. He was killed instantly.

With Donnie gone, we inherited his cat, Audrey. He had only brought her to our home for a few visits over the years, and she had spent each visit hiding under a bed. She was skittish and shy, a gray feline beauty whom he had acquired from a shelter when he lived in Memphis, Tennessee. He called Audrey a "prissy-miss" and said she only tolerated petting on her own terms—when *she* was in the mood for it!

Audrey arrived in our home just a month after we had adopted MoJo, a stray from our local shelter. Audrey spent all her time hiding under a bed or sofa. MoJo, being a domineering male, stalked her constantly. I wanted so much for Audrey to get to know us, but she was wary of coming out for longer than it took to gulp down her morning meal.

One thing I noticed about Audrey was that she loved music. Whenever music played, she would poke her head out and look around as if she wanted somehow to be a part of it.

"Just think of all the music she has been exposed to," I said to my husband. "It must comfort her because the sound is so familiar."

My son had loved music of all kinds. Not only did he play guitar every day, he also had friends over to play different musical instruments. I know that he had many CDs—everything from classical to bluegrass. He and I shared a love of good acoustical bluegrass music.

Audrey had been with us approximately three weeks when a good friend of mine lost the little dog she'd had for years. I offered to give her MoJo, knowing that it would help her with her grief. I knew I would miss MoJo, but also knew that his absence would permit Audrey to come out from hiding and get to know us a little better. I wanted so much for her to feel at home with us—and for us to love her openly and have her give back that love.

Then it happened. One evening, after MoJo was gone from the house and I had been attempting for a few hours to coax Audrey out of hiding, I had an idea. I pulled out one of Donnie's recital CDs and began to play it on our CD player. My husband had spent many hours transferring all of Donnie's guitar recitals from tape to CDs so that we would always have his music with us.

The music began playing, and my eyes filled with tears as I imagined my son seated before me with his guitar. He was never happier than when performing. His head would sometimes fall and rise to emphasize a note, and, in

my mind's eye, I saw him with a glint of sunlight accentuating the blond hair that tumbled over his forehead. I
turned up the volume, letting the music swell louder and
fill my soul.

Within minutes, I felt it: Audrey rubbing on my leg and
purring! Then she walked in circles around the room as if
on a search mission. Where was her beloved Donnie? She
heard him and she remembered him—I just knew she did!

I walked gingerly by her so I would not frighten her into
hiding again, and I retrieved his quilt from the closet. It
was a quilt I had made him and he had slept on, using it
as a sheet on the mattress in his apartment. I had not
washed it. I carefully spread the quilt out on the floor and
called to my husband to come see what was transpiring.
By this time, tears were rolling down my face, and I felt my
son was with us as never before.

Audrey walked on the quilt and suddenly dropped and
rolled. She rolled over and over, rubbing the side of her
face into the quilt repeatedly, as if to say, "Hey, I loved
your son; now, I love you, too." Happy tears were shed
that day—the day that Audrey accepted the love we
wanted so desperately to show her. I truly believe she
grieved his absence in her own way and, suddenly, realized the connection we had to this wonderful young man
when she once again heard him perform on his guitar.

Our music-loving tabby blesses our lives each day. She
and I now share that "bluegrass connection." When I put
my favorite bluegrass CDs on, she comes running to purr
and rub her love all over me while the songs are playing!
It is amazing to witness the actions of this cat who is
undeniably stirred by music. She can also sense when I
am sad and thinking about how much I miss my son.
Certain pieces of music still bring him to mind, and she
will come to me and glide against me, extending her soul
in comfort. The tears roll down my cheeks as I *feel* my son

near me through his cat. I know she is in my life for a reason—to continue to comfort me and bond me to him with her love.

Beverly F. Walker

Coco's Cat

"She looks bored," pronounced my daughter, home for a short visit from college.

We both studied the longhaired gray cat I'd adopted the previous week from the D.C. Humane Society. Ever since I'd brought her home, Coco, who had been the most vivacious cat at the shelter, had been listless and apathetic. I tried changing her food, gave her vitamins, played with her more in the evenings. Nothing seemed to pique her interest.

"Maybe she needs a pet," smirked my know-it-all daughter.

A few nights later, I was startled awake by a long, mournful wail coming from a dark mound on the sill of my open bedroom window. "Coco, for goodness sake, what *is* your problem?" I said as I scooped her up and plopped her in her usual nighttime spot at the end of my bed. As soon as I'd turned off the light, she jumped back down and resumed her wailing position. I won that round by depositing her on the other side of a closed bedroom door, but her scratching kept me awake most of the night.

For the next couple of days, Coco spent most of her time on the windowsill, alternately mewling and wailing—all the while, glaring accusingly at me.

"Let her out," advised my daughter, over the phone from her college dorm.

"Are you serious?" I said. Busy Wisconsin Avenue ran right in front of my apartment building. "She wouldn't last long enough for me to double-lock my door."

After a few more days of listening to an emotionally distressed feline—one who was now on a kitty hunger strike—I was ready to take my daughter's advice. But my second-floor apartment was too high for a cat to come and go. I made a reconnaissance trip to the courtyard in back of my apartment building and looked up at my window, barred for inner-city security. Coco stared down at me in silent appeal.

I widened my gaze. An old, wooden ladder was half-hidden behind some shrubs. I leaned it against the building under my window. There was still a five-foot gap, but it was worth a try.

I tried not to think about other city critters that might find the makeshift entrance inviting as I opened the window just enough for Coco to slip under. She had no trouble jumping down to the top of the ladder. As I watched her disappear around the corner of the building, I prayed she'd be able to make the jump back up again—and that she'd be safe.

I know it's irresponsible to let house cats outside, especially in a busy city, but Coco's need to go out was so intense, I couldn't help but believe she knew what she was doing. Even so, I probably glanced out that window every quarter hour for the rest of the afternoon.

Just as I was starting to worry, I heard the rattle of the mini-blind covering the open window. Coco jumped down to the floor, then turned to stare back at the window. Almost immediately, a black-and-white head pushed aside the blind. Coco gave an encouraging meow, and the newcomer jumped down. The cats touched noses as I stared in disbelief.

The visiting cat wasn't very clean—her spots were more gray than white—and she was extremely thin, except for her belly, which showed obvious signs of late-stage pregnancy. I couldn't imagine how Coco had induced her to make that last five-foot jump onto the sill, let alone enter a strange apartment. But there she was, looking around my bedroom while Coco gently licked her neck and back.

"This is not a good idea," I grumbled as I put out a second dish of food and introduced the visitor to the litter box. "Tomorrow, she has to go to the Humane Society. After all, that's the responsible thing to do with stray cats, especially pregnant stray cats." Both cats ignored my comments.

The next morning, I pulled my cat carrier from under my bed and went looking for the stray. She wasn't in any of the rooms of the apartment. Finally, I noticed Coco sneaking into my hall coat closet. When I opened the door, I found the visitor cat stretched out in a box of winter garments nursing four tiny fur balls. Okay, forget the Humane Society. How heartless would I have to be to turn out a new mother and four adorable babies?

Polly, as I now called her, and her babies stayed in the closet for a couple of weeks, until the babies got big enough and brave enough to venture out into the apartment. During that time, it was apparent Polly wasn't exhibiting natural maternal behavior. She didn't even groom herself, let alone her babies. Coco assumed responsibility for cleaning, cuddling and playing with the kittens. Polly merely served as wet nurse, showing no interest in her offspring, as Coco taught them how to wash and defend themselves, and to use the litter box. In fact, Polly showed little interest in anything and spent most of her time staring into space. As soon as the kittens were weaned, I took her to my vet for spaying and shots. In the course of his examination, he discovered Polly was deaf and possibly brain-damaged.

On the other hand, the kittens were as active and curious as kittens everywhere, getting into everything and getting bigger each day. I decided I would keep Polly and started looking for adoptive homes for the kittens. Within a week, I found homes for all four.

The day the last kitten left, Coco retreated under the couch and refused to come out for her evening meal, occasionally emitting soft kitty moans. The next morning, she was still there, and no amount of coaxing could budge her. I thought about taking a sick day from work, but I was afraid that "my cat's depressed because she lost her foster kittens" was not a legitimate excuse for absence. I rushed home after work and, when Coco failed to meet me at the door, looked under the couch. There was only empty space and some shed fur. I made a tour of the apartment and finally found both cats curled up face-to-face in the box of winter clothes in the hall closet, Polly with both paws around Coco's neck. Coco looked up when I opened the door, but Polly just continued licking Coco's face. Both cats were purring loudly.

Coco and Polly still live with me and are never very far away from each other. Coco never eats her food until she's sure Polly is beside her at her own dish, and she faithfully grooms her daily. Polly remains unresponsive to my attention. She seems happiest when cuddled up against Coco.

I guess my daughter was right: Coco did need a pet, someone to take care of. And Polly and her kittens would never have survived for long on their own. How Coco knew this, I'll never know. And, somehow, by some instinct, Polly recognized when Coco was grieving and was able to offer the comfort she needed, comfort that could only come from another cat.

Sheila Sowder

The Power of Love

His friendship is not easily won, but it is something worth having.

Michael Joseph

When I first saw the big gray-and-white cat in our yard, I knew right away that he was a stray. He was fierce-looking—a wounded warrior with a huge head and shoulders and a badly scarred body.

I started putting out food for him each day, and, even though you could see that he was starving, he wouldn't come near it if anyone was in sight. Because of one dead eye, which gave him a malevolent appearance, all the neighbors who saw him were afraid of him, even the cat lovers. Winter came, and he still wouldn't trust me or my family. Then, one day, it happened—a car hit him. I realized this when I saw him dragging himself through the snow to the food dish. I knew then that we would have to humanely trap him. It took some ingenuity, but we finally did it.

He spent a week with the veterinarian getting treated for his injuries, and also being neutered, de-wormed, de-fleaed, having his shots, being bathed, etc. We were eager to bring him home to join our family, but, when we arrived at the veterinarian's office to take the cat home, we were met by a very serious doctor who told us that we should put the cat to sleep immediately. Our big stray was so ferocious and mean that he would never, ever become tame, let alone a pet.

I wasn't convinced. I have always had great faith in love's power to tame even the wildest beast. I thought to myself, *I've been praying for this cat since the day I first saw him. I'm not giving up that easily!*

I told the vet, "I want to try. I'm taking him home." We named him Paws.

We opened the cat carrier under the bed in the guest-room, where we had put food, water and a litter box—in the farthest back corner so Paws would feel protected—and we left the room. Three days went by, and we did not see any sign of the cat. The only way we knew he was under the bed was that, when any of us walked by the open bedroom door, we heard deep growling and hissing.

I wanted to touch his heart, to somehow let him know that he was safe and loved. I devised a plan to reach him safely. I put on my husband's large hard hat and a pair of his welding gloves. Lying on the floor, I slid under the bed toward Paws, with my face to the floor and only the top of my head, protected by the hat, facing him. I reached out to stroke him, all the while gently repeating over and over again, "Paws, we love you, we love you, we love you."

He acted like the Tasmanian Devil—snarling, growling, howling, hissing, hitting his back on the underside of the bed as he tried to scratch and bite me. It was scary—but I knew he couldn't hurt me, so I just kept going. Finally, my gloved hand reached his face, and I was able to stroke him, still telling him how much we loved him. Ever so slowly, he began to calm down. He was trembling with fear as I continued to stroke him and speak to him in the same soft tone for a few more minutes. Then I slid out from under the bed and left the room.

The first step had been made. I was pleased but wondered how long this campaign would have to go on.

Several hours later, I came back upstairs and went to my bedroom. I noticed a cat on the bed, then did a double-take. It was Paws—all stretched out on the pillows and purring up a storm! I clapped my hand over my mouth. I literally couldn't believe it.

That dear cat became the love of our household. He often had three of our other cats licking and grooming him at one time, two dogs snuggled up next to him throughout the day, and, best of all, every night he would assume his special place to sleep—on my pillow with his beautiful, scarred, furry face nuzzling mine.

Although Paws finally succumbed to cancer, his legacy—my continued and steadfast belief in the power of love—lives on.

Barbara (Bobby) Adrian

"Child" Proof

My husband and I had just returned from the grocery store when a blood-curdling feline scream from outside rattled our front door. I was terrified that one of our two inside cats had slipped past us on our way in and now was in trouble.

When I threw open the door, a strange cat—and I'm not using the word *strange* loosely—casually padded into the foyer. "Hey, you don't belong here," I told the dusty white animal as I reached down for him. Too late. He was on the run now, into the kitchen.

Our two pampered felines studied the interloper, who looked back and forth between them and the tempting bowls of food on the kitchen floor, as if to ask, "Were you going to finish that?"

Before anyone could answer, he buried his head in the nearest food bowl.

"Hey, fur ball, that's enough," I said, putting him and the confiscated cat chow out on the patio. "Nobody gets in the house without a pass from the vet."

Not only was I not in the market for another cat, but, more importantly, for the first time in years, our household was free of feline leukemia—and I wasn't taking any chances. The scruffy-looking cat was patient. He hung around the patio, basking in the sunshine and eating the food I supplied on cue every time he tapped his paw against the window.

We chatted when I brought him his food, or at least, I chatted. He pretty much nodded his head and swished his tail. He was solid white except for a gold tail and one gold ear. I named him Bogus because he didn't look quite real. He looked like two cats put together into one. I should have suspected that naming him was the same as adopting him, but it took another week of searching for his owners before my husband and I took him to the vet for his official checkup.

We started to realize how clever this cat was, and so did the vet, when Bogus nudged a bottle of vaccine off the table. Then he knocked the syringe out of the vet's hand. Finally, the vet declared Bogus healthy except for sunburned ears, which he assured us would heal on their own without the need for a follow-up visit.

Like that first night, as soon as we opened the door and let him into the house, Bogus made himself at home. He would cozy up to our other cats, then steal their favorite sleeping spots. He was always first in line when dinner was served, and he picked the best lap to sit on at any given moment.

All was well except for one bad habit—well, maybe more than one—toilet-tissue demolition. In a matter of minutes, he could shred a double roll of Charmin.

But we're smarter than the cat, my husband and I told ourselves. We hid the paper in a cabinet over the toilet. It took Bogus about ten minutes to find it. Now, we had streams of toilet tissue flowing out of the cabinet, down the wall, over the bathroom floor, across the hallway and onto Bogus's favorite pillow—one he'd stolen from one of the other cats, of course.

That's when I discovered the child-safety aisle at the market. Among the handy supplies designed to protect children from such hazards as might lurk under kitchen sinks or behind electrical outlets, I found the perfect cabinet lock.

"See this?" I waved the package in a very curious cat's face. "This will keep you out of the toilet tissue once and for all." Bogus watched as I struggled to remove the plastic packaging from around the simple gizmo that I was certain would save the Charmin from his obsession.

Twenty minutes later, with the help of heavy-duty shears, I managed to free the childproof lock from its wrapping. It was a narrow, U-shaped plastic contraption that fit over the cabinet knobs with a sliding lock that tightened it on one side, making it impossible for any child, furry or otherwise, to open the doors. I was impressed. Now, if it just worked as well as its packaging . . . Bogus blinked his gold eyes at me from the bathroom doorway.

"There you go, big guy," I laughed as I patted his head and rubbed his gold ear. "Let's see you open that cabinet now."

I settled down in my favorite chair and picked up the novel I'd been reading. *Bang, bang, bang,* came the sound of the cabinet doors as Bogus tested the new lock. I flipped the page and laughed out loud as the banging grew more intense.

Suddenly, the noise stopped. An eerie silence . . . the soft padding of paws on the hardwood floor of the hallway . . . the thump as Bogus landed next to me. I looked down at the childproof lock he'd dropped in my lap.

That's when I knew: I could childproof my home, but I couldn't Bogus-proof my heart. And I wouldn't have it any other way.

Valerie Gawthrop

"... Anyone know who ate some of my jalapeno chopped liver sandwich spread?!"

The Uncles

Many years ago, we had a cat named Curly. The one thing that people remembered about him was his gorgeous, long black-and-white fur. As a kitten, he was just one big ball of fluff, accented by long curly hairs sticking out of his ears—hence the name.

And, of course, if you'd been around our house long enough, you'd know he was the "top cat" of our group of felines. Self-appointed, of course. This meant that he would have preferred his brother Grayspot to set off for parts unknown and never return. Ditto for Yellowcat, an old stray who was always hanging around. Along with this status went a responsibility that Curly took very seriously: care and concern for all the younger cats.

It all started when Mama Cat, an attractive young stray, decided that the space under our storage shed was the perfect place for her soon-due family. Our other cats accepted her as warmly as if they'd known her all their lives. Soon, she introduced her three new kittens to us: Ginger, a friendly, inquisitive, ginger-colored longhair; Blue Eyes, a beautiful tawny shorthair with big blue eyes; and Stripes, their dark, drab littermate.

All of them loved to play with their "uncles," Grayspot

and Curly—especially Curly, who delighted in their merry antics. Unfortunately, they imitated their overly wary mother and refused to have anything to do with us humans. All five felines—kittens and uncles alike—slept together in the cozy nest under the shed, at least until the day the uncles remembered they couldn't stand to be near each other. After that you never saw the kittens with more than one uncle at a time.

Then, one day when the kittens were about four months old, Stripes suddenly became very ill. After two days of constant diarrhea and vomiting, he was so dehydrated that I thought he was already dead. All the other cats were concerned—Curly most of all. What Stripes needed, of course, was a vet's care, but his mother refused to let me near him. Without fluids, little Stripes was a goner. When he collapsed in the backyard a long way from the water dish, there seemed to be no hope.

While I was inside finding a suitable bag for the inevitable burial, I glanced out the window to see something startling. Curly was headed across the backyard toward the water dish. So was Grayspot. But these sworn enemies were walking very slowly—*side by side!*

Then I saw the reason. *Supported between the two of them was poor little Stripes!* Inch by inch, Curly and Grayspot moved forward, carrying the sick little kitten with them— all the way to the water dish. And they continued to hold him upright while he drank the life-giving liquid.

After that, Curly never left Stripes's side until the kitten was completely well. Unfortunately, that meant he also caught whatever it was that had made his little friend so ill. He recovered, but his strength never returned.

That year, our rain came early and in torrents. With the kittens rapidly growing, there was now room for only one adult in their safe, dry nest. Curly insisted that Grayspot sleep there with the little ones; Curly stayed just outside, in the driving rain, and refused to let me budge him. Already weakened in his chest area, he quickly succumbed to pneumonia and died.

I don't know how Curly convinced Grayspot to help Stripes that day—perhaps Grayspot volunteered. Curly's beautiful coat was memorable, but his amazing compassion, self-sacrifice and unconditional love are what I remember most about him—and which still fill my heart.

Bonnie Compton Hanson

A Perfect Match

One Sunday afternoon in the late fall, a few months into our relationship, my boyfriend and I went to the local animal shelter together to adopt two cats, one for each of us. The shelter was a dingy concrete building, unremarkable except for the large window flanking the entrance where the cutest of the shelter's residents—usually a litter of kittens or puppies—appeared daily. On the wall facing the street, a window at eye level showcased other strays, usually cats who, unafraid of heights, seemed to enjoy peering down at pedestrians.

The volunteer in the reception area, a shoebox-sized room crammed with a dented tan-and-black metal desk and a half-dozen mismatched folding chairs, explained the adoption process. Satisfied that we were serious candidates for adoption, she directed us to the door in the wall, half-hidden behind the cartons of donated pet food and bags of generic kitty litter, leading to the cat room.

At the end of the narrow hallway filled with the sounds of whining and barking, scratching and mewling, the cat room—a room no bigger than the reception area—glowed green under fluorescent lights. Cages lined the walls from floor to ceiling. On the left side, several families were clustered around the cages containing litters of kittens. Two volunteers in blue tunics were taking cats out of cages for people to hold.

My boyfriend and I separated. Bypassing the crowd around the kittens, I headed for the cages on the right side of the room. Index cards on the front of the cages listed the name and description of the occupants: Flossie (four years old, spayed female, family moved) was a luxuriant white cat with a squashed face and sapphire-blue eyes; Jojo (six months, male, owner allergic) was a stringy cat with black and orange splotches; Sam (two years old, male, stray) was a burly Maine Coon cat; Yin and Yang (one year old, male and female, too much work for owner) were a pair of mewling, undernourished Siamese. The last cage on the right at shoulder height appeared to be empty, although it had a card: Morris (one year old, male, stray).

I peered into the cage. The same blue-gray as the metal walls that surrounded him, Morris melted into the shadowy corner of the cage. Only the brilliant shield of white fur on his chest and the stripe of white across his nose reflected the dim light. His yellow eyes, flecked with brown and gold, glowed as though lit from within. He sat on his haunches, erect and motionless, like the stone statues of cats that guarded the pyramids of ancient Egypt.

"Hey, Morris," I whispered. "Hey, guy," I cooed, sticking my fingers in the cage and wiggling them. He blinked and inclined his head slightly, considering me.

A volunteer, a sallow woman in her mid-twenties with a stringy brown ponytail, appeared at my shoulder. She consulted her clipboard.

"Excuse me," she said, reaching across me to pull the card out of the holder. She checked the card against her paperwork, made a notation on her clipboard and fit the card back in the metal slot sideways, short end up. She turned to go.

I turned with her, withdrawing my fingers from Morris's cage.

"Excuse me," I said. "What does it mean when you turn the card like that?"

She looked around at the family of noisy children behind her. Turning back to me, she said, in a voice just above a whisper: "It means he's the next to go."

"He's being adopted? That's great!"

"Well, no," she mumbled, looking down at her clipboard again. "He's next to, you know, go."

I didn't know. I looked at her, but she wouldn't meet my eyes.

"He's been here ten days already," she said. "We can't keep him any longer."

"So, what happens to him?" I said, although I suddenly understood.

"If no one adopts him by the end of the day, he'll be put to sleep." She sighed. "He's an adult cat, and families want kittens. And he's not very friendly. He just sits in the corner."

A father with two children, standing in front of the kitten cage, called to her, and she excused herself. My eyes prickled and my throat felt tight as I watched her open the door to the cage, pluck two squirming kittens from the pile, and hand one to each of the shrieking children.

Across the room, my boyfriend was bent over, poking his fingers through the bars of a cage where two handsome ginger-and-white-striped cats vied with each other for his attention.

Something quick and light brushed my right ear, and I turned. Morris was sitting at the front of his cage, one white-tipped paw extended through the bars. I moved closer to the cage, and he reached out again, tapping my left ear with his paw.

"Excuse me," I called over my shoulder to the volunteer.

"Can I hold him?" I asked as she came up beside me.

"Morris?" she asked. "Sure." She swung open the door and reached her hand in, but Morris had backed into his corner again.

"Let me try," I said as she backed away.

"Morris," I called softly. "Hey, Morris." He edged forward, and I lifted him out of the cage. He settled himself in my arms, his front paws on my chest. The tears that had been burning the back of my eyes threatened to overflow, and I bent my head low over him. He reached his bony, pointed face up to mine, and, with a purr that was almost a growl, licked my ear. My chest constricted. Tears ran down my cheeks.

I heard my name and turned. My boyfriend was still standing in front of the same cage. He had one of the orange cats in his arms.

"Hey, look at these guys," he said. "Snickers and Reeses. But we'll change their names. He'll be Calvin." He stroked the purring cat. "And he'll be Hobbes." He indicated the cat in the cage.

"No," I choked. "I want this one."

"What?" he said, staring at me. "C'mon, these guys are perfect. A matched pair."

"No!" I said, wiping my cheek on my shoulder. "They'll put Morris to sleep if I don't take him."

"Morris? Look, you can't rescue every cat in here. Besides, these two are so cute. . . ." His voice trailed off as he smiled encouragingly.

"I'm not leaving him," I said. Morris reached up a paw and patted my face.

My boyfriend opened his mouth, thought better of whatever he was going to say, and closed it again. He sighed.

"Okay," he said. "Mine'll be Calvin. Yours can be Hobbes."

"Morris," I said. "His name is Morris."

My boyfriend shook his head, motioning for the volunteer.

"Calvin and Morris," he grunted. "Great."

Throughout the winter, Morris and Calvin played together often, but Morris never liked my boyfriend. Morris proved to be a good judge of character. By spring, my boyfriend was gone. Fifteen years later, Morris is still with me, as loving and lovable as the first day I met him.

M. L. Charendoff

Conversation with a Cat

You are my cat, and I am your human.

Hilaire Belloc

About eight years ago, my girlfriend Gale and I bought a cabin in Flagstaff, Arizona, to use as a summer getaway. The cabin needed extensive renovation, so, during that first summer, while Gale worked in Tucson, where we lived at the time, I traveled to Flagstaff for a week or so each month to make the necessary repairs.

One warm afternoon, while I was working on the deck, I heard a meow. Looking up, I saw a half-grown cat standing thirty or forty feet away from me near our woodpile. I figured she was one of the feral cats that lived in the area. Studying her for a moment, I meowed back. Encouraged, the cat meowed again. I replied, briefly wondering what we were saying to each other. A few more mews were exchanged before she finally skittered off into the woods.

She obviously enjoyed our conversation because she came back. Every day that week, I saw her running through the yard or sunning herself in a protected spot near the woodpile.

I have always had a soft spot for cats—we had two at home in Tucson—and so I began to leave food out for her. If I was around, she wouldn't go near it, but if I was inside, she'd come and lick the bowl clean. I tried holding food out to her in my hand, but it was still too frightening for her. She needed her space, so I gave her a wide berth.

Something about this particular cat touched me. I wanted to convince her to let me pet her. I could see that a whole person was just too much for her to handle, so while she ate her dinner on the porch, I put some cat food on my fingers, lay down on the floor just inside the door, and stuck my arm and hand with the food on it out the door—in clear view from her food dish. It took a few days of this dinnertime routine, but soon she was licking the food off my fingers with no problem.

Next, I brought her food bowl out to the porch and, instead of leaving, sat near her while she ate. She quickly made the connection that the big, scary human also meant delicious food. She was wary, but her hunger was stronger than her fear.

She was fairly unremarkable in appearance. Her short, smooth coat was white with patches of charcoal gray that was almost black. Her face was mostly white, but she had a dark spot above one eye and around one ear. Her back was all dark gray except for her one unusual marking: a small patch of white, shaped like an arrowhead, in the middle of her spine.

One day as she had her nose buried deep in her bowl, I reached over and ran my hand along her back. She startled, but didn't bolt. I continued to pet her and talk to her while she finished her food.

We had made definite progress, but this was where it stopped. She let me sit near her and pet her during meals. She would even come up on the porch and hang around if I was sitting on a chair reading, but she wouldn't come inside and wouldn't let me pick her up or hold her. We'd hit a wall, and she wouldn't go an inch further.

Still, we had a connection. If I left to run errands, as soon as my car pulled into the drive, my standoffish cat would come running to greet me. I decided to name her Moki, after the Moki Dugway, a spectacular stretch of road that winds through the red rocks and desert of southern Utah. Something about the arrowhead on her back seemed to resonate with that area.

For the next few months, whenever I went back to Tucson, I paid Jessica, a neighbor's daughter, to put out food for Moki while I was gone. Jessica told me that Moki ate her food, but wouldn't let Jessica near her. She reserved that privilege for me. And so our pattern continued: Every time I pulled into the drive that summer and fall, Moki seemed to sense my presence and came running.

Then, one October afternoon, I pulled in, but Moki didn't come. I was uneasy, but not alarmed. Perhaps she was off hunting. A little while later, Jessica's mother knocked on my door. "I have some bad news," she told me.

One evening, my neighbor explained, when Jessica came over to put out food for Moki, somehow the family dog got out of the yard and followed Jessica over to my house. Moki was waiting near the woodpile for her dinner when the dog came up behind her and attacked her. Jessica screamed at him to stop, but the dog shook Moki violently before Jessica could reach them. A moment later, the dog dropped the cat, and Moki took off, bloody and injured. She didn't know where Moki was—or how she was—but she wasn't hopeful about an injured cat's chances in the predator-filled woods around our houses.

I immediately jumped in the car and went looking along the woods by the road. I called and called, but heard and saw nothing. Moki, if she was alive, was long gone. That visit I spent part of every day searching for Moki. All that I found was some fur by the woodpile, a horrible reminder of what had occurred. Deeply saddened, I left Flagstaff a week later, sure I'd seen the last of Moki.

Winter passed, and I made one or two trips to Flagstaff to work on the cabin. There was never any sign of Moki. I was surprised at the pain I felt at the loss of this cat who had kept such an unbending boundary between us. I put the memory of Moki in a compartment in my heart and tried to forget about her.

When May rolled around again, I made another trip to Flagstaff to put the finishing touches on the cabin where I hoped Gale and I could spend some time together that summer.

Late one afternoon, as I was working inside with the door open to let in the spring breeze, I heard it: a faint meow. I dropped what I was doing and ran outside.

There she was, coming toward me as fast as she could— on three legs. Her fourth leg was still there, but she wouldn't put any weight on it.

I knelt down and petted Moki gently so I wouldn't frighten her, but I was so happy to see her, I found myself picking her up and holding her close to me. She didn't struggle. Instead, she purred loudly as I carried her inside.

I called Gale to share the good news. She thought I should get Moki to a vet as soon as possible. That night, Moki slept with me without ever leaving the bed.

The next morning, I took her to the vet. He X-rayed her leg and said that it had been broken and had knitted badly, but he didn't recommend putting her through the trauma of re-setting it. He felt that, in time, once the leg was fully healed, she would begin using it again. I asked the vet to spay her and give her shots and worming medicines. The following day, when I picked her up at the vet's office, Moki snuggled in my arms as if she had always done so. The wall between us had disappeared.

Moki and I have remained close. In fact, there haven't been very many occasions over the last eight years when we've been apart; she even travels with us on vacations. I don't know how she survived that snowy winter, alone and injured out in the cold, but I'm glad she did. I don't know which one of us was happier at our reunion; today, I can't tell you which one of us is more attached to the other. Gale says that Moki looks at me with "Nancy Reagan eyes." Moki is clearly my cat, and I am clearly her person. And life is sweeter because of it.

You just never know where a conversation with a cat might lead you.

Hoyt Tarola

Always Room for One More

One day last spring, we were driving home from a Saturday afternoon's shopping trip. It was four-thirty, peak traffic time on the major four-lane road through town. I was tired and gazing without focus at the shops and houses passing by. My husband Fred, who was driving, suddenly said in an outraged voice, "What was that?"

"What?" I asked, suddenly alert.

He looked to our right and yelled, "It's a kitten!"

He had seen a small, fuzzy ball tossed from the right side window of the car in front of us. Too stunned to take note of the car's license plate, Fred swerved into the first available driveway, put the car in park and ran back to where he'd seen the kitten land by the curb. I sat in the car imagining the worst. What chance would a kitten have in that kind of traffic?

A few minutes later, Fred returned and handed me an eight-week-old white bundle of fur, with orange stripes behind each ear and an orange rump. The kitten was trembling and looked dazed, but did not seem injured. Then I noticed he was missing his tail. *Oh no,* I thought, *he's been run over.* Looking more closely, I saw that he had been born that way.

"He's part Manx," I said. I held him close to me, petting

him and talking in soft tones. Turning to Fred, I said,
"Now what?"

We already had longtime housemates: two adult cats in
their early teens. At Christmas, we had added a young
part-Persian stray who had been hanging around the
antique mall where Fred worked. It had taken three
months for the resident cats and the newcomer, Pooh, to
get accustomed to each other. Now we were bringing
home another? And to a house not much larger than a
two-bedroom apartment, no less.

Fred said, "Let's just take him home and get him calmed
down. On Monday, I'll take him to the pet-grooming
shop." The woman who ran the shop had a soft heart for
stray cats and took them in until she could find homes
for them.

We snuck the kitten into the house and put him into
one of the small bedrooms, along with food, water, kitty
litter and an old towel to sleep on. It didn't take long for
the other cats to discover the interloper. One by one, they
planted themselves in front of the closed door, demanding
silently to know what was going on. Squeek, the dominant older cat, was clearly dismayed and gave me glower-
ing looks every time I walked by the bedroom door. He
wanted me to know that there simply was no more room
in the house or in his heart to accept another cat. "It's
okay, old man," I said, leaning over to stroke his silky
head, "we are only keeping him for the weekend."

By Sunday, the kitten had gotten comfortable with his
new arrangement and was looking for entertainment. I
found myself checking on him frequently, petting him and
dangling a string for him to attack. When I picked him up
to hold him, he purred intensely and rubbed his nose
affectionately on mine.

"Don't get too attached," Fred warned.

"No problem," I said, "I can't manage another cat." Two

cats had seemed easy. Two cats to locate. Two cat dishes to wash. Two cats to brush and medicate when needed. Eight paws worth of nails to trim. Two cats who sometimes shared the bed at night. Then the third arrived. Suddenly, my morning routine was overturned. Where was each cat? Who had been fed, and who hadn't? Why was I always running out of clean dishes for them? While the older ones slept, the young one wanted me to come out and play. Life had gotten a lot busier with the addition of just one. I couldn't imagine adding a fourth.

Sunday night, Fred and I reassured one another of our decision not to keep him. "It will be too hard on the older cats," I said. "They are already stressed by Pooh."

"Yes," he agreed, "and there is the added expense of cat food and vet care." Three cats were quite enough, we concluded.

Monday morning, I said good-bye to the kitten and left for work. As I drove away, I thought about the fact that the tiny face with the huge amber eyes would not be there when I got home. I started to cry. "Stop that," I admonished myself out loud. "You can't take in every stray who comes your way." Still, I could not shake the heaviness from my heart.

I fretted all morning and couldn't focus on my work. I found myself wanting to call Fred and tell him to forget taking the kitten to the pet shop. Each time I reached for the phone, however, the prior night's words of reason stopped me.

That night, I arrived home to find that the kitten was gone, safely ensconced in a cage at the grooming shop, according to Fred. I felt like a traitor. "He trusted us," I said despondently, "and now he sits alone in a cage. How frightened he must be. Who knows if anyone will adopt him or how long it will take." Fred didn't respond and was uncharacteristically quiet all evening.

My mood was no lighter the next morning. I could think

of nothing but the kitten. By midafternoon, I had made a decision. I called home and said to Fred, "Go get the kitten. How much work is one more, anyway?"

"No need," Fred replied. "He's right here in my lap. I couldn't stand it, so I went back and got him this morning." He had given the shop owner a donation to help with the other stray cats, thanked her and told her we'd decided to keep him. She had smiled and said, "It doesn't surprise me."

"We are nuts," I said.

"I know," he responded, laughing.

Skeeter is now a happy established member of the family. Yes, there was a period of adjustment for both cats and humans. Squeek still reminds him with an occasional cuff to the head that Squeek is the boss cat and has full ownership of the new cat bed. Pooh, at first cautious, is now delighted to have a playmate to chase around the yard. Shadow, the elder cat, has become the surrogate mother, giving the kitten long loving licks. They often sleep together, Shadow's front paw cuddling the kitten.

Somehow, my routine has adjusted itself—or I've adjusted to it. The cats have their own feeding schedule so that there are never more than two of them in our tiny kitchen at one time. They seem to understand the two-cats-on-the-bed-at-one-time rule and they rotate occupancy. Skeeter has established an evening ritual of racing first to Fred's lap and then to mine to give each of us an affectionate glad-you're-mine buss on the nose.

All new life brings teachings—or reminders—of past lessons lost. In this case, I am reminded that, even when the head says "impossible," the heart can always find room for one more.

Roberta Lockwood

Disney's World

He was my soul mate, but none of my friends shared my adoration of him. Disney was a cat so bonded to me that he regarded all other people in the world as intrusive enemies.

When I first met the four-week-old orphaned kitty at the League for Animal Protection in Long Island, New York, he won my heart immediately by climbing up my back and nestling against my neck. With high hopes for a frolicking, fun-loving and entertaining new housemate—and to commemorate my recent visit to Disneyland—I named him Disney.

Placing the twelve-ounce gray tabby in a cardboard carrying case, I set off for home and our new life together. Disney, determining from the start that there would be no barrier between us, crawled out of the box and into my coat pocket. This need for physical closeness remained a pattern throughout our life together.

Upon arriving at my apartment in Queens, I set about bottle-feeding the little critter. However, Disney indicated that he was ready to be a big boy and weaned himself on the spot. Exploring my tiny apartment, he found and used the litter box, then settled down for the night in bed with

Flicka, my golden retriever guide dog, and me.

I wanted my adorable kitten to be well socialized, so I brought him to work with me at Kings Park Psychiatric Center at least twice a week. After resting quietly in the carrier as I walked to the train station, Disney curled on my shoulder during the hour-long train ride to Long Island. Yet, despite every effort to shape him into a loving, caring and outgoing cat, by the time he reached puberty— even after being neutered—Disney wanted no part of any person other than me. When Disney finally wore out his welcome on the job by growling and hissing at patients and fellow workers, he had to be left at home.

After that, Disney poured his heart and soul into his relationship with Flicka and me. Each evening when I returned from work, he greeted me by flinging himself into my arms, putting his paws around my neck and licking my face. Totally tuned in to my every mood, my furry roommate followed me around the house, taking advantage of every opportunity to sit on my lap or maintain physical contact. If I cried, he tried to lick the tears away. When my beloved Flicka was diagnosed with terminal cancer, Disney's opportunity to minister to my unhappiness reached its peak.

Although Flicka had been diagnosed, she was still working. My new guide dog, Ivy, another golden retriever, came to live with us for her training as Flicka's successor. Disney was ecstatic about this new canine buddy. Ivy learned that Disney enjoyed being nuzzled and flipped in the air, and this soon became their favorite game.

When blind friends visited my apartment, Disney warmly welcomed their guide dogs, but made it apparent by his continuous hissing that my human guests were a considerable annoyance. My friends quipped that they maintained our friendship despite Disney. Disney's well-deserved reputation as a misanthrope caused me to become even more bonded to and protective of my one-woman feline.

After Flicka's death, Ivy smoothly took over the role of guide. Wanting to provide companionship for Disney during the long days I was away at work, I adopted another cat. Disney quickly adjusted to the addition of Tevye, our new feline family member.

However, when I brought home Ed, my new husband, Disney's adjustment was less than tranquil! Always ready to make friends with members of the animal kingdom, Disney immediately welcomed Ed's black Labrador guide dog, Perrier, but resented Ed's intrusion into our lives.

Sensing that this particular intruder was permanent, Disney did not display his usual hostility by hissing and spitting. Instead, he would not allow Ed to touch him and never voluntarily climbed into his lap. Worse, Disney would take advantage of Ed's blindness and lack of familiarity with cunning feline tactics by swiping any unguarded food on Ed's plate. In contrast, I was never a target of his marauding ways.

When we moved to Fresno, California, Disney was in his element. Sitting on the kitchen windowsill, he was able to monitor the comings and goings of our neighbors. Should any friend or neighbor enter the house, Disney greeted them with hisses and growls. We joked that if anyone broke into our house, it would be Disney, not the dogs, who would scare away the intruder!

As our friendship network expanded, Disney's infamous reputation spread. When people entered our home, our dogs gleefully greeted them, and Tevye explored their bags and belongings, but Disney disdainfully glared at them. Everyone learned to give him a wide berth.

Since Disney was not hostile to new dogs, he became useful in the training of assistance-dog puppies. Fresno-based puppies being socialized to become future guide, service and hearing dogs were brought to our house to learn proper cat etiquette from our miniature tiger. Disney taught them that sniffs and occasional licks were permissible, but nipping, chasing and frenetic activity were not. We were surprised to learn that feline smacks, hisses and snarls could control the most exuberant canine behavior. When these puppies later assumed their careers as assistance dogs, their new partners marveled at their perfect cat etiquette.

At the age of twelve, Disney began displaying signs of failing health. We made the 150-mile trip to a specialty veterinary practice, where they made the diagnosis of intestinal cancer and said Disney would have to be hospitalized for a week following surgery. I could not imagine how my wild cat would cope in a strange environment completely cut off from me. Realizing we would both suffer separation anxiety, I cuddled my striped boy and tearfully left him with the vets.

Disney, labeled a classic example of Feline Hysterical Syndrome by the veterinarians who had treated him in the past, was far from an ideal patient. His weeklong stay turned out to be traumatic not only for Disney and me, but also for the hospital staff.

Inconsolable at home, I phoned first thing in the morning and last thing at night for progress reports. Disney was progressing medically, but was virtually impossible for the staff to handle without sedation. Toward the end of his hospital stay, I asked the doctor if Disney was one of the worst patients she ever had. After a short pause, she said, "No, he isn't *one* of the worst; he is *the* worst!"

Anxious to be reunited with my soul mate, we again made the long trip to the specialty hospital. Intimidated by this ferocious patient, the staff debated how best to wrestle him from the hospital cage into his carrying case. I assured them Disney would not hurt me and would calmly allow me to lift him out of the cage. The hospital staff was astonished when I picked up a raging Disney, who instantly became a clinging, loving kitty-marshmallow. Hearing my voice, he flung himself into my arms, put his front paws around my neck and covered my face with kisses. The entire hospital staff came running to witness this miraculous transformation.

At home, as the days stretched into weeks, Disney regained his strength but not his fierceness. We had been told that Disney's surgery would not cure the intestinal cancer, and so I cherished each remaining day with my "passion kitty." Our bond became even greater. He rarely left my side and slept in the crook of my arm at night, with his paw touching my face. In the morning, he followed me into the bathroom and sat on the sink while I prepared for the day. He developed the habit of standing on my foot until I reached down to scoop him into my arms.

When his health again began to fail, I faced one of the most difficult times of my life. In the past, when I had lost my guide dogs to death, I knew another golden retriever would have a similar temperament and could assume the guiding role. Now, I found myself in anguish, knowing that there would never be another Disney.

After his death, friends, although personally glad he was gone, lovingly extended a hand to me in my profound grief. One memorable phone call broke the spell of bereavement. A distant friend, who had never met Disney, tried to console me with the thought that my beloved soul mate was now happily sitting on God's lap. The idea of a content little Disney relaxed and purring was so absurd, my tears instantly turned into laughter. I assured my friend that if Disney were on *anyone* else's lap—divine or otherwise—he would certainly be hissing!

Toni Eames

What Was That Sound?

I volunteer regularly with the Peninsula Humane Society & SPCA, outside San Francisco, socializing cats. When I first met Boots, the little gray feline was one of twenty-seven cats rescued from a hoarder in a condemned house. A flea-infested four-year-old who weighed less than five pounds, he tore my heart.

His socializing card noted, "Boots is getting worse. He needs attention." Did he ever! When I first reached in the cage for him, it took minutes to gently pry his claws from the shelf to which he clung. When I finally held him on my lap, his whole body trembled; he was paralyzed with fear. Having had twenty-six other cats to compete with, it was obvious this runt never received enough affection or attention.

Then Boots did something unusual. Fear tensed his skin, slicked back his ears and curled his tail tightly around his body. Next, terror loosened his bladder all over me. I saw his face for only a second. He looked apologetic, as if saying, "Sorry, but I just don't know what you're doing!" Then his face was gone, tucked inside my arms and hidden from sight.

So that he would feel secure, I wrapped him inside a large towel. Eventually, he stuck his head out, assessed the situation and retreated again. That was the best he had to offer, and his best was good enough for me.

Each day, I returned to the shelter to spend time with Boots. With the passing days, he seemed to feel better, though his fear of being held was still obvious.

While I was at the shelter, socializing Boots and his mates, the hoarder often came to visit. (Legally, it was allowed.) She walked with shelter staff past the cages and even identified each cat by name. She wasn't intentionally cruel, but, like most hoarders, she was either emotionally or mentally unbalanced. She did transfer custody of many cats to the shelter so they could be adopted.

But Boots was in a bad situation. He wasn't socialized enough to be put up for adoption. And given his slow rate of progress, he would probably have to be euthanized because of space constraints.

Even though my husband Rog and I had been a one-cat family, we decided to adopt Boots. We were moving into a new house and figured the time was right. The hoarder transferred custody, allowing him to be adopted. Once we brought him home, the first action we took was to rename him. We wanted to give him a strong identity to separate him from his old life. Rog suggested Bodacious, and I agreed.

We immediately ran into difficulties. After spending six months in the shelter, Boots knew that routine. But here in our house, Bodacious was terrified all over again. At times, I wondered if we'd done the right thing in adopting him. For the first month, he hid out in my office closet. Neither friendship nor food could coax him out. He'd already experienced starvation; food wasn't incentive. And he didn't understand affection well enough for that to encourage him either. We simply had to wait.

When he did venture out of the closet, a sudden turn of my head would send him back into hiding. If he was nearby, and I lifted my hand to reach for the phone, he was gone in a flash.

One day, he made an appearance at the top of the stairs, but when Rog and I noticed him, he disappeared. But his flights grew shorter, and Bo grew bolder. An expert in cat massage, I experimented with every technique I knew, searching for the magical touch that would relieve this frightened feline. I'd learned that slow caresses, especially under the chin and cheeks, worked extraordinarily well to soothe cats and accelerate the bonding process.

Baby steps of progress occurred. Those incredibly slow caresses were appreciated. We also discovered that Bo tolerated being brushed with a long-handled bath brush because the handle allowed for a "connection without contact." Or maybe it reminded him of his mom's raspy tongue. Whatever the reason, he'd always sit for brush massage.

Bo found "safe spots" where he could be approached. Our bed and his pet bed were safe havens. And, one day, when my husband flipped up the leg-rest on his side of the loveseat, Bo planted himself between Rog's legs. It was Bo's first demonstration of being territorial.

Our resident cat, Champion, a mellow twelve-year-old, became Bo's role model, demonstrating how to deal with affection and attention. Bo watched the way we petted Champion and saw that it was safe. He took comfort with "one of his own" and started shadowing Champ throughout the house. Their feline bonding developed into a loving relationship.

One night, Rog and I were on the loveseat, Bo between Rog's legs. My arm rested against Bo while Rog caressed him under his chin. Suddenly, we heard a noise. We looked at each other, brows furrowed—what was that sound? It was a new house, and we still weren't accustomed to all the different sounds. The noise grew louder.

Still confused, we looked around. Then turning to Bo, we realized *he* was its source. Our confusion turned to amazement and delight: Bo was purring! He'd never purred before and already he was at high volume.

This was the beginning of Bo's unending feline symphony of contentment. While Champion taught me about "power purring," Bo exhibits "full-body rumbling." He's an extreme purring machine. It's a joyous sound, and my heart warms each time I hear him.

Eventually, Bo comforted us when Champ went to animal heaven. Then he became the top cat when we welcomed another shelter specialty, Minka, to our home.

Over time, we discovered Bo's gorgeous white belly. Today, he often flips over, belly up for attention. This vulnerable position indicates ultimate trust—what a huge step for such a frightened cat! He still spooks easily, and an unexpected movement can still send him away, but it's never very far, or for very long. And while he may never quite be bodacious, he's much improved.

As I write this on my laptop, it's early morning. Minka is sprawled on the table next to our loveseat, planning his feline day. Bo is nestled, comfortable in his favorite spot between my legs.

It took him a few minutes to get there, though. First, he interrupted my typing, ferociously head-butting my chin, then waltzing on the keyboard, oblivious to the crazy onscreen patterns created by the pressure of his white paws. Then he tried scrunching into the tiny space between my belly and the laptop itself. Now, settled between my legs, once again I hear that full-body rumbling emanate deep from within him. A contented belly full of food, kept company by a heart full of love—what a fine combination.

Now, he's back, blocking my view of the screen, totally oblivious, yet absolutely joyous in a moment of feline freedom. And me? I'm thrilled. My writing can wait; moments of freely flowing love are priceless.

Maryjean Ballner

What I Did for Love

The call came at ten o'clock on a warm August night.

"Can you foster-sit a kitten who can't walk?" asked Laura, the humane-society volunteer. The word *kitten* is equivalent to a guarantee of fostering in our house, and the fact that he couldn't walk just sealed the deal. Without a thought, we agreed to be the temporary guardians of a handicapped cat.

He arrived a few minutes later, scared, shaking and covered in his own mess.

"We found him on Grove Street," Laura said, "so we named him Grover."

Job one was to clean him up. He was tiny enough to fit in one hand, so the bathroom sink seemed a logical choice for his bath. While gently rubbing the shampoo into his smelly fur, Laura answered our as-yet-unspoken but obvious question of what was wrong with him.

"He might have been hit by a car," Laura explained. "We'll wait a couple of weeks to see if he gets better." We didn't have to ask what would happen if he *didn't* get better. With an all-volunteer humane society supported solely by donations, we had to make difficult but pragmatic decisions about the animals we invested our time and money in.

Over the next two weeks, we watched with pity as Grover's hind legs continually played tricks on him, first moving in odd directions, then jacking up his rear end as if it were on a hydraulic lift, sometimes resulting in his literally being end over end. He often landed with a thud in his food or water dish, either frustrated or soaking wet. On top of all that, the poor little guy had seizures whenever he tilted his head back too far. There was virtually no change in his condition during those first crucial days in our care, and we knew what that meant.

What did change, though, was *our* attitude. What began as pity soon grew into admiration as we recognized characteristics we often find sorely lacking in many of our fellow humans: trust, patience, persistence, courage—along with a surprising *lack* of what is often all too evident with those same humans, a complaining nature. It simply wasn't in him to grumble about his plight in life. Instead, he seemed inordinately grateful that we had found it in our hearts to help him.

The two weeks of waiting had not yet fully passed when we realized that even a little handicapped cat deserved a chance, whether he had been hit by a car or was simply born this way. And we were determined to give him that chance.

Over the next few weeks, life with Grover challenged our heretofore mundane routine. We found ourselves learning a new language: "Grover-speak." We quickly became adept at determining which cries meant, "I'm hungry," and which meant, "Hurry! I can't make it to the litter box in time!" The second cry always brought an instant reaction as we dropped whatever we were doing like a hot potato. Scooping him up, we would rush him to "his" room, where there waited a specially designed litter box atop a shower curtain that would catch any "overspray." He would struggle to find a comfortable position on his side to do what other cats do so naturally in a much more private and dignified manner.

All along, we knew we were just temporary caretakers of this special kitten, and so began our search for the perfect home for a little guy who many would consider imperfect.

In the meantime, we researched what might have caused this strange condition. From our research, it seemed as if Grover was born with cerebellar hypoplasia, a genetic condition caused by the mother cat contracting distemper while pregnant. Whether or not any or all of her kittens would be affected, and to what degree, appeared to be simply a matter of chance—and Lady Luck had obviously chosen to ignore Grover.

Our next step was to confirm this diagnosis. Off we went to Ohio State University Veterinary Hospital—two hours by car, each way, from our home. There, Grover was given his very first nickname, "Pud Pud," which we assumed must be short for "Puddin," in response to his sweet temperament. Several veterinarians and veterinary students observed Grover's walk, examined him, and asked us a litany of questions about his everyday activities, after which they confirmed that Grover suffered from cerebellar hypoplasia.

During this period, we received two inquiries about adopting Grover, one from a vet and one from a family two states away. We determined to find Grover the perfect new home by Thanksgiving. This brought a simultaneous sense of relief and sadness, each in equal measure. Thanksgiving was not far off, but we knew that the home he found would not be ours.

There were other things to worry about during the waiting period, though. All the sharp edges in our home that might hurt Grover as he struggled to travel from place to place had to be dealt with. We found some scrap pieces of bubble wrap and promptly wrapped the corner of the brick hearth, the "meanest" corner in the house in Grover's esteemed opinion. My observant nature soon required a trip to the office-supply store for two giant rolls of the cushiony bubble wrap, most of which soon decorated the chair legs, wall corners, lamp bottoms, desk edges and anything else that might harm our temporary boarder.

Grover was now old enough to be neutered, a decision that required another two-hour drive, this time to MedVet, in Columbus, Ohio, an animal-emergency hospital that specialized in nonroutine care. After speaking to the surgeon who would take care of Grover, and being assured that they would use every necessary precaution to ensure his safety—including the use of "people" anesthesia—we entrusted him to the capable hands of the doctor. Then came the seemingly endless wait until Grover appeared once again, totally alert and looking none the worse for wear after his brief hospitalization.

So, after adapting our daily routine to fit his, modifying an entire room so he had a space of his own, making two four-hour round trips to have him diagnosed and neutered, "decorating" our entire home in bubble wrap and moving his favorite chair in front of our bay window so he could watch the birds, Grover was adopted.

Three Thanksgivings have come and gone since Grover found his forever home—and, as I write this, he sits beside my desk in his favorite chair.

And when next Thanksgiving comes, we will give thanks again—for the privilege of sharing our lives with a little handicapped cat named Grover.

Linda Bruno

2

CELEBRATING
THE BOND

Time spent with cats is never wasted.

Colette

Beautiful Music

Everything a cat is and does physically is to me beautiful, lovely, stimulating, soothing, attractive and an enchantment.

Paul Gallico

I fell in love with Ricky's mother first. Topanga was a calico Devon Rex—an unusual-looking athletic breed of cat with large ears, enormous eyes and a distinctive single coat of wavy, chenille-like fur.

Thump! The calico beauty landed on my shoulder and began to purr into my ear.

I looked at her. Topanga looked at me. The purring got louder. It was the most beautiful cat music I'd ever heard, and I fell head over heels.

"If this cat ever has kittens, let me know," I told Leslie, the breeder.

"Steve," Leslie said with a grin, "she's pregnant."

As a professional pet journalist, I like all animals. At that time, my wife Robin and I shared our Chicago condo with two dogs, Chaser and Lucy, and although I'd been around hundreds or maybe thousands of cats through my work, I was currently cat-less. I couldn't resist the thought of one of Topanga's kittens.

From the beginning, our white kitten Ricky charmed friend and stranger alike. Lucy and Chaser had always gone places with me, and Ricky was no different. Ricky soon had fans everywhere: the vet's office, the pet store, the bank, the dry cleaner, even the radio station where I worked. His endearing gremlin look and sparse, baby-fine fur—Rex kittens often look like candidates for Rogaine—never failed to draw a curious, friendly crowd, and, consequently, the little guy learned from day one that people loved him. I was his biggest fan of all.

My Ricky-admiration bumped up another level, though, when he turned eight or nine months old. Our dog Lucy did animal-assisted therapy, and I purchased a toy piano for her, thinking people would get a kick out of her plinking on the keys. To begin her training, I thought it best to close ourselves in my study to avoid distractions. Within three or four minutes of Lucy's first clicker-training piano lesson, Ricky managed to open the door. He walked across the room and performed a perfect sit right next to Lucy, right in front of me. He couldn't have said it any clearer: "I want in on this, too."

By the end of three training sessions, Ricky hit the piano keys. Within ten days, Ricky was playing Chopin—okay, I'm being generous, but he did compose unique, individual compositions, which I refer to as modern jazz. If I doubted it before, Ricky made it clear he was one cool cat.

At first, I was just having a good time. I taught Ricky how to come when called and to jump through or over objects—hula-hoops, prone kids, even strange dogs doing a "down/stay." He'd give a high five—well, four—if you asked him.

I'm not sure when I realized we were breaking barriers. You aren't supposed to be able to train cats. Suddenly,

Ricky was the teacher, showing by example that a cat can be so much more than a snoring feline lump on the sofa. Ricky's appearances on local and national television—or on the front steps of our condo building—playing original piano compositions touched people in ways I never thought possible.

At one outdoor concert, a ten-year-old boy with Down syndrome walked by. He was enthralled by the piano-playing feline. He stared at Ricky for several minutes, then spontaneously began to laugh. We're not talking little giggles here; I mean full-blown belly laughter.

His mother was stunned. She told me quietly, "Billy's father passed on two weeks ago. Everyone tried to get him to talk, to react, but he wouldn't."

Billy, who was still in stitches, began to pet Ricky. Then Billy sat down and snuggled with Ricky, now purring in his lap. I don't know what secrets Billy shared, but he whispered to Ricky for several minutes. Just before he and his mom departed, Billy looked at Ricky and said, "I love you," then he kissed Ricky. Ricky just had this extraordinary ability to reach people.

When Ricky's yearly vet visit rolled around, his veterinarian requested a piano concert for the staff. They were packed in tighter than sardines to hear Ricky play, *ooh*ing and *aah*ing through his entire performance.

Afterward, as the doctor began Ricky's physical, I will never forget the look on her face as she listened to my cat's heart. "Steve, I hear a murmur—and it doesn't sound good."

She referred me to a nearby heart specialist, one of the best in the country, and I held my breath until the day of the appointment. I looked at the ultrasound, listened to what the specialist said, but didn't really hear the words. As a pet journalist, I knew about hypertrophic cardiomyopathy, which made it worse. I felt numb. Most likely,

Ricky had only a limited amount of time left.

Once back at the car, I took Ricky out of the carrier, and sat in the parking lot holding him and weeping. I loved my dogs, but Ricky was my best friend. Working closely with him during training had forged a special bond—a mind/heart connection born from "reading" and understanding each other on an almost mystical level. Our relationship had become like superglue, tighter than you could imagine.

Ricky didn't know he was sick, thank goodness. Over the next months and years, he made regular trips to the cardiac veterinarian for ultrasound checkups, and, although the disease progressed, it did so slowly. Ricky learned to leap onto my shoulder each day and "ask" for his heart medicine—the only cat I ever met who actually *liked* taking pills.

While visiting the heart specialist, Ricky became fascinated by the dog cookie jar on the reception counter that went, *"Woof, woof."* He taught himself to open the jar and would take out the treats, lining them up on the edge of the counter, and then, one by one, he'd push them off the counter to the waiting dogs sitting patiently below. Even ill, he was still Ricky, doing the unexpected.

In fact, the first time he pulled the dog-biscuit stunt, the receptionist was so startled that she ran to the back of the clinic, insisting everyone come up front to see Ricky feed the dogs. Ricky never stopped changing people's perceptions of what cats could do.

Eventually, the time came when going to the vet lost its appeal. As Ricky's illness intensified, I remained in denial and didn't want to think his time was as short as it was. One day, he sat next to me in my office, perched on the radiator doing his favorite thing—eating. Then he looked up at me.

And he fell over.

My wife Robin thought he just fell, but I knew. I knew
—and I grabbed him and ran down the hall. Neighbors
say they heard me scream in the elevator as I went down.
Robin called and told the vets to expect us. They tried, but
couldn't save him. . . .

It's been over two years, but I still think of Ricky every
single day. I can't imagine I'll ever again have a cat who
takes as much of my heart as he did. Though he only lived
for a short time, he packed an awful lot of living into his
six years. Ricky was the best ambassador ever—for Devon
Rex cats and for cats in general.

Steve Dale
As told to Amy Shojai

[EDITORS' NOTE: *In June 2002, the Winn Feline Foundation
(www.winnfelinehealth.org), which supports feline health
research, announced the creation of THE RICKY FUND, set up to
accept donations specifically for studies related to feline hypertrophic cardiomyopathy. Steve Dale, nationally syndicated pet
columnist and radio-show host, worked with Winn to create this
fund in memory of his Devon Rex, Ricky.*]

That's My Cat

February 1991. Operation Desert Storm is raging; our country is at war. Here at home, my house is strangely silent—the result of both the absence of my eleven-year-old son, Zach, who is spending the weekend with his father, and the void left by the death of my mother, who will never again interrupt me with an ill-timed phone call. As if war, separation and death are not enough, Valentine's Day lurks around the corner, with no lover or beloved in sight.

This is the clincher. At age thirty-seven, I have yet to experience a Valentine's Day that comes through on its Hallmark promise. For whatever reason, when February 14 rolls around, boyfriends take a hike or I receive valentines from admirers I wish had stayed secret. This year, my sense of abandonment is profound.

Out of this mire of despair, I have an idea: Forget the man. I will get a cat.

A long-haired, pink-nosed, calico female cat is what I have in mind. But, suddenly, the image of a black male cat pops into my head. Just as suddenly, I reject the thought. *No black cats and no males,* I decide. *Black cats are too mysterious, too sleek and aloof. And male cats, too independent and too likely to spray.* Bottom line: A black, male cat doesn't seem cuddly enough.

And so, on this fateful day in February, I call the local humane society and ask if they have any calico female cats. "You're in luck!" the voice at the other end of the line says. "We have a calico female kitten just waiting to be adopted."

"Great!" I say. "That's just what I'm looking for."

After hanging up, I immediately launch into a nest-making frenzy—vacuuming, dusting, cleaning and organizing. It never occurs to me that a little kitten wouldn't know the difference or even care. Mothers nest, so that's what I do.

With the home fires now burning brightly, I launch my blue Mazda in the direction of the animal shelter, all the while thinking about my mother. My mother always occupied a lot of my time, but her recent death has made her an even more frequent companion, unlimited now by the constraints of time and space.

My mother hated cats for as long as I could remember—until, that is, one walked into her life. It was Christmas in northern Michigan, and my brother Michael, my son Zach, and I had convened at my mother's house to celebrate the holidays.

There was a scratch at the door. My mother opened it. In walked a cat, a huge presence of a cat with long, black-and-brown-mottled fur coated with a dusting of snow. He entered the house like he had been there before. He had an enormous head with round yellow eyes and a broad, flat face. Looking up at my mother, he meowed, as if to say, "Merry Christmas" or "So nice to see you again." His face reminded us of a mug shot on a most-wanted poster, so we named him Muggs.

He was the only cat my mother ever loved, and he only stayed the week. When my brother and I were getting ready to return to our own homes, apparently, so was Muggs. My mother was convinced that he embodied the spirit of my brother Ricky, who had died at the age of five. Who were we to argue? Somehow, it made sense. Muggs returned the following year, same time, same place, only to leave at the end of Christmas week, this time never to return.

Driving up to the humane society, I decide to name my new cat Muggs, in memory of my mother and in deference to her hope that death isn't the end. Right now, I want to believe that, too.

I park my car in the shelter's circular driveway and crunch through the snow to the door. A spry older man in a light-blue shirt greets me at the reception counter. "Hi there! What can I do for you?"

"I've come for the calico kitten," I announce.

"I'm sorry, miss. The calico was just adopted about an hour ago."

I feel as if I have been sucker-punched. That cat was supposed to be mine. Why didn't I run over the minute I got off the phone?

"Hey!" the attendant said, brightening. "Her brother is still here."

"No," I say. "I don't want a male cat." My despondency is as thick as quicksand and just as slippery. "Okay," I say finally. "Do you have any other cats I could look at?"

"Do we have other cats?" he replies with a wry grin.

He guides me down a long narrow hallway to a room with cage after cage of cats: sleek cats, fluffy cats, dainty cats and chunky cats. Tigers, torties, white ones and gray ones. And they all just sit there, or lie there plastered against the back of their cages, staring coolly at me with complete indifference. *Cats are so good at that,* I suddenly remember. *What was I thinking?*

And then I hear something: a strange, low vibration and the tinkling of a bell. As I proceed down the row of cages, the vibration and bell get louder, until I finally identify their source. There, in the last cage at the end of the line, is a tiny black kitten, batting a plastic jingle ball around its cage and purring at the top of its little kitty lungs. *Ah,* I think, *this must be the calico's brother.* Imagine that, a black male cat.

His antics amuse me, and I find myself stirred by his show of life. But then, as if propelled by some counter-magnetic force, I turn abruptly away from his cage, searching in earnest for what I really want.

Except that, now, compared to the vibrant little one, the other cats seem even more lifeless, like four-legged zombies or feather dusters on sticks. The purring and jingling black kitten emanates a presence that tugs and beckons, reeling me in. *Come see! Come see me!* And so I do.

"Oh my, little one. What are we going to do?" I ask out loud, quietly, as he rubs against the bars of his cage, leaning toward my touch. As if on cue, the attendant appears and says, "Want to hold him?"

"Okay," I breathe, knowing all the while that I am losing my grip on something and sinking fast. Not into quicksand this time, but into something softer, darker, more comforting, like the sleek black velvet of this little one's body in my arms.

As the kitten crawls up my jacket and against my neck, purring loudly into my ear, I read the sign at the side of his cage:

Black male cat.
Purrs like a motorboat.
Name: Muggins.

I am not making this up.

"So, what do you think?" grins the attendant, holding the cage door open.

"I think," I say through my tears, "this is my cat."

Mary Knight

"Well . . . I did ask for a sign."

The Wisdom of Socrates

*The soul is the same in all living creatures,
although the body of each is different.*

Hippocrates

One frigid January morning in 1995, I found a dog curled up on my front lawn, his nose tucked tightly under his tail like a sleeping swan. He was a tiny thing, white with splashes of black and tan, and a black "mask" ringing his eyes. He looked like a little bandit as he lifted his head, tilting it quizzically to the side with the right ear up and the other flopped over. He rose, trotted over to me and plopped down on the front steps as if to say, *"Finally,* I'm home!*"*

I walked around the neighborhood, trying to find where he had come from, with no success, so he spent a week at the local shelter. No one called about him, but someone claimed him—me. What to name him? I already knew. He had been wise enough to pick my lawn to sleep on so I would name him after one of the wisest men in history: Socrates.

I, however, wasn't wise enough to anticipate the reception from my two cats at home: Samantha, my big, gray eight-year-old tiger tabby, and her "daughter" Sabrina, my six-year-old white patchwork calico. Samantha took an instant dislike to the bouncing boisterousness of the Jack Russell terrier-mix. Chasing him into the kitchen, Samantha backed Socrates into the corner and scratched him from the middle of his forehead to the tip of his nose!

At that moment, Sabrina walked in.

Sabrina was a delicate beauty: huge light-green eyes, fine bones, aristocratic face, lean body and long legs. If she were human, she'd have been a prima ballerina. Snow white with calico markings splashed on the top of her head and on her side, she possessed a long tail perpetually at attention, curling into a question-mark tip. It looked like it had been dipped in calico sauce.

She sized up the scratched but spunky Socrates and sauntered seductively up to him. Touching the tip of his nose with her own delicate one, she curled her tail around his head as she wove through his legs. The little enchantress! Smitten by the spell she cast on him, from that moment on, Sabrina was his girl. She, in turn, looked to Socrates as her protector. She ran to him during thunderstorms. If she protested when I clipped her nails, he was there to investigate. If she screamed because Samantha or Wesley, my newest cat, pounced on her, Socrates chased them away. When Sabrina developed diabetes and had to endure insulin shots twice a day, Socrates was always by her side, ensuring that his girl wasn't hurt.

Then, in October 2002, Samantha passed away from cancer. During her illness, Sabrina sensed Samantha was in trouble. Sabrina shadowed Samantha—and Socrates shadowed Sabrina. When I took Samantha to the vet for overnight tests, Sabrina hung over the side of the sofa, head and front paws dangling down, staring blankly into space. Socrates sat below her, nuzzling her and cleaning her face. But as soon as he was finished, satisfied at a job well done, she'd heave a sigh and hang her head once again.

Her despondency grew after Samantha died. As Sabrina stared into space, the ever-concerned Socrates brought Sabrina his toys and his treats. When that didn't work, he sat and watched her, head between his paws. Nothing lightened her sadness. Then, every once in a while, Sabrina seemed like her old self, cuddling up to Socrates in his bed or following him around the house. Before long, Sabrina started losing weight rapidly and was diagnosed with chronic kidney failure. Although no longer diabetic, she was wasting away from dehydration, even with twice weekly fluid therapy. After every treatment, I'd bring Sabrina home to find Socrates waiting at the door for her, welcoming her as she stepped out of her carrier, bumping heads and touching noses. He followed her everywhere, knowing something was wrong but not understanding what.

Sabrina's light began to dim.

I stayed with her round-the-clock during the last three days of her life, making her comfortable as her breathing became shallower. Socrates kept vigil, watching with sad brown eyes. Concerned, he tiptoed to her. He gently placed his paws on the bed where she lay, gazing at her with love and longing. She opened her eyes to look at him, but couldn't expend the energy to move.

I made the agonizing decision to release her from her suffering. Cradling her in my arms, I explained to her that everyone loved her and would miss her. What were we going to do without her? She looked up at me as if she understood. She sighed and turned her head to look at her beloved Socrates, who was sitting quietly by the bed. I placed Sabrina on the floor, and she slowly, delicately and gracefully walked to him and touched his nose. We prepared for our last journey together.

Socrates didn't understand why his girl did not come

home that night. He sat stoically in front of me while I sobbed on the sofa. Heaving a sad sigh, he plopped down with his head on his paws, staring at her carrier in the hope she'd appear.

Over the next week, Socrates went from room to room looking for Sabrina. He sat in front of the door, waiting for her. He sat in front of her carrier. He jumped up on the couch to inspect her usual lounging spot. No Sabrina.

During this time, my wonderful vet called. "I'm calling to find out how you are."

"I'm hanging in there," I replied.

"I'm also calling to ask you something. Don't say 'no' immediately. I know this is tough. Do you remember the two kittens, the sisters, who were brought in a few weeks ago? The ones you met—the calico that looks like Sabrina and her tortoiseshell sister?"

"Ye-e-e-es," I slowly answered.

"They're yours if you want them. Just think about it. Don't answer now . . . just get back to me," the doctor said quickly, hanging up the phone.

I mentally ran through the litany of excuses: *It's too soon after Sabrina. I've had no time to mourn. What am I going to do with two babies? (Separating them was out of the question.) How's Wesley going to react? How's Socrates going to react . . . ?*

I mulled it over for almost a week.

"I'm naming them Serena and Esmerelda," I announced to my roommate six days after my vet had called.

"You're going to take them *both*?" She gaped at me.

I made the call.

A few days later, I brought them home—two tiny babies about fifteen weeks old. Serena, the smaller of the two, was Sabrina's carbon-copy spirit daughter: fine bones, long legs, white fur with a few calico patches, and the same dipped-in-calico-sauce patchwork tail. Esmerelda, stockier and more muscular than her sister, was the reverse: totally patchwork, save for a white bib on her chest, a white tummy and four white-mittened paws.

As I carried them into the house, Socrates bounced over to peek in the cage: "Babies! Kittens! Oh, boy! Oh, boy!"

I held him as my friend opened the cage; they came out slowly, bellies hugging the floor. Not able to hold back any longer, Socrates bounded up to them. Esmerelda, her sister's protector, gave her fiercest imitation of a spooky, spitting Halloween cat, all spiky fur and hisses. Serena cowered behind her—until she peeked through Esmerelda's legs and spotted Socrates. And he spotted her.

Having had enough of Socrates's enthusiasm, Esmerelda dove for protection behind the sofa. Serena, however, stood still while Socrates sniffed and snuffled her. And then . . . Serena began to weave around his legs. She twirled her tail around his head. She sniffed his chest. And then, she rubbed her face against his face. Serena had claimed Socrates for her own.

The babies, now adolescents, are double doses of high-octane energy, keeping Socrates—now ten years old with a bit of gray around the muzzle—in great shape. Serena runs in one direction; he chases her. She stops and spins around to gallop back across the floor; Socrates streaks after her. My very own Bugs Bunny cartoon! Curiously, the kittens' influence goes beyond playtime. Socrates has now begun to groom himself like a cat, licking his front paws to clean his face and ears.

The other day, Socrates was curled in his usual head-tucked-under-tail napping position in his fleecy bed. Serena caught sight of him sleeping as she stealthily came down the stairs. She slowly approached the snoozing Socrates and sat in front of him. Studying him for a bit, Serena began to clean his face. Startled, Socrates's eyes popped open and his head lifted a little. Serena, unperturbed, waited patiently for him to put his head back down. Seeing Serena, Socrates gently rested his chin on the bed. Sighing happily, he closed his eyes and grinned, enjoying his special calico girl's attentions.

Syndee A. Barwick

In a perfect state of catatonia

Saving Private Hammer

My company, Team Hammer, crossed the border into Iraq in April 2003 as the lead element of the 4th Infantry Division. As the last maneuver battalion, we jumped from hotspot to hotspot in central and northeastern Iraq until September, when we finally set up operations at an airbase in Balad, fifty miles north of Baghdad.

It was in November that I first noticed three kittens running around the base. Someone told me that they had been born under a shipping container about six or eight weeks earlier. There were dogs around the base—drawn by the food—but no other cats. Two of the kittens behaved like typical ferals and weren't interested in being around us soldiers.

That wasn't the case with the third kitten. He made himself conspicuous by constantly being underfoot in the large tent we used as a dining facility. You couldn't miss the little cat. He was as playful a kitten as I had ever seen—in fact, we called his antics "dinner theater." He chased after anything and everything, pounced on boots and batted wildly at anything that dangled. He was a complete clown and a welcome distraction from the battles raging around us. We named him Hammer, and he became our mascot. When I told my wife about the cat, she sent me a bright-red collar and "dog tag" for Hammer. It read: Pfc. Hammer, HHC 1/8 Infantry, Balad, Iraq.

Hammer was involved in almost everything that happened on the base. He ate with us, slept with us, went on missions with us. We fashioned a harness and leash out of parachute cord to keep Hammer safe when he left the base with us. He loved riding in the truck and was always one of the first to jump in when the door of a truck was opened. During artillery attacks, soldiers tucked Hammer inside their body armor for safekeeping. Everyone vied for the chance to have Hammer sleep with him; usually, the one who fed him at night got to have the warm and furry feline as a bunkmate.

For me, Hammer was a little piece of home. Our family had five cats at the time, and it felt so good having a cat with me—a living, breathing, purring daily reminder of my loved ones back in the States.

Even the "cat haters" loved Hammer. One of those was a soldier who had been badly injured. We snuck Hammer into the hospital to visit him. He was in the ICU and hooked up to a lot of monitors. He was so surprised. We put Hammer in his arms, and, although he wouldn't admit it, it was obvious Hammer made him feel better. The monitors gave him away. We could see that his blood pressure and heart rate improved while he held the cat.

Just down the hall were two Iraqi children who had been burned when the clay oven in their home had exploded. We brought Hammer to see them, and, although they couldn't speak English, their wide smiles and sparkling eyes made it clear that the cat was a special and welcome visitor.

Hammer was special to a lot of people. We called him our on-site stress therapist. When we returned from a mission, tired, dirty, stressed and jittery from all the adrenaline pumping through our systems, Hammer was there for us. He jumped into laps, rubbed against ankles and did whatever it took to get our attention. We knew we'd have to go out again in four or five hours, and it was important to relax. Hammer was the greatest at taking our minds off things and helping us feel comfortable and at ease.

Hammer was the pest-management officer for our base as well. Although he no longer had to hunt for food—we kept him well-fed—he continued to keep the mouse and rat population under control, which was important for maintaining our fresh food supplies. Hammer was simply doing his part.

As the weeks went by and the time approached for our company to return home, I couldn't imagine leaving Hammer behind. Everyone agreed that he was part of our company. He had done so much for our spirits; we wanted him to come back to the U.S. with us. At the end of January, I started sending e-mails and making phone calls—trying to arrange for Hammer to leave Iraq with the rest of Team Hammer in March.

It was a nerve-racking time for me. When Jordan closed its borders, our best chance of shipping Hammer home was lost. We set our sights on getting Hammer sent home via Kuwait City and the International Veterinary Hospital. Unfortunately, this would take funds we didn't have.

Alley Cat Allies and Military Mascots responded to my plea, and, with their help, we began asking for private donations to get Hammer home. But the time for our departure was fast approaching, and our plan for Hammer wasn't coming together as quickly as I'd hoped. I was getting worried—I knew Hammer's chances for survival were slim to none if we didn't get him home. It was coming down to the wire, and we began trying to find safe places for Hammer to stay in Iraq. We even had a wild plan to try to get a private plane chartered for the little guy.

Then the call came: The money was there! I was told to bring Hammer to Kuwait City to get his health certificate in preparation for his long journey home.

The final obstacle was getting Hammer across the border. The border patrol stopped every vehicle and searched it for contraband. Taking an animal across the border was in the gray area—some border guards would allow it, and others wouldn't. If the patrol were one of the ones who wouldn't, they would make us leave Hammer on the side of the road. But since this was Hammer's only opportunity to leave Iraq, we felt it was a chance we had to take.

Driving to the border, I was nervous. Hammer, in his handmade harness and leash, was oblivious to any tension and looked out the window at the passing countryside. As we pulled up to the border, we stopped, and the border-patrol guards began their search of our truck. Hardly daring to breathe, we watched as they made their way to the seat where Hammer was perched. They looked at the cat, but didn't say a word. They finished their search and signaled us to drive on. As we left the checkpoint, we breathed a huge collective sigh of relief and all high-fived each other—including Hammer. We'd made it!

In Kuwait City, we brought Hammer to the veterinary hospital where he was vaccinated, neutered and thoroughly vetted. Our company had to leave Kuwait before Hammer was ready to go, but he was scheduled to take a KLM flight to San Francisco and then on to Denver, where I would meet him at the airport.

Once home, I kept in touch with the hospital in Kuwait, and, finally, Hammer was okayed for departure. He was met in San Francisco by a volunteer from Pets Unlimited, a nonprofit veterinary hospital and shelter. The volunteer kept him overnight and then accompanied him to Denver. Pets Unlimited even donated a soft-sided carrier for Hammer to travel in.

When Hammer and his escort arrived in Denver, my family met them at the airport. The volunteer told me that Hammer had been quiet for the whole trip, but, as they walked toward us and Hammer heard my voice, he immediately began to purr.

It was an emotional reunion for me. Mostly, I felt relief. We had done it: Hammer was home—and he was safe. I held my old friend in my arms and savored the comfort of being together again.

For the most part, Hammer has adjusted well to civilian life. Although he was a cat who had lived with a lot of danger and learned to take it in stride, he found some things in his new surroundings pretty scary. He had never been around little children before, and his first encounter with my three-year-old grandson sent Hammer scurrying under the bed for cover. He soon accepted that these miniature people were all right, and today he has no fear of anyone who visits us.

He has also come to realize that our hamster, Zeus, is not a rodent that needs exterminating, but one of the family. As Zeus rolls around the house in his "hamster ball," Hammer watches with interest, but with no predatory gleam in his eyes. The other cats and dog have accepted Hammer, and he fits in well with the pack.

Some habits die hard, though. When it's time for bed, Hammer, used to sleeping with the enlisted men of Team Hammer, heads for what we call the "boys' room," where he, another male cat and my teenage son all bunk down together for the night.

Half a world away from Iraq, Private First Class Hammer is still on duty—lifting spirits and making people smile.

Rick Bousfield

Billu the Beauty, Henry the Hero

An animal's eyes have the power to speak a great language.

Martin Buber

Of my two cats, I always thought Billu would be the one to make a name for himself. He's the smart one, the orange-and-white calendar cat in the making, the extreme extrovert who flops over for a belly-rub and makes friends with anyone who visits the house. *Hi! I'm Billu! That's BEE-lu! Good to see you! Don't I have a beautiful belly?* Yet it was his brother, Henry—the "slow" one, the big-pawed, black-lipped tabby—who, in the summer of 2003, saved my life.

I was staying at our summer cabin by a lake in New Hampshire, a place I had been coming to since 1950, the year I was born. One afternoon in late July, I was sitting in the yard reading. The day was sunny; the humidity was low; lake water lapped tranquilly at the shoreline. When I heard Henry's characteristic chirp, I looked up to see him perched in the bathroom window, watching me quite intently. I found that odd—Henry never sat in that window and was rarely, if ever, awake at that time of day.

He cried to me several times, and, after I sang out, "Hi, Henry," I continued reading. He kept crying. My right arm and leg, I noticed, were strangely numb, asleep. I decided to get them moving by going for a swim. The lake water did the trick; the numbness disappeared. I said nothing to my husband.

But something was wrong, and Henry knew it. He paced around me all evening long, and, that night, he slept on the pillow next to the left side of my head, something I couldn't remember him ever doing. Usually he stretched out along my side, while Billu draped himself over my ankles. I woke up several times during the night, feeling absolutely awful: nauseated, dizzy and disoriented. *You're in for a nasty stomach bug*, I thought foggily.

By morning, the nausea was gone, but the numbness had returned. Henry kept butting my shoulder. When I stood up, I fell, but I was able, somehow, to stand again and walk normally. By now, Henry was wailing. Shrill and ceaseless, his message finally got through to me: Something was terribly wrong. I realized I had to get myself to a hospital—after, of course, feeding the cats.

Then I proceeded to make one of the stupidest decisions I've ever made: Since I didn't want to alarm my husband, I didn't wake him and drove myself to the ER—fifteen miles in my stick-shift RAV4. Miraculously, I made the drive without incident, and, some three hours later—after I'd given my insurance information to no fewer than seven people and been ushered into three examining rooms, where I was told to "wait"—I learned what I think Henry had sensed, or perhaps smelled, the day before: Over the past twenty-four hours, I'd had a "gradual" and cumulative stroke.

The ten days that followed remain vague in my memory. After a day or so, I was transferred to Brigham and Women's Hospital in Boston, where I stayed for a week. A clotting disorder, antiphospholipid antibody syndrome, lay at the root of my condition. The doctors assigned to my case seemed genuinely moved by the story I told to them (with a fair bit of mispronunciation and bizarre grammatical constructions) of Henry's warning. "He . . . him . . . save I think my life."

Maybe my husband could bring Henry down for a visit, one doctor suggested. But my husband and I agreed: *no*. He doesn't travel well, and he's too shy; he'd be terrified. I'd see him soon enough.

It's been a year now. As stroke victims go, I have been almost unbelievably lucky: I talk normally; I am writing again. I still get tired daily, but fatigue gives me a good excuse to cuddle and nap with the cats. I think I have a lot of years left. So, I hope, do Henry and Billu, who will both turn five in November. As always, they'll get a party. I'll sing "Happy Birthday" to them and buy them some treats. My guess is that they'll show their love for me the way they do every day: Billu will flop over and show me his beautiful belly, and Henry will chirp, jump into my lap and gaze up at me.

"How did you know?" I ask him sometimes. His purr, low and rumbly, is the only answer I get. But that's all right. As we look into each other's eyes, the difference between us fades away. We sit like that for a while, gazing at each other, no longer a cat and a woman, but simply two creatures who'd do anything for each other, anything in the world.

Cori Jones

The Cat Burglar

Ruth called the veterinary hospital where I worked and said that her cat hadn't been acting right for several days. "Could a vet come to my house and look at Puff?" the elderly woman asked the receptionist.

The receptionist had asked the standard questions: Can you bring Puff in? Can someone bring the two of you in? Can we come get you?

Ruth had answered, "I don't drive. I don't have any friends or family to give me a ride. I don't want you to come get me. I want you to come to my house. My cat is under the bed. He won't come out, and I'm worried sick about him. Please come!"

Now, house calls might have been common in James Herriot's time, but they are rare in today's veterinary world, so even my mentor, the experienced partner at our practice, couldn't offer much in the way of coaching. He just said, "You'd probably better bring Puff back to the hospital so that you can examine him properly, run any necessary tests and observe him for awhile."

So, minutes later, after finishing the day's surgeries, this recent veterinary-school graduate pulled out of the parking lot and headed out to make his very first house call.

When I got to Ruth's modest ranch house in the rural outskirts of Twin Falls, Idaho, my eyes searched for clues as to what I might find inside. I saw corrals, broken-down and empty; an old car with two flat tires and ten-year-old license plates; a doghouse with a chain, but no dog. This woman is definitely on her own, I concluded.

At my knock, the door opened a crack, and I heard, "Doc, is that you?" I was greeted by a caricature of a formerly robust ranch wife: withered, weathered and worried. "Let's go see Puff," she implored.

As I walked through the house, dodging a litter box, a pet bed, scratching posts and dozens of cat toys, I noticed current pictures of Puff on the refrigerator. I also noticed older pictures of family on the television. "Is this your family?" I asked.

Ruth replied, "Yes, my husband died almost twenty years ago, and both my children died in car accidents when they were very young." It was clear that Puff was the only family Ruth had.

Ruth led me to the bedroom where Puff was hiding under the bed. I bent down to look and saw a cat in distress—eyes dilated, breathing shallow and rapid. To a veterinarian, these signs said, "This cat has used up at least eight of his nine lives."

As I began to extract the cat from under the bed to examine him, he let out a long, mournful meow and began to struggle. As I continued to pull, the cat began scratching me. Then Ruth grabbed a nearby broom and began hitting me on the rear end, yelling, "Don't hurt my cat!"

"I'm not!" I probably screamed, since the cat's claws were digging into the flesh of my hand. "I'm just trying to get a good look at him!"

Luckily, this chaotic scene was cut short when Puff finally popped out. I lay the ball of longhair fluff on the bed and began to examine him. Mostly white, Puff's coat featured an iridescent shimmer. Too sick to struggle any further, Puff lay quietly as I ran my still amateurish, recent-vet-school-graduate hands over him, from the tip of his nose to the end of his bushy tail. I found that, underneath the flowing fur, was a skeletal frame. Remembering my mentor's words, I told Ruth that I needed to take Puff back to the veterinary hospital for tests, treatments, observation and consultation with my partner.

Ruth hesitated. This was not because she didn't want the tests done or because of the costs involved. With Puff gone, Ruth would be all alone. And from the expression on my face, she feared, rightfully so, that Puff might not ever come home from the hospital.

Finally, after a tearful good-bye, I put Puff into a pet carrier I had brought with me and headed back to the clinic. I had just entered the clinic and gotten Puff onto the table to draw some blood for tests when the receptionist poked her head in the back and exclaimed, "The police are up front. Ruth called them and told them that you stole her cat!"

I told her to send the officers back to me. I explained what had happened: Ruth was all alone, this was her only child, and, yes, in a way I had been a "cat burglar," but that she had asked me to help her cat. Puff needed urgent medical attention that could only be given at the hospital. With understanding smiles, the officers agreed to pay Ruth a visit and try to comfort her.

My veterinary team drew blood and took radiographs. We needed a diagnosis before we could begin treatment. The tests came back showing that a powerful, chronic infection was causing Puff's kidneys to fail. The prognosis was grim.

We started Puff on potent antibiotics and IV fluids, and put him on a special diet that allowed his kidneys to go on cruise control. But despite our best efforts—and the almost hourly phone calls from Ruth asking when she could bring Puff home—Puff continued to slip away.

Three days after pulling Puff from under the bed, I sensed death gripping him as I prepared to leave the hospital after my evening rounds. I rechecked the charts to make sure Puff had received all his medications and fluids; I rechecked the lab work, looking for anything we had missed—or for a sign of hope. But nothing looked encouraging. There seemed to be no hope as I checked on Puff and found him practically motionless where he lay on the blanket that was covering a heating pad. The cat was fighting for his life. I called Ruth and tried to prepare her for the devastating loss I knew was coming.

Ruth said, "Isn't there anything else you can do, Dr. Becker?"

I remember thinking, *There's nothing else I can do medically; Puff's a goner, and Ruth will be alone.* Out loud, I said the only thing that came to me, "I'm going to ask people to join in praying for Puff."

When I got home, I called the prayer chain at our church and told them about Ruth and Puff. They promised to lift them up in prayer and made plans to ensure that our church ladies would immediately start regular visits with Ruth, as I told them of the day, not far off, when Ruth would truly be all alone.

Shaking my head, I told my wife Teresa that being without Puff was going to kill Ruth. Then I walked outside onto the patio, and, looking up at the night sky, in full realization of my own impotence and helplessness in this drama, I asked a greater power for compassion and assistance.

Next morning, I walked into the veterinary hospital, filled with trepidation. Imagine my surprise when I was met by a wildly smiling, nearly-delirious-with-happiness veterinary technician, who informed me, "Puff is not only alive, he acts like he's ready to go home! He's eating, drinking, urinating and meowing incessantly."

When I saw Puff, I couldn't believe my eyes. Could this be the same cat that I'd left late the night before, so sick he'd have to get better to die? Incredibly, when I drew more blood, the lab tests revealed that the kidneys were working again. Puff's eyes danced with expectation. I translated his meowing: "Take me home to Momma!"

I raced to the phone to give Ruth the good news. "Puff is going to be okay," I blurted out as soon as she was on the line. "During the night, the medications and prayers healed him, and I'm going to make my second house call and bring him home to you just as soon as I finish my morning treatments."

Ruth said few words, but the muffled flow of tears spoke volumes.

When I got to her house, the door flew open as Ruth rushed as fast as her crooked, old legs would take her, scooped Puff out of my arms and kissed him all over his face. Puff kissed her back.

She invited me into the house for a cup of coffee to celebrate the homecoming. As I lowered myself into a chair at the kitchen table, I watched as Ruth went over to the cornucopia of treats spread on the counter and asked Puff which one he wanted. Apparently, he answered because Ruth said, "I figured you'd ask for that one, Puff."

Ruth thanked me over and over for saving Puff. Inside, I was thanking her. For I knew, as a fledgling veterinarian entrusted to take care of precious, four-legged family members, that I had discovered for myself a powerful new treatment tool. It was a tool they didn't teach me in veterinary school, but one that could be deployed anytime, by anyone, in any dosage, at no cost, and with no side effects—the power of prayer.

Marty Becker, D.V.M.

Ling Ling

We had been traveling for four months. My husband, Tyler, and I had backpacks and another month of adventuring ahead of us. At that point, we were in Thailand, spending a week in Prachuap Kiri Khan, a town of about thirty thousand people, 250 miles south of Bangkok. Prachuap isn't a Western tourist destination, which was part of what attracted us, and the city is dotted with dozens of elaborate temples, putting it at the top of the list of Thai tourists' domestic vacation spots.

One of the first places we visited was the town's predominant temple, constructed atop a hill overlooking the quaint town and the sparkling Gulf of Thailand. A winding set of stairs led to the ornate structure, maybe four or five hundred steps in all. At the base of the stairs, hordes of monkeys splashed in a water fountain crafted in the shape of a giant, smiling primate. One by one, the monkeys would clamber atop the statue's head and jump into the water below, squealing and tussling with each other, the cool water an evident relief on that hot day.

But one monkey abstained from the commotion of her compatriots. As my husband and I got closer, we saw the monkey was cuddling a white kitten with orange tabby patches. The kitten couldn't have been more than eight weeks old. The monkey groomed the cat with gentleness and devotion, stroking her tiny orange head. We weren't the only passersby to stop and stare at this unusual inter-species affection. Some Thai tourists watched and cooed, and one man put a banana in the hands of the monkey, who held the little kitten gently between her legs while she peeled the fruit.

The other monkeys weren't as docile. Some were down-right ferocious. As aggressive monkeys made advances, as if to steal the pet, we watched the monkey with the kitten snatch up her ward by the scruff of her neck and head for cover.

"Does this seem okay?" I asked my husband.

We worried that the kitten would be hurt, or worse. She looked healthy, but living with a belligerent troop of mon-keys couldn't be an ideal environment. We watched the Thais around us for signs of concern, but they seemed undisturbed by the kitten-toting monkey. As guests in their nation, we felt we should follow our hosts' cues. And the monkey clearly cared for her kitten.

The day before we were due to leave Prachuap, we decided to visit the temple on the hill once more. We told each other we wanted to take more photos, but we both knew our real motivation was to check up on the little cat. At the fountain at the base of the stairs, there was no sign of the kitten, but about halfway up, we found her in dis-mal condition. A dominant male monkey held the limp ball of white-and-orange fur by her hind leg. At first, we thought the kitten was dead. But, when the monkey put the cat down to shriek at another monkey trying to sneak up behind him, we saw the kitten meekly try to get up.

"Tyler," I said to my husband, "I want that cat."

My hero set to action. With the force of a bionic man, Tyler pulled a four-foot-long leafy branch off a nearby tree and held it in front of him like a shield. Armed and determined, he waited for his moment. The monkey knew he was being watched. The kitten had become a pawn in a nasty match of keep-away, and the monkey knew Tyler wanted in on his game. An audience of monkeys gathered around for this human/monkey rumble. Then, we got a break.

A group of Thai tourists was heading up the hill with bunches of bananas. The crowd of monkeys instantly forgot about the standoff and teemed around the Thais, screeching and grabbing for the fruit. But the male with the kitten stayed put with his prize. Tyler pretended he wasn't watching, standing nonchalantly with his big stick. The monkey looked at Tyler, then at the tourists and their bananas, then at Tyler again. The monkey couldn't help himself. Leaving the kitten, he went for the bananas.

With the speed of Flash Gordon, my husband snatched up the tiny cat. The monkey turned back instantly and snarled, showing glistening yellow fangs, and lunged for Tyler, who fended him off with his stick. Turning on his heel, Tyler made off down the stairs, kitten in one hand, weapon of defense in the other. I took off after him, and what seemed like the entire hill full of monkeys made pursuit. If you've never been under attack by a swarm of screaming primates, picture Dorothy in *The Wizard of Oz*, when the winged monkeys chase her. The Thai monkeys were swinging maniacally through the trees lining the stairs; the air was full of barred fangs and high-pitched shrieks.

At the bottom of the stairs, we ran across the street, barely glancing for oncoming cars, and, somehow, the monkeys gave up the chase. It seemed there was some sort of monkey demarcation line; the primates stayed on the wooded hill, while the town belonged to the humans. We sat on the grass in the shade of a tree in front of a little

store and looked over the tiny kitten, who was too weak
to be afraid. I went in for milk, which the cat lapped right
out of my hand. I shuddered to think of the last time she
had food or water; it had been six days since we'd seen the
kitten with her kindly monkey guardian. When she had
her fill, the cat lay in the grass and went to sleep. Tyler and
I watched the heave of her little chest, certain each breath
was her last.

An hour or two later, with the kitten still sleeping, we
made our way back to our hotel. Tucking her inside my
shirt, we snuck her into our room. We weren't sure what
the house rules were on pets, and we weren't stopping to
ask. We opened a can of cat food we'd picked up at the
store, and, to our delight, the kitten ate. She drank more
milk, used our makeshift litter box and fell asleep in a basket we'd lined with my sarong. We were amazed at her
resiliency; clearly this little cat was a survivor.

But what were we to do with her now? As much as we
wanted to, there was no way that we could take the cat
we'd named Ling, which is Thai for *monkey*, with us.
Traveling around Thailand with a kitten in tow would not
have been feasible—or very comfortable for the cat. And
international travel would have been extremely complicated. No, we would have to find a safe and loving place
for Ling right here in her native land.

We had eaten a number of times at a restaurant in town
where we had noticed a sleek, healthy-looking cat hanging around. It turned out the cat belonged to the kind Thai
family who ran the restaurant. Perhaps we could convince
them to adopt Ling.

We bought a beautiful basket and put cans of cat food,
milk and even some Thai currency inside. Then we set Ling
in the middle of the basket and went into the restaurant.

Through a combination of hand gestures and cartoon
drawings, we told the family Ling's story, while their

five-year-old daughter sang "Ling, Ling" in delight and petted the kitten's orange head. Ling purred in response with equal delight.

Eventually, they understood that we were asking them to make Ling their own, and they agreed. As we left for the train station, I gave Ling one last look and felt a bitter-sweet pang of regret—knowing we'd done what was best, even though it was hard to leave her behind.

When we returned to our home in Colorado, we decided it was time for us to get our own cat. Before long, two beautiful kittens, rescued as strays, came to us. We named the brother cat Sanook, which means *funny* in Thai, and the sister cat Suay, which means *pretty*. They are Ling's cousins in spirit, our own "Thai" cats here in America.

Theresa Dwyre Young

The Ashram Cat

The greatness of a nation and its moral progress can be judged by the way its animals are treated.

Mahatma Gandhi

In southern India, situated in the rolling hills and fields outside the city of Bangalore, there is an ashram. A traditional part of Indian culture, an ashram is a spiritual center where people go to meditate and sit in the presence of their spiritual teacher, or guru. The guru at this particular ashram is a man named Sri Sri Ravi Shankar. Known to his devotees as Guruji, Sri Sri is a youngish man—still in his forties—who radiates love, joy and a gentle humor. Like Mother Teresa and the Dalai Lama, Sri Sri is deeply committed to aiding humanity. Worldwide service projects, teaching programs and meditation courses are organized from the ashram, making it at once a haven of serenity and a bustling center for positive change in the world.

Sri Sri is frequently away, traveling to almost every country on Earth, teaching, lecturing and meeting with leaders of government, business and religion in the course of his humanitarian work. When he is at home at the ashram, he is at the hub of the activities there. Speaking to groups and individuals who come to see him and hear him speak, he rises early and stays up late.

A guru's personal living space at an ashram is called his *kutir*. Sri Sri's *kutir* is a small, simple cottage that sits off to the side of the property, surrounded by trees and a beautiful garden. Brightly colored birds roost in the branches of the trees, and fragrant flowers line the edges of the lawn. When Sri Sri is at home in the ashram, he often sits on the verandah of his *kutir* at night, enjoying his garden. On some nights, groups of people sit with him, listening to him speak on a variety of topics or asking questions for him to answer. This personal attention from the teacher is called receiving *darshan* and is treasured as being highly beneficial to the student's personal growth. Sometimes, no one speaks for long periods of time, and the silence is enjoyed together; the teacher's presence alone is a powerful gift of *darshan*. When it is time to sleep, Sri Sri rises from his seat on the verandah and goes inside his *kutir*. *Darshan* is over. And, quietly, his guests take their leave.

* * *

Late one night, just after an evening session in the garden, Sri Sri heard a noise outside his door. Thinking that someone wanted to speak to him, he opened the door, but didn't see anyone. Then he looked down to see a small gray cat.

In India—especially in the countryside—animals like cats and dogs do not commonly live in the house as pets the way they do in Europe and America. In rural India, most dogs and cats are feral and live as scavengers in the small villages.

The gray cat on the floor in front of Sri Sri didn't run

away the way that feral cats do, but instead sat calmly looking up at him. Sri Sri took the warm milk that he had been about to drink and set it down in front of the cat. The cat sniffed the milk delicately and began to lap it up. When the cat was done drinking, it walked to the edge of the porch, sat down and began to groom itself.

Sri Sri sat down in his chair. The cat finished its grooming, folded its front legs beneath itself, curled its tail around its body and closed its eyes. The night air was warm and soft. All was quiet except for the rustling of the leaves and the steady purr of the cat.

The man and the cat sat together, enjoying the peace of the night for a while. Then the cat stretched, stood up and jumped onto the garden wall. With one small meow, the cat leaped down on the other side of the wall and was gone.

This became a regular routine. Late at night, after everyone had gone, the little cat—a female—appeared on Sri Sri's verandah for milk and *darshan*. Sri Sri always greeted the cat with a soft, "Hello, my dear," and a smile.

The cat never came around when there were other people in the garden. The cat also seemed to know when Sri Sri was home and when he was away. Sri Sri asked people to give the cat milk when he was gone, but when someone else waited at night to offer it, the cat never came around. Clearly, the cat was after more than milk.

One night, when Sri Sri and the gray cat were sitting on the porch, the cat came close to Sri Sri's chair and sat looking up at him gravely. Sri Sri watched the cat for a moment, then said, "I think you need a name."

After sitting quietly for a few minutes longer, Sri Sri spoke again. "I already call you My Dear, so that will be your name."

My Dear slowly blinked her eyes a few times, then walked back to her spot on the edge of the porch and lay down. Another important Indian tradition—the giving of a spiritual name by the teacher—was complete.

*   *   *

Most nights, My Dear continues to sit with Sri Sri on the verandah, but only when no one else is there, and the cat and he can sit together undisturbed. Many people envy My Dear's private *darshan* with Sri Sri, but the cat asks little for her privilege and adds her own meditative presence to their evening get-togethers. With the passing of time, My Dear, the ashram cat, has become a part of the peace that pervades the *kutir* garden.

Shirley Harmison

Ariel and Pongo

Ariel, my cat, has two good eyes, four working legs and has never thrown herself into the path of a rattlesnake to save my life. There is, in fact, nothing extraordinary about her. Or so I thought.

In a household of ten pets, she has only distinguished herself by her relationship with my blue-and-gold macaw, Pongo. It has always surprised me that my cats, who regularly chase birds outside, have always kept their distance from him. Perhaps it's because macaws are so large and intimidating, but I like to think the cats know that "Mommy's bird" is off-limits.

Ariel, however, has a special fascination with Pongo. She sits at the base of his cage and looks up at him as though he were a god. In a way, he is. Food falls from his perch into Ariel's waiting mouth—cheese, chicken, whatever I feed him. I don't know whether it's the usual bird messiness or if Pongo is actually sharing his meals. Sometimes, Ariel will even stand on her hind legs and reach up into the cage with her paw. Although Pongo screams if any of the other cats do that, he accepts it from Ariel.

Once when I was leaving on a vacation, I arranged for

Pongo to spend two weeks at First Flight, a local bird store that accepted boarders. I always used a large cat carrier to transport him outside the house. He'd managed to chew some large holes in it, but it still served its purpose. I put the carrier on the kitchen counter and went into the living room to get Pongo. He walked readily into his carrier (his only pet trick); I latched the door and carried it to the car, placing it on the front passenger seat.

On the half-hour trip to First Flight, Pongo peered around, chewed a little on the plastic and held onto my finger with his claw. No squawks, no complaints.

We entered the bird store, and I put the carrier down on the counter. When I opened the door, Pongo walked out— a little quicker than usual, I noticed.

We settled him in his cage, and I picked up the carrier to leave. It was still heavy. How could that be?

I looked in and saw Ariel peering out at me. She had obviously climbed in before we left the house and traveled the fifteen miles in the carrier with Pongo. Neither had made a sound during the entire journey. Packed in together, neither had bitten or clawed—not a single feather or drop of blood was shed. Who would have believed it? No one in the bird store did.

In a world filled with warring nations, these natural enemies had forged a relationship that defied the odds. If birds and cats can get along, maybe there's hope for the rest of the world.

P.S. When I picked up Pongo two weeks later, he paused and looked into the carrier before he got in. He may be a bird, but he's not a birdbrain.

Kerri Glynn

Reunion

Strawberry Shortcake had only recently come to live with me. Her previous home was with a friend who'd relocated out of state. When he asked if I'd adopt her, I heard myself say yes before I'd even processed the implications. The next day, Strawberry was mine—lock, stock and litter box. Although I'd periodically kept her when my friend was away on business, it was one thing to enjoy a good cat's company on occasion, and quite another to become her permanent caregiver. Nevertheless, we were getting along famously and had settled into a comfortable routine.

As summer stretched into fall, however, Strawberry's flea allergy flared up. This being the days before the marvelous once-a-month flea treatments, a trip to the vet was the only solution to her discomfort. We needed to establish a relationship with a vet, anyway, so I chose the one closest to my rural home. I promised Strawberry it would be a fast trip as I bundled her into her cardboard carrier and trudged to the car. Normally pretty talkative, she uttered only a few plaintive meows as we headed down the driveway, then was silent.

The vet had a country practice, and his large parcel of farmland adjoined an even larger state wildlife-management area—a dense forest where black bears, deer, turkey, bob-cats, foxes and other wild creatures roamed. During the mile and a half drive in from the highway, the land on both sides of the empty dirt road was either rolling pasture dotted with cattle, or deeply shaded woods. Although Strawberry was quiet during the fifteen-minute ride, I figured she was nervous. "It's okay. I'm not leaving you there," I promised the green eyes peering through the cardboard cutouts. "It'll be over real quick, and I'll be right beside you the whole time."

We rounded a bend, and I saw the vet's two-story red barn located in the middle of a fenced cow pasture. The metal livestock gate was closed, and, not seeing any other way in, I parked outside it. Setting Strawberry's carrier on the grass, I labored to lift the gate, release its lock and push the clumsy thing open. Once she and I were in the pasture, I had to reverse the process to close the gate.

Large Holstein cows and Angus steer grazed everywhere, but only a few seemed curious about a woman toting a red-and-white cat carrier toward the barn. Once inside, the vet, a short, trim, middle-aged man dressed simply in jeans, boots and a plaid shirt, looked up, smiled and said, "Be right with you."

Strawberry had all but dissolved into the darkness of her carrier, and I had to peer hard through the peepholes to make out the paler markings of her gray-and-beige, longhair tabby coat. As still as she was, though, I knew ears, nose and brain were working hard to process all the different smells and sounds of this strange place.

Within minutes, the examination, diagnosis and shot had been completed, and Strawberry was back in her carrier. Since we were Doc's last appointment, he followed us out, turned out the lights and secured the door. Strawberry and I headed across the pasture, but Doc was going in the other direction, so I paused and turned to say good-bye.

Without warning, the bottom of Strawberry's carrier fell open, dumping her right on the grass. It happened so fast that she still had her legs tucked beneath her.

As I reached for her, the vet said, "Don't let her get away!" But Strawberry's reflexes were at least triple mine, and that silky fur slipped from my grasp. I watched in horror as she shot across the pasture, under the barbed wire fence, across the dirt road, up a bank and into the woods. In a heartbeat, she was gone.

Doc hustled over the barbed-wire fence, but my feet felt stuck to the ground as I called, "Strawberry . . . Strawberry . . . c'mere, Strawberry," struggling to make my voice sound normal.

"She'll never come to me, but I'll try to watch where she goes," Doc yelled over his shoulder. "Drive up into that area over there."

Seconds passed like hours as I collected the broken carrier and ran toward the car. I cursed the gate out loud when it fought my frantic efforts, then cursed everything in general as I jockeyed the car across the street.

"Last I saw her, she was up in that area and still going," Doc said, pointing into the forest. "Walk up that hillside," he advised. "Maybe she'll come to you. I'll stay here because she'll never come to me."

My heart pounded. *How will I ever find her?* I wondered, as I charged into the thick, dark woods. Briars and underbrush tore at my bare legs and sandaled feet. *But how can I just lose her like this?*

"Strrra-a-a-a-awberry . . . Strrra-a-a-a-awberry," I hollered every few steps, forcing my voice to sound normal. But my chest was tight with fear, and sweat beaded across my forehead as I continued the sweep through the trees.

Finally, reaching the spot where Doc had last seen her, I stopped and called. Nothing. The only sounds in the woods were my voice and my footsteps. I scanned the ground, the rocks and logs, even high into the trees. I had to admit she was gone.

Back at my car, I reported to Doc: "I never saw or heard a thing."

"Well, we've had two other cats get away like that," he said. "One was found—the other never did show up."

Just then a low rumble and a puff of road dust announced the arrival of a blue pickup. Doc turned and waved to the attractive woman behind the wheel. "That's my wife, and, I'm sorry, but I've got to leave. I'm afraid I wouldn't be much help anyway, since I'm the last person your cat will ever come to. But, look, why don't you go home and come back in a couple of hours. Maybe she'll come then. Or maybe she'll show up at the office. If you don't catch her tonight, we'll just keep an eye out and call you if we see her."

There was an hour of daylight left by the time I was home, had changed my clothes and loaded cat treats, the repaired carrier, and a jacket, pillow and thermos of water into the car. What-ifs flooded my mind, but I refused them lodging. Surely, Strawberry would retrace her steps, and I would be there when she did, even if it meant sleeping in the car. My house—my life—would be too empty without that little heartbeat. I was going to find Strawberry and bring her home. Period.

I sped along the dirt road, tires thumping over stones and gravel, and pulled a hard left into the parking area. Rolling down the window, I hollered up into the woods.

"Stra-a-a-a-awberry . . ."

What was that sound? I cut off the engine and leaped from the car.

"Stra-a-a-a-awberry . . ."

"MerrOOOOOWL," came the distant reply. It was the oddest, most mournful sound—not one I'd ever heard a cat make—but it had to be her. I rushed into the woods, stopping every few yards to call.

"*MerrOOOOOWL,*" she answered, call for call. I paused in the stand of trees where I had quit my search earlier that day.

"Strawberry . . . c'mon baby girl . . ." There was still no sign of her.

"*MerrOOOOOWL . . .*"

Suddenly, movement atop a rise about thirty feet ahead caught my eye. I could make out the familiar coat, then the ears, then the eyes.

"Good girl! C'mon right here!" She walked very steadily toward me, carefully picking her way among the briars and underbrush.

"*MerrOOOOOWL . . .*" With every fourth step, she repeated the cry.

I knelt down and shook her can of cat treats. When Strawberry was about ten feet away, up went the tail in her familiar greeting. She greedily ate the treats, and I talked to her while petting her all over. She wasn't any the worse for wear, and had only snagged a few burrs in her long, silky fur.

When I picked her up, she relaxed into my arms, purring loudly, and wriggled around to be tummy-to-tummy. Her front claws hooked securely into my blouse, and she clung to me like a marsupial. For several minutes we just hugged, grateful to be reunited.

At bedtime, Strawberry hopped up on my chest and, purring loudly, tucked herself neatly into a loaf shape facing me. I pulled my hands from under the covers to pet her and gently scratch all her favorite places. In those quiet moments, the magnitude of the near loss crashed down on me. "I need to talk about this, Strawberry," I said, tears filling my eyes. "I was really scared today, and you must have been, too. I thought we'd never see each other again. I'd never have you waiting for me at the door. Never again hear your purr. . ." She watched my face intently and purred even louder. "You are so precious to me."

She scooted up closer to my head, stretched out both front legs and took my face in her paws. We looked in each other's eyes, and, in that moment, realized the depth of our bond. As I turned out the light, we each drew a deep breath and drifted off to sleep.

Strawberry lay across my heart for the rest of the night.

Karen S. Bentley

Can You See Me?

When she was little, my sister used to poke her fingers beneath the bathroom door and wiggle them.

"Can you see me?" she'd ask.

"Go away," whoever was inside would answer.

She would shove her hand further beneath the door.

"Now? Can you see me now?"

"Yes, I see you now. Can you go away for a few minutes?"

The hand would disappear, and there would be a light thud as she leaned her small body against the door.

"When are you coming out?"

We were all happy to see that phase end, and I thought my days of being stalked through closed doors were over.

As an adult, I admit to giggling when friends moaned about how their children never left them alone, even when they were in the bathroom.

"Should've had cats," I informed them smugly.

But my life of bathroom solitude has been upended. Both my cats have recently decided that they can't abide a closed door, be it a closet door, bedroom door or—you guessed it—bathroom door.

They scared the daylights out of me the first time. I awoke in the middle of the night and groped my way to the bathroom. Half-asleep, I had just closed the door, when suddenly, *Whump!* The bathroom door flew open, and a small tabby cat stood illuminated in the doorway. She gazed steadily at me before turning away. My heart raced. I felt like I'd been given a warning visit by the kitty Mafia: *Keep the door open, or else.*

I alerted my husband the next morning. "Better lock the door when you're in the bathroom."

"Why?"

"It's the cats," I said, looking over my shoulder. "They don't like closed doors."

"Uh-huh," he said slowly. "And I should be concerned . . . why?"

But Mister Oh-So-Smart wasn't laughing when the cats body-slammed the bathroom door open while *he* was inside. I was upstairs when I heard his call for help.

"Would you get the cats out of here?" he asked. "I'd like some privacy."

So we started locking the door. That's when tiny paws began to appear underneath the door.

It was cute for a while. A tiny white paw would slide beneath the door and tap the floor.

Can you see me?

But then there was the talking. Finding that the door wouldn't budge and, unable to reach us from beneath the door, the cats would sit outside the locked door and "talk" to the person inside.

"Mrow. Rowr-rowr. Mow?" When are you coming out?

The best, though, was coming home early and finding both cats sitting outside the bathroom where my husband had locked himself in. He was talking back to them.

"Rowr? Meow, meow," said the cats.

"Yeah, I know. I hate when that happens," he answered through the closed door.

"Purr, rowr-meow."

"Really? So what did you say back?"

"Mow! Psfft! Meow."

"Ah, ha-ha," he said. "You are so clever."

"Honey?" I knocked. "Everything okay?"

There was a moment of silence. "I have no idea what you're talking about," he called back.

I wasn't letting him off that easy. I squatted on the floor and wriggled my fingers beneath the door. "Can you see me?" I asked.

"Go away," he said.

I scratched on the door. "So when are you coming out?"

"The minute I do, I'm having you committed," he warned. "Go away!"

And so it went. We had pretty much resigned ourselves to the situation when luck struck.

One day, I went into the bathroom and didn't close the door. No cats appeared. Excellent. I shared my discovery that night with my husband.

"I broke the code!" I said. "We need to adopt an open-door policy. If you don't close the door, they take no interest in what you're doing."

He seemed less than thrilled. "But I like closing the door."

I sighed. "Close the door and have an audience, or enjoy the peace of an open one. It's your choice."

"I miss our life before cats," he said.

He had a point. It was nice when we had some say over the ajar status of doors in our home. Still, even with all the bother, it's nice knowing you are so important to someone that every minute apart counts.

"Mrow?"

Yes, I'll be out soon.

Dena Harris

Mayor Morris

In his younger days, our cat Morris, now sixteen years old, was the mayor of our neighborhood. A stray I adopted from our local animal shelter when he was about a year old, Morris settled into life as an apartment dweller quite easily, content to give up scavenging for meals and dodging dogs and cars for food from a can and a sunny square of carpet to nap on. Yet as happy as he was to have a home, Morris never completely gave up his love of the outdoors. He would sit for hours by the open bedroom window in our apartment, his nose pressed to the screen, sniffing the air and watching the activity in the park three stories down. At first, I thought he wanted to be out in the fresh air and sunshine, but soon, I realized that it was the hustle and bustle of the outside world that he missed.

When my husband and I moved to our first home—a red-brick row house on a tiny street in Philadelphia—Morris would sit with us on our stoop or lounge in our miniscule front yard greeting the neighbors and holding court. In the spring, he'd sit on our elderly neighbor's stoop, a pace or two from our own door, supervising her attempts to plant flowers in her patch of dirt. On Halloween, he'd wait at the front door for the trick-or-treaters, his amber eyes glinting in the candlelight from the jack-o'-lanterns. And when our daughter started walking, he'd station himself on the sidewalk in front of the house, keeping a watchful eye on her as she clattered past him, up and down the street, behind her push toys. Morris never seemed to want to venture more than a few feet from his own front door.

A few years later, expecting twins and suddenly needing much more space, we bought a house in a nearby suburb, on a quiet street that wound around in an elongated oval, beginning and ending at the top of the hill. The only traffic was the morning and evening rush of a half-dozen cars taking neighbors to and from work, and the mail and UPS vans making their occasional deliveries.

One midsummer morning, when we had been living there a few months, I walked to the end of our driveway to collect the newspaper, Morris trotting at my heels.

"Is that your cat?" someone called, as I bent to retrieve the papers.

I straightened up. A trim woman in her fifties wearing bright-pink walking shorts and a sleeveless button-down shirt was crossing the lawn toward me. I knew she lived in the house to the right of ours with her husband and a twenty-something-year-old son, but I had not yet met her. I had not met many of our neighbors since I had been closeted in the house for most of the late spring and early summer, first on bed rest, then taking care of my newborns.

"Yes," I said as she stepped onto my driveway. "This is Morris. And I'm Meg. It's nice to finally meet you."

"It's nice to meet you, too," she said, introducing herself and shaking my hand. "And it's nice to know your name," she said, squatting to scratch Morris behind his ears. "My husband will be happy, too," she said, gazing up at me. "Now he'll know what to call him," she said.

My face must have shown my confusion because she laughed.

"My husband and your cat—Morris—have breakfast together on our patio every morning," she explained, standing up. "One morning just after you moved in, my husband went out with his coffee and the newspaper and found Morris sitting in one of the chairs. They had a lovely chat. Now, Morris waits for him on the patio every morning. My husband reads the paper to him, and they discuss world events, don't you Morris?"

Morris had apparently made more friends in the neighborhood than I had in the few months we'd been living there. Every morning he'd meet our neighbor on his back patio for coffee and conversation. Then he'd spend some time playing with the poodles in the house to the left, sitting in the grass at the edge of our driveway just beyond the boundary of their invisible fence, while the dogs ran back and forth, barking and wagging their tails.

When the fall came, he began ambling to the foot of our driveway every afternoon to wait for the school buses to drop the neighborhood kids at the top of the street. He'd greet each kid as they came down the hill past our house, accepting pats and scratches behind his ears. And on Halloween, he took up his place next to the pumpkins and greeted the trick-or-treaters.

Shortly before Thanksgiving every year, our neighbors to the right would travel to Florida, where they spent the winter. Morris took this as a sign to retreat into the house for the winter. In April, when the weather grew warm again, our neighbors would return, and Morris would resume his daily round of social activities. But one spring, our neighbors didn't return. Instead, a for-sale sign appeared in front of the house. Our neighbors had decided to stay in Florida, their son told us when he came by one afternoon to check on the house.

"Oh, by the way," he said, getting into his car, "my dad said to say hi to your cat. He really misses their conversations."

I knew Morris missed those conversations, too. He still waited on the patio every morning for his friend to come out for breakfast.

The house sold quickly, to a Korean family with two teenage daughters and an elderly grandmother. They were friendly neighbors. The girls always stopped to talk to our children when they were playing outside, and the parents would wave and chat for a few minutes whenever we happened to be picking up our newspapers or getting into our cars at the same time. But the elderly grandmother never said a word, ducking her head and looking the other way the few times we'd seen her in the front yard. I'd overheard her granddaughters speaking to her in Korean and suspected that she didn't know any English.

One summer morning, I was watering the plants on our back deck when I heard the soft quavering voice of the elderly grandmother on her patio below. She was speaking quickly and quietly, a steady stream of words in Korean. Occasionally, she'd pause as if asking a question, but I heard no voice answering back. *She must be talking to herself,* I thought. Quietly, I peered over the deck railing. She was sitting at the wrought-iron table with a cup of tea. Morris, in the chair next to her, was listening intently as she talked to him.

The mayor of the neighborhood had done it again! Morris had a new breakfast companion, and our elderly Korean neighbor had a new friend.

M. L. Charendoff

"Can't talk now—I'm working."

Trash-Pickin' Kitty

When I adopted a kitten from a local animal shelter, I knew I was in for a real test of my patience. I had raised two other cats, big boys now, and felt sure I was ready for the chaos a new kitten would bring back into my life—and my heart. I did all the right things, like buying top-brand, expensive cat food; a big, soft bed and all the best cat toys available. But I soon began to notice that this playful and demanding little being named Lucy had her own ideas of what was best for her.

She only wanted table scraps, she would rather sleep on *my* bed than hers and she scoffed at her store-bought toys, preferring to amuse herself for hours by stealing balls of paper out of my office wastepaper basket. As a writer, I often tried to discourage her from bothering me when I was in my office working, but, try as I might, she would sneak in and overturn the trash can, running off with a mouthful of my old notes and tossed-off ideas. I would yell at her, scold her, try to encourage her to play with her "real" toys—the ones that cost me an arm and a leg—but I could not change her. My patience was wearing thin.

Determined to turn her into a good little kitten, I started locking Lucy out of the office when I was working, only to find her sitting outside the door with big, sad eyes when I came out for a breather. Sometimes, she would dart in between my feet and go straight for the trash can before I even knew what was happening. Then I'd raise my voice and lightly tap her rump, causing her to drop the wad of paper in her mouth and slink off into a corner. I hated to scold her, but she had to stop!

The tables were about to be turned.

Not long thereafter, I realized I had accidentally thrown away a great and very timely story idea, along with a magazine editor's name and contact number, given to me by a supportive writer friend. Frantically, I searched through my half-full trash can, only to realize I had emptied it—and the story idea—the day before in time for the trash pickup. Defeated, I struggled to remember what I could of the idea that I had fleshed out, and figured I could always call my friend—until I realized she was in Europe for two weeks on vacation! I doubted she had the magazine editor's name and phone number with her on her travels.

Resigned to the fact that I would lose the lead completely—or get the info I needed only after someone else had probably covered the story—I resolved never to write ideas on scraps of paper again. Instead, I would type and save them on my computer immediately.

I sat there thinking about all the other ideas and notes I had probably tossed out prematurely or accidentally when I heard a sniffing, rooting sound and turned to find Lucy pulling out a wad of paper from my trash can. I went ballistic, chasing her out of the room and up the stairs to her little cozy corner, where I noticed a handful of other balls of paper on the floor. She hid under a chair and watched me as I picked up the scraps, swearing under my breath. But then I stopped dead—as I noticed one particular paper ball with my handwriting on it. As I unfolded it,

I shook my head in disbelief! It was my story idea, and the magazine editor's name and number!

I grabbed Lucy out from under the chair and hugged her tight, smooching her and praising her. She looked at me in total shock, then snuggled her little kitten nose into my chest. I hoped that meant she forgave all my impatience and rude behavior. For, in that instant, I knew that a trash-pickin' kitten is the best kitten a writer could ever have.

No more would I try to change her or scold her for being herself. I love Lucy—just the way she is.

Marie D. Jones

Volunteer of the Year

Last spring, a very special volunteer in our charitable organization nearly lost his life to a reckless driver. Our relationship with this volunteer had begun long before with a chance visit. Like most visitors, he first entered our offices through the front door—what was unusual is that he walked in on four legs!

Our charity is nestled in a residential community a block from the beach in the beautiful city of White Rock, British Columbia. We often leave the front doors open to catch a bit of the summer breeze blowing in from the ocean. One afternoon eleven years ago, an orange-and-white tabby cat appeared. He was so overweight that we thought "she" was pregnant. First, he stuck his head inside the door to see what was inside. When nobody chased him out, he walked past the counseling reception office, through the empty waiting room, then boldly marched up the stairs to the administration offices.

He made friends with all the right people: our executive director, Martin; our volunteer coordinator, Valerie; and our executive secretary, Maureen. Valerie talked with the neighbors and discovered that our visitor's name was Tigger. A social worker who lived across the street from our office had taken him in when his family moved to another province. Lonely, he came into our building to be with people. One or two counselors thought it was unprofessional to have a cat in the building, but he had friends in high places. Martin received letters from counseling clients saying how comforting it was when Tigger jumped into their laps and curled up, purring. He was also a regular visitor to our playgroup for developmentally delayed infants. Some of these children said "kitty" as their first word. In light of his valuable service, Valerie formally added Tigger to our volunteer list.

After a year, the social worker moved away, and Tigger moved in with a retired couple next-door to us. The gentleman passed away soon afterward, and his widow, Olive, told us that caring for Tigger helped her to cope with the loss. However, he did not forget about us. He continued his visits and brightened the day for many clients and staff, also creating a bond between Olive and many of our employees. Valerie gave Olive a special plaque with Tigger's picture and a bronze plate engraved with "Volunteer of the Year."

Last spring, Tigger was hit by a car. A neighbor discovered his broken body, and he was rushed to the veterinarian. His injuries were terrible. The veterinarian held out little hope for Tigger's survival and advised that the kindest thing would be to let him go. Olive could not bear the thought of putting him down without trying to save him, so she told them to make every effort. Many of us went to visit him during the weeks that he was in the hospital.

On my first visit, the receptionist led me into the back. The smell of antiseptics, medicine and animals hit me as soon as I walked through the door. Along two of the walls were several cages with animals in various states of distress. Tigger was lying on a metal table in the center of the room. Seated beside it, a veterinary assistant was giving him a shot of antibiotics and painkillers. She invited me to come closer.

An IV tube protruded from his little paw. His face was a mess. His jaw, which had been broken in two places, was wired shut. He had a broken pelvis, and his hind legs were in casts. He looked so small and fragile. The assistant asked if I wanted to stay and feed him. Carefully, she placed him back in his cage, settling him down on a soft blanket. There was a dish of soft food in one corner of the cage. I picked up a small spoon, scooped up a tiny bit of the food and held it to his mouth. He could not lift his head, although he tried. He stuck his tongue out a little to get a taste. Intravenous feeding would be necessary for a while longer.

For the first week, we did not know if he would make it, but, each time he had a visitor, his spirits seemed to lift. By the second week, we were very hopeful. By the third week, the veterinarian had to limit visits, saying, "We've never had a patient with so many visitors. It does seem to have made a difference, but he needs his rest."

After a few weeks of recovery and careful observation, Tigger was able to go home. He was honored at our annual volunteer-recognition luncheon in April, and the local newspaper ran a story on him, complete with photos.

Although Tigger no longer comes to the office, he will always have a very special place in our hearts. We are so delighted that we, his friends and colleagues, were able to give this little creature the will to live in return for the pleasure and service he's given so freely over the years.

Edi dePencier

To Find a Friend

You can't own a cat. The best you can do is be partners.

Sir Harry Swanson

During the summer of 2003, the Mustafa Hotel in Kabul, Afghanistan, was thronged with journalists, aid workers, American embassy personnel and businessmen. It offered a wide range of amenities—and a place to find peace after a hard day of stark encounters with the grinding desolation of this war-ravaged city.

As a freelance journalist based in Kabul for my second straight year, I felt reduced to a state of profound depression by circumstances both personal and political. I longed for peace. But what I needed most was a very special friend, a sort of cosmic messenger to miraculously appear and reconnect me to all the goodness and beauty of the universe.

I had such a friend in Kabul the year before. Though now safe at home in America, I had rescued the darling little tuxedo kitten, Queen Soraya, from Kabul's devastated streets, saving her from a stark fate. Now, I needed some fellow inhabitant of Earth to do the same for me.

I was heading toward Pashtunistan Square, a once-grand public space in front of the presidential palace, when I saw him. Right in front of me on the broken sidewalk, as if he had appeared out of nowhere, was a tiny, handsome, tiger kitten, calmly surveying the grim scene of beggars, street kids and *burqa*-shrouded women. Well-groomed, alert and self-possessed, he was the only whole and healthy thing amid the battered vista.

I scooped him up like a parched man reaching for his first sip of water and plopped him into my briefcase among my clippings and notes. He accepted this with perfect equanimity, as if he had been waiting for such a thing to happen. After I zipped him inside, he pushed his pink-and-black nose through the breathing space left open at the end, his darling kitten snout pointing the way back to the hotel.

Once in the garden of the hotel, I proceeded to examine him. The kitten sported intricate black tiger stripes on a field of gray—and his underside was covered with spots. "So you are not only a *babur*, you are also a *palang!*" I said to him, using the Dari (an Afghan dialect) words for *tiger* and *leopard*. "You must be very hungry. I will fetch you a meal fit for both."

I fed him my own poor fare—a U.S. Army ration Meals Ready to Eat (MRE)—and pondered what name to give this special little boy who had come into my life when he was most needed. I settled on Dost Mohammad Khan, after the nineteenth-century king of Afghanistan who had been overthrown, but had returned to lead his people to independence and justice. *Dost* also means "friend," and, indeed, I needed one badly. After obtaining permission to keep him with me—he could stay in the hotel garden—my kitten and I began our life together.

Oh, what fun Dost and I had that summer! He was the

most agile, bouncing, playful and happy kitten I had ever seen. He brought sunshine back into my life with his antics, his every movement directed at a joyous affirmation of life. No rose garden could hold him, though. He continually and literally pushed boundaries, racing along the adjoining hotel rooms and darting in any doors left open for curious exploration.

Dost became the darling of the hotel, but no one appreciated his presence more than I. Any hour of the day, Dost met me with welcoming meows so sincere and pure, it was obvious he considered me as special as I did him. He'd grab my pant leg, begging to be held, and then would furiously rub his little pink-and-black nose against mine. I began sneaking Dost into my room at night to indulge in late-night play sessions. Then we'd sleep side by side until he awakened me the next morning with a loving rub against my nose, and I'd sneak him back to the garden for his MRE breakfast.

But sunshine again turned to darkness the day Dost went missing from the hotel.

I looked everywhere, I asked everyone, but no one had seen him. The hotel is a closed and secure compound, with only one way in and out. The little darling of the hotel would not have been allowed to make such an exit by those who knew him. What had happened? I lay awake in my room that night unable to sleep—alone once more, and overwhelmed by feelings of solitude and powerlessness.

The next morning, I learned that workmen doing renovations—not part of the close-knit Mustafa family—were annoyed by his kitten antics, and, to get him out of their way, had often tossed Dost onto the first-story roof that flanked the garden. This last time, he'd obviously jumped to the adjacent alley to resume his explorations of the city of his birth. My dear friend was once again forced to survive without the nurturing hand that desperately needed *his* nurture.

There was only one thing to do: I had to spread the word.

I placed an ad in *The Kabul Weekly,* a widely read bilingual journal, describing Dost and the circumstances of his disappearance. I included a reward of 2,500 afghanis (about $50) for his return, the equivalent of a month's pay in a city racked by unemployment and desperate poverty.

"I hope it is not a joke," the editor said, very seriously.

"On my honor, it is not," I answered. "We *feringhee* (foreigners) have very strong feelings about cats."

Knowing that it would not be enough to simply print an advertisement that many would ignore or regard with derision, I resolved to take more aggressive steps in the search. All Kabul had to know about my quest.

I enlarged the advertisement, made hundreds of copies and posted flyers everywhere: in front of embassies and United Nations offices; opposite the central, blue-domed Pul-i-Khisti mosque; across from Kabul's only synagogue and its two Hindu temples; at kebab stalls and teahouses; and along the fabled commercial boulevards of Chicken and Flower Streets. People took time from pressing business to read about the lost cat. Those who could not read—tragically, a majority of the Afghan population—were told of my quest by those who could.

"His name is Dost!" I heard a woman in a fringed sky-blue *burqa* tell a ragged little boy outside the Mustafa. "He is the kitten of a very great *feringhee* who loves him very much and will pay much for his return."

The extent of my greatness was certainly exaggerated by the lady, and the reward was only big in Afghan terms, but she was right about the love part.

The tens of thousands of dirty, ragged children who constantly wander the streets seeking money seemed a promising resource to help retrieve my beloved little wanderer. The only issue was one of conscience: Was it right to use the street children of Kabul toward a personal end, and would I be hurting or helping them in any way?

Most of these waifs are not orphans, but have families dependent on them for survival. There are two schools of thought as to how to deal with the street kids. One is that, as long as the situation in Afghanistan remains so grim, the way of compassion lies in giving them a little something to ensure that they and their families will live to see the better day that the international community is striving to bring about. The other is that individual charity actually hurts them by rewarding the choice of a life on the streets, when they would be better off in school. My own position came to be a compromise between the two, which influenced me to enlist their aid in finding Dost.

I explained my mission to a couple of boys I knew and gave them flyers to pass on to their fellow waifs. I repeated this action on street corners around town. On the whole, the kids were energized by the task I had given them, inspired in no small part by the prospect of the life-transforming sum of money. The fun and play were just as important to them, though—looking for a lost cat relieved the daily drudgery of begging or selling wares, and reintroduced a childlike element back into lives devoid of such innocent endeavors. I took solace in this, and joy in the new sense of wonder I had given them.

My quest to find my friend thus became a citywide phenomenon, the talk of teahouses and kebab stalls, the subject of concerned, quizzical, as well as condescending comments. Yet, after two weeks of heroic striving, there was still no sign of Dost, and I began to feel that I would never see my precious kitten again. How could my campaign that had become the talk of Kabul have failed to yield even a single sighting of my little friend? As I listlessly sipped green tea in my room at the Mustafa, there was a knock at the door, and I opened it to find one of the hotel boys standing there with a Cheshire cat grin on his face.

"Mr. Vanni, there is a little girl downstairs who is asking for you," he beamed. "I think she has some good news for you."

I raced down two flights of stairs into the lobby, where I beheld a sight that I will remember and treasure for the rest of my life.

There in the entrance, bathed in the particular crystalline light of a Kabul afternoon, stood a tiny schoolgirl wearing the universal Afghan girls' school uniform of black trousers, black jacket and white headscarf. She gently rocked something wrapped in a blue shawl, cradling it in her arms like a new mother. Her light-brown oval face seemed perfect in its innocent beauty, save for a scar on one cheek, which was completely obscured by her radiant smile. As she held out the bundle toward me, a little feline head popped up.

"Do-o-o-o-ost!" giggled the girl.

There he was, magnificent in his tiger-leopard uniqueness, once again singing that joyous meow of recognition that had come to be the sweetest music in the world to me. A few moments of passionate nose rubbing and a quick glance at those special markings dispelled all doubts. Dost was back. I had found my little friend.

"Where did you find him?" I handed the girl her richly deserved reward, which I imagined would help her buy schoolbooks and provide for her family.

She spoke no English, so one of the guards interpreted.

"She found him where she lives, in Khair Khana," he said. "She was on her way to school, and he was just there on the sidewalk, watching everyone pass."

"Khair Khana!" I exclaimed as I held Dost up in front of

my face. "That's all the way over on the western part of town, miles away! Dost, how did you get all the way over there?" I laughed with that special relief that follows an averted disaster.

A vigorous and self-affirming meow was the only description he offered of what must have been an epic two-week odyssey of dodging cars, avoiding dogs, negotiating rubble and scrounging for food. After profusely thanking the blushing child and giving her some candy as an extra mark of my gratitude, I triumphantly bore Dost up to my room.

There was no question of his returning to live in the rose garden after such a close call and long agony. I resolved that he would stay safe in my room until I took him back with me to America. I wanted to give him a new life and fill his world with sunshine, as he had done for me here in this beautiful, yet heartbreaking place called Kabul.

Vanni Cappelli

[EDITORS' NOTE: *This award-winning story first appeared, in a different form, in* CAT FANCY *magazine.*]

READER/CUSTOMER CARE SURVEY

REFG

We care about your opinions! Please take a moment to fill out our online Reader Survey at **http://survey.hcibooks.com**.

As a **"THANK YOU"** you will receive a **VALUABLE INSTANT COUPON** towards future book purchases as well as a **SPECIAL GIFT** available only online! Or, you may mail this card back to us and we will send you a copy of our exciting catalog with your valuable coupon inside.

(PLEASE PRINT IN ALL CAPS)

First Name _____ MI. _____ Last Name _____

Address _____ City _____

State _____ Zip _____ Email _____

1. Gender
- ❑ Female
- ❑ Male

2. Age
- ❑ 8 or younger
- ❑ 9-12
- ❑ 13-16
- ❑ 17-20
- ❑ 21-30
- ❑ 31+

3. Did you receive this book as a gift?
- ❑ Yes
- ❑ No

4. Annual Household Income
- ❑ under $25,000
- ❑ $25,000 - $34,999
- ❑ $35,000 - $49,999
- ❑ $50,000 - $74,999
- ❑ over $75,000

5. What are the ages of the children living in your house?
- ❑ 0 - 14
- ❑ 15+

6. Marital Status
- ❑ Single
- ❑ Married
- ❑ Divorced
- ❑ Widowed

7. How did you find out about the book?
(please choose one)
- ❑ Recommendation
- ❑ Store Display
- ❑ Online
- ❑ Catalog/Mailing
- ❑ Interview/Review

8. Where do you usually buy books?
(please choose one)
- ❑ Bookstore
- ❑ Online
- ❑ Book Club/Mail Order
- ❑ Price Club (Sam's Club, Costco's, etc.)
- ❑ Retail Store (Target, Wal-Mart, etc.)

9. What subject do you enjoy reading about the most?
(please choose one)
- ❑ Parenting/Family
- ❑ Relationships
- ❑ Recovery/Addictions
- ❑ Health/Nutrition
- ❑ Christianity
- ❑ Spirituality/Inspiration
- ❑ Business Self-help
- ❑ Women's Issues
- ❑ Sports

10. What attracts you most to a book?
(please choose one)
- ❑ Title
- ❑ Cover Design
- ❑ Author
- ❑ Content

TAPE IN MIDDLE; DO NOT STAPLE

BUSINESS REPLY MAIL

FIRST-CLASS MAIL PERMIT NO 45 DEERFIELD BEACH, FL

POSTAGE WILL BE PAID BY ADDRESSEE

NO POSTAGE
NECESSARY
IF MAILED
IN THE
UNITED STATES

Chicken Soup for the Soul®
3201 SW 15th Street
Deerfield Beach FL 33442-9875

FOLD HERE

Comments

Do you have your own Chicken Soup story
that you would like to send us?
Please submit at: **www.chickensoup.com**

3

A FURRY R_X

Cats are a tonic, they are a laugh, they are a cuddle, they are at least pretty just about all of the time and beautiful some of the time.

Roger Caras

Laser, the Therapist

The moment he reached his little paw through the cage bars at the humane society, I was a goner. I wasn't looking for another cat—I already had two—but was just stopping by to give the animals some attention. When the shelter volunteer, apparently knowing a sucker when she saw one, asked if I would like to hold him, there was no longer any doubt. He came home with me that day.

He was a gorgeous cat, a five-month-old blue-point Siamese with eyes like blue laser beams: thus, his name. Right from the beginning, it was obvious that Laser was an exceptional cat. He loved everyone—the other cats, visitors to the house, even the dog who later joined the household.

I first heard about animal-assisted therapy several months after we adopted Laser. While most of what I heard was about dogs, it occurred to me that Laser would be perfect for this type of work. I signed up for the training class, and, after completing the preliminary requirements, Laser and I passed the test to become registered Delta Society Pet Partners.

While he had always been a little lovebug at home, Laser found his true calling when we began to go on visits. Whether it was with sick kids at the children's hospital, seniors with Alzheimer's disease, or teens in a psychiatric unit, Laser always knew just what to do. He curled up on laps or beside bed-bound patients and happily snuggled close. He never tried to get up until I moved him to the next person. People often commented that they'd never seen a cat so calm and friendly. Even people who didn't like cats liked him!

One young man, who had been badly burned in a fire, smiled for the first time since his accident when Laser nestled under his lap blanket. A little boy, tired and lethargic from terminal leukemia, rallied to smile, hug Laser and kiss his head, and then talked endlessly about Laser after the visits. Several geriatric patients with dementia, who were agitated and uncommunicative prior to Laser's appearance, calmed down and became talkative with each other and the staff after a visit from my therapeutic feline partner. It has been our hospice visits, though, that I consider the most challenging and rewarding of all our Pet Partner experiences.

One day, I got a phone call telling me about a hospice patient at a nearby nursing home who had requested a visit by a cat. At the time, only one cat—Laser—actively participated in the local program. Even so, my first inclination was to make some excuse not to do it. I have always had issues with death and dying, and a hard time talking about it to anyone, but I quickly realized how selfish I was being—the poor woman was dying, and all she asked was that I bring my cat to visit. I said yes.

A few days later, we made our first visit. Mrs. P. was ninety-one years old, and although her body was weak, her mind was still very sharp. It was a little awkward at first (what do you say to a perfect stranger who knows she's dying?), but Laser was a great conversation catalyst. He crawled into bed with her and curled up right next to her hip—exactly where her hand could rest on his back.

She told me stories about the cat she and her husband had years ago.

"See you next week," she said as we got up to leave.

We visited every Sunday during the three months that followed, and a real friendship developed between us. Mrs. P. would excitedly exclaim, "Laser!" every time we appeared at her door and "See you next week!" every time we left. She had been gradually getting weaker, but, one week when we arrived to see her, I was distressed to see that her condition had deteriorated significantly. Still, she smiled and said, "Laser!" when we walked into the room.

She complained of being cold, even though the room was warm, and when Laser cuddled up close to her, she said, "Oh, he's so warm—it feels so good." We had a nice visit, even though Mrs. P. wasn't feeling very well. Her hand never left Laser's back. As we left, she said her usual, "See you next week," and I hoped that was true.

The next Saturday, a phone call informed me that Mrs. P. was going downhill rapidly, and that she probably wouldn't live more than another few days. I asked if we should still come for our visit, and the nurse told me that she thought that would be wonderful.

When we arrived, it was obvious that Mrs. P. was dying. She was fading in and out of consciousness, but when she noticed that Laser and I were beside her bed, she smiled and whispered, "Laser."

She was having a very hard time breathing, so I told her not to try to talk; we would just sit quietly and keep her company. Laser took his spot on the bed next to her hip, and Mrs. P. rested her hand on his soft back. Neither of them moved from that position for the entire length of our visit. This time, when we got up to leave, Mrs. P. whispered, "Thank you." She knew that there would be no "next week" for us.

A couple of days later, I got the phone call telling me

that Mrs. P. had died. I was sad—our weekly visits had been so wonderful—but I was glad that she was no longer in pain. I remembered how I had considered declining to make the hospice visits and was so grateful that I had not.

In our seventh year as a Pet Partner team, Laser and I still make visits to several facilities. Laser, the little cat that nobody wanted, is as beautiful on the inside as he is on the outside, and he continues to brighten the lives of everyone he meets.

Nancy Kucik

Five Hundred Flowers

I love cats because I enjoy my home; and little by little, they become its visible soul.

Jean Cocteau

I am what is sometimes referred to as "a woman of a certain age." Single and childless, I have lived alone for most of my adult life. Up until six years ago, I hadn't even had a pet.

At that time, I was living in an apartment—which didn't allow pets—where I commuted an hour each way to the Los Angeles high school where I teach English. Although I had always wanted a little house of my own, with a yard and a garden, I somehow never took the necessary steps to make that dream come true. One year followed another, and as so often happens, I just continued in the comfortable, if somewhat unfulfilling, rhythm of my life.

Until "the week of the cats."

It was late May, and the school year was almost over. My classroom, which is a little bungalow, sits off by itself on the school grounds. One Tuesday afternoon, I heard a piteous meowing coming from underneath the classroom floor. It took me almost four hours to coax a small, but vocal, gray tabby kitten from its hiding place. The kitten was hungry and obviously needed help. Although I knew it wasn't allowed, that afternoon after school I took the kitten I'd named Maximus home to my apartment, smuggling him upstairs so I wouldn't get in trouble with the manager. I wondered what in heaven's name I was going to do, now that I had a kitten in my life, because from the very first I knew that whatever happened, I was going to keep him.

Two days later, one of my students, knowing that I had rescued a kitten, came to me and begged me to take her little girl kitten. She had brought it home, but her parents wouldn't let her keep the cat, a Russian blue, and she didn't know what to do. I figured I was already breaking the rules with Maximus, so what was one more? My student brought me the "little girl"—who turned out to be an adolescent boy cat: my Grey Boy.

The weekend came and went. Things were going well. I was enjoying my two new apartment-mates, and so far no one had complained or turned me in. Then, the next Tuesday, another little gray tabby kitten—an orphan, possibly Maximus' sister—was placed in my arms by a fellow teacher. I knew taking her home would be pushing my luck, but I did it anyway. When I carried Pearl into the apartment that afternoon, it was clear my life was about to change. I had a family now and needed a home to put them in.

My cats were just the catalysts I needed to finally go for my dreams. I began looking to buy a house in earnest. Within a week, I found one, and just two months later, we moved in.

It was a wonderful time in my life. I loved my new home, and coming back each day to my trio of sweet and loving cats was a joy beyond description. This happy state lasted about a year—until the morning I found Pearl dead. I wasn't sure what had killed her. I thought it might have been a stroke or aneurysm as she didn't have a scratch on her body.

I stared at her small, still figure, feeling as though my heart would break, but I *had* to go to work. I picked up Pearl and put her in the backyard. I would bury her when I came home that afternoon.

It was a miserable day; I was distraught, and my students were particularly unruly. When I dragged myself home after work, overcome with fatigue and grief, I wasn't sure I could actually face the sad task that lay ahead of me. Barely holding myself together, I asked my neighbor to help me dig the hole. When it was ready, I put Pearl into it and then completely broke down. As I sobbed hysterically, I was aware that Grey Boy was staring at me with an unusual amount of focus. Then I gave myself over to my grief, and Grey Boy quietly walked away.

Eventually, I fell silent. As the sun began to set, I sat at the picnic table in the backyard, staring at the ground and simply feeling the aching pain in my chest. My darling Pearl was gone, and nothing would be the same.

I looked up and noticed Grey Boy trotting toward me, holding something in his mouth. I couldn't tell what it was. He came directly to where I was sitting and, stopping a foot away, dropped the item in his mouth at my feet.

It was a single pinkish-purple flower shaped like a trumpet. Grey Boy tilted his head to look up at me and then, seeing that I had observed his gift, turned and trotted away.

Surprised, I inhaled sharply, and then sighing, I breathed, "Oh, Grey Boy." He had never done anything like this before.

The tears slid down my cheeks as I reached down and picked up the beautiful blossom. I held it in my hand and cried again, but this time my tears felt healing. I sat there for an hour, holding Grey Boy's gift and slowly recovering my equilibrium.

Pearl's death was harder on me than I ever could have imagined. For the next three months, I felt just terrible. During that period, Maximus stayed close, and Grey Boy continued to bring me flowers—about five hundred of them! On the weekends when I was home all day, he brought them morning, noon and night, and several times in between. On workdays, he would bring flowers to me before work and when I returned in the evening. It seemed whenever I turned around, Grey Boy would be coming to me to deliver another flower. He didn't stay— after he dropped the flower and saw me pick it up, he walked away.

Then, after about three months, as I started to feel better, Grey Boy suddenly stopped bringing the flowers. And he has never done it again, not once.

What touches me the most about the five hundred flowers is that during those three months, Grey Boy was grieving, too. He was quieter than usual, and I often noticed him sitting and staring at Pearl's grave. But my Grey Boy *knew* that I needed his help—and he never wavered from his self-appointed mission of mercy.

Bev Nielsen

A Dickens of a Cat

"Gwen, I think it's ovarian cancer, and I think it's spread everywhere. I'm so sorry," my surgeon told me. "Go home and get your affairs in order. We'll operate as soon as possible."

Surgery revealed that I did, indeed, have an aggressive form of ovarian cancer. Lying in the hospital, I feared for my future. I feared I might not have a future. I feared I would be unable to care for myself. And since I was recently divorced, I feared being alone. How could I cope with chemotherapy, my job as an editor and caring for my home?

"Mom, I think you need a pet," my daughter said as she walked me up and down the halls of the hospital.

"Why do I need a pet?"

"I don't want you to be alone."

"Oh, Wendy, how can I take care of a pet? I'm not sure I can take care of me."

"Cats don't require much care."

"I'm a dog person," I answered, with an "and that is that" finality.

But that night, after she had gone home, I began to think. She and I were so focused on my cancer and whether I'd live or die that we thought of little else. Perhaps a pet would not only give me some company, but would also give us something else to focus our attention on now. Pets have always given me joy, and the doctor had already told me that the very best therapy was going to be a positive attitude.

I drifted off to sleep thinking about the kind of pet I might want. In the morning when Wendy came by, I shocked her by saying, "All right, I've decided I want a cat. I want you to go to the animal shelter and get me a tuxedo cat. Since I'm a book editor, I think I should have a very literary-looking cat. His name will be Charles Dickens. Make sure he looks the part. He should have a white bib, mittens and socks, and a mustache would be good."

She didn't make it to the shelter that day because after eleven long, tiresome days in a hospital bed, I was suddenly discharged to go home. But the next afternoon, Wendy got a "mommy sitter" and went to find my cat. I could hardly wait for her to get home. When the garage door opened, Judy, my "sitter," went to see what Wendy had chosen.

Judy carried a young, bright-eyed cat to my bed. He had the compulsory white bib, mittens, socks and a one-sided mustache. I couldn't believe it. I had told Wendy what I wanted, but I never dreamed she would find the exact cat I'd described. "Hello, Charles Dickens," I said.

He said, "Meow."

Dickens had a history. As a frightened stray, he had found his way to a Colorado Springs back porch during a rainstorm. Soaking wet and freezing cold, he shivered next to a glass door. The lady of the house had compassion. She took him in and fed him, but she could not keep him. The next day, she wept as she took him to the pound and told the attendants, "Make sure whoever gets him calls me."

That evening, after Dickens had settled in, I called her.

She told me, "I'm about to have a baby, and I already have three cats. I wanted to keep him, but there was just no way. So I prayed God would send him to someone who needed him and would really love him."

In that moment, I realized that Dickens had not come to me by chance. "Your prayers have been answered," I said, and then I told her my story and ended with, "I need him, and I already love him."

All that first day and the next, Dickens went over my house with a "fine-toothed nose." He poked into every crevice and cranny, investigating everything. Then he began to sneeze and sneeze and sneeze. His nose was running, and his eyes were dull. Dickens was sick. Wendy took him to the vet.

"Is he going to die?" I asked when she brought him home.

"The vet doesn't think so. He's started him on some antibiotics and thinks Dickens is old enough and strong enough to survive."

Poor Dickens. He was very sick. He lay on the foot of my bed on a hot-water bottle for days. I had wanted to refocus our attention on something besides my illness and upcoming chemotherapy, and I surely did. All we could think about was whether *Dickens* would live or die.

After about eight days, Dickens had his turning point. He sprang up from the hot-water bottle with a gleam in his eye. "Well, hello, cat," I said. And I could see in an instant that I had correctly named him. He was going to be a rascally dickens all right. He crouched around corners waiting to spring at me as I passed by. He attacked my feet under the covers. He played until he dropped exhausted at my side.

Then I started my chemotherapy. Wendy went with me for the first four-day round of treatment. I didn't learn until later how frightened she had been. I didn't realize what it was costing her emotionally to see her mother in this dire situation. Neither of us knew when (or if) I, like Dickens, might have *my* turning point.

I tolerated the first round of chemotherapy fairly well, and I thought I could make it through the remainder of the twenty-four treatments on my own. "Go home and get on with your life," I told my daughter.

There were lots of nights during the six months that followed when I would wake from a deep sleep, nauseated beyond belief. By that point, Dickens was sleeping in the crook of my arm. When I awakened, he'd jump to the end of the bed and wait. When I would get back into bed, he would once again snuggle down beside me. This little creature God had sent my way blessed my long, lonely nights.

Some days, Dickens raced me up the stairs. At my pace it wasn't much of a race. He romped and played and made me laugh and laugh. I tolerated the chemotherapy pretty well, and I am sure one reason was because Dickens gave me a cheerful heart that was "good medicine."

Then, finally, I finished chemo. All I had to do was wait—wait and pray and hope that the cancer was in remission.

In October, my surgeon said, "We can't find any cancer from the outside, and we'd like to take a look inside." I agreed surgery would be a good idea.

This time, my son Mark came to stay with me and to take care of Dickens. After only an hour in surgery, I heard the voice of my delighted surgeon saying, "It's gone. There's no cancer anywhere."

This was *my* turning point! I was going to live! I went home to be greeted by a very happy cat, and while I couldn't lift Dickens (he now weighed fourteen pounds, and I was not supposed to lift anything over ten), I sat down, and he crawled onto my lap. "Well, cat," I said, "it looks like I'm going to stick around for a while. We both made it. We're survivors." Dickens didn't say much. He just stretched a little and purred and purred.

Dickens and I have a new problem now—one we like. We're getting older. We retired this year, and now I spend all my time at home with him. It's been ten years since I heard those fateful words "ovarian cancer." Today, these two survivors are living life to the fullest.

Gwen Ellis

Puffin's Gift

On a hot, stifling day in early August, I made the decision to get a cat. My shadow, a beautiful Belgian sheepdog, had passed away, and I needed a new animal to love. I'd never been around a cat, but my new landlord didn't allow dogs. Ron, my fiancé and a veterinarian, persuaded me to adopt a cat.

Reluctantly, I left my air-conditioned car and walked into a veterinary clinic that gave temporary shelter to stray cats. As I opened the door, a blast of hot, pungent air enveloped me, and I fought the urge to go home. A weary technician led me back to the cages. "Picked a bad day to come," she complained. "Lost our air a few hours ago, and now all we have is one fan."

It wasn't doing much for the cats. I looked at them in their small cages. Not a tail twitched; no eager eyes met mine, begging for a home. Some were asleep; others, limp and quiet, were paralyzed by the heat. Unable to decide which comatose cat to bring into my life, I turned to leave, feeling only a little disappointed. After all, I was a dog person.

"Meow."

I looked at the technician, and we turned back.

"Meow!" A gray paw stretched out between the bars, and emerald eyes demanded my attention.

"I'll take that one," I said without hesitation, then wondered what I had just done.

After a brief exam, they handed her over to me, and we drove to the clinic where Ron worked. He performed a more thorough exam to assure me that the cat was healthy. He showed me how to hold her, which wasn't easy because she had been on the streets for so long that she was just as scared of me as I was of her. I named her Puffin after my favorite Maine seabird, and, flush with Ron's approval, I took her home to my orderly, neat apartment in the city.

I can do this, I thought, and, after I'd closed all the windows and doors, I unlatched the door of her carrier. Puffin flew out much faster than her namesake and tore through the apartment, a blur of gray fur. It was the beginning of a very long week. The new scratching post wasn't satisfying, and she took to my old couch. When both sides were bare, she started on the legs of the antique dining-room table that had originally belonged to my parents. When she wasn't tearing through the apartment or clawing up the furniture, she was lying in wait for the inevitable moment that I opened the front door, eager for escape.

Ribbons of scratches covered my arms from our battles at the front door. After all, she had been an outdoor cat, ten months old, who already had given birth to a litter of kittens. "Give her time," Ron pleaded. But the only time I really enjoyed Puffin was at night when she curled up into a ball next to me on my quilt, purring us to sleep.

Ron and I married two years later, and the three of us moved into a condo in the suburbs, near the new clinic Ron purchased with a partner. Puffin now had two floors to roam and didn't seem as tempted to escape. But, when we settled into our new home, she began to boldly claim her territory. The second-floor landing became her perch, and I became her mouse. Whenever I tried to go upstairs, Puffin would crouch at the landing, waiting until I was within reach, then lunge at my ankles with a sharp bite. It wasn't long before I invested in a pair of Nike high-tops. I would have given anything for a gentle dog who didn't bite, scratch or attack.

Five months later, we had wonderful news: I was pregnant. It started out smoothly with the usual fatigue and a little morning sickness. Every afternoon, I returned home from teaching, put on my high-tops and prepared for my face-off with Puffin at the top of the stairs. When I reached the second stair from the top, Puffin would lunge at me, biting, as I ran into the bedroom. Safe on the bed, I pulled off my shoes and crawled under the quilt for a nap. Puffin followed suit, curling into my legs and softly purring us off to sleep.

At thirteen weeks, I had a miscarriage. Ron drove me home from the hospital late in the day, trying his best to keep up our spirits. "I just need some time to be alone," I told him, urging him to go back to work.

"You're not alone," he reminded me. "Puffin will take care of you until I get home." I looked at him incredulously, shaking my head. If only I was coming home to my dog.

Ron went back to work, and I went inside. Our home felt dark and lonely. With a deep breath, I slipped into my high-tops and started to climb. Puffin's eyes glinted green from the top of the stairs. She stood poised, alert and ready to attack. Her eyes narrowed, and I tensed. "Please, Puffin, not today," I begged, tears starting to form. It was all too much. I collapsed on the staircase and started to cry.

Puffin hesitated, then sat down. Wiping my cheeks, I slowly got up and made my way to the top, unimpeded by my cat. She let me pass, licking a paw. I walked to the bedroom, removed my shoes and fell onto the bed. Puffin leaped onto the quilt, staring into my teary eyes. I held out my arms, and, for the first time, she came to me and licked my face with her tiny, rough tongue. I smiled and rubbed her ears. She turned and purred, then snuggled into my belly, her heartbeat making up for the one I had lost. We drifted off to sleep.

Twelve years later, Puffin sleeps on our bed in a new house. Her best friend, an adopted border collie, snores softly on a pillow below. Suddenly, the door bangs open, and our five-year-old daughter, Julianne, leaps on the bed, eager to pet her cat. Puffin's green eyes narrow, Julianne laughs, and the chase is on. Little pink Nikes run as fast as they can.

Jennifer Gay Summers

Friends for Life

I met Chris when another volunteer in our feral-cat assistance group moved away, and I took over her feeding duties. Chris was a large black tomcat with a mangy tail and rheumy eyes; the tip of one ear was nearly torn in half, no doubt the result of a long-ago street fight. But, in spite of his intimidating appearance, Chris had the loving disposition of a kitten. He communicated in a unique way: a rapid flow of modulated mews that sounded as expressive as human conversation. Unlike other ferals in my charge, Chris lived not in a colony with his own kind, but all alone on the litter-filled grounds of an abandoned drive-in theater near San Francisco International Airport, a commercial area where my husband and I operated a café that catered to local office workers. Chris, probably someone's abandoned pet, had settled in this forsaken landscape, inside a rusty oil drum that lay amidst the rubble.

Mondays, Wednesdays and Fridays, before or after work, I attended to my feeding rounds, leaving the drive-in for last. The feeding station was next to a hole in the fence that ran alongside the road, and Chris never seemed to stray too far from it. As soon as I got out of the car and called, "Chris!" he would appear at full trot, gushing happy meows.

Chris and I became the best of friends. Even when it was past his mealtime and he must have been famished, instead of lunging at his food, he purred loudly against my legs, demanding attention first. When I squatted down to stroke his bedraggled fur, he lifted himself up on his hind legs and placed both front paws on my shoulders, until his big yellow eyes were level with mine, our noses practically touching.

As my bond with Chris grew stronger, so did my resolve to find him a loving home. With five cats in our own household, adopting him was out of the question. According to my family, who was always frowning upon the cat hair on my clothes and the felines sprawled all over the scratched living-room furniture, I was well on my way to becoming one of those "crazy cat ladies" that you read about in the newspaper. My husband had already issued an ultimatum: "One more cat, and I'm out of here!" But, in spite of my best efforts, nobody wanted an older stray with battle scars and runny eyes. And bringing him to a shelter would have been an automatic death sentence.

The onset of autumn, with its storms and lower temperatures, didn't make things any easier. Soon, I was stopping by the feeding station every day, just to make sure that Chris was safe and sound. Every time I headed for the drive-in, I feared finding Chris dead or injured at the side of the road; or, even worse, not finding him at all. But, happily, he always showed up, within seconds of my calling his name.

Ironically, the life in grave and imminent danger was not his, but mine.

That fall, I found a lump in my breast, and, suddenly, I was faced with a human's most dreaded enemy: cancer. By the time I discovered it, the malignancy had grown to the size of a golf ball. When the doctor broke the news, I could tell by the look on his face that he was not very optimistic: I had a very rare and aggressive form of cancer, with few recorded studies of its response to standard treatments. Worse yet, mine was no stage I, caught-just-in-time lump, but an advanced growth that called for an immediate counterattack with all the weapons in modern medicine's arsenal: a barrage of chemotherapy, daily radiation, surgery—which could be successful, provided that some microscopic malignant cell had not already migrated to vital organs in my body.

In the wake of the initial despair, I realized that fighting such a formidable foe would require all my physical, emotional and spiritual resources. I refused to dwell on the statistics that pervaded most cancer literature and Web sites, and focused every moment of my day on positive thinking and activities that would promote my healing. I would not stand by idly. I started a regimen of exercises designed to strengthen my immune system. I meditated daily, visualizing a healthy me in a bright near-future. I switched to an organic diet of whole grains and fresh vegetables, and took massive doses of herbal supplements to boost my body's natural defenses.

By mid-November, my hair had begun to fall out, and the chemotherapy had sapped my strength. I quit going to the café, but, although I had found someone to substitute for me on my feeding rounds, I tried to go see Chris at least once a week; I just didn't have the heart to say goodbye to him. I called the other volunteers almost every day to check up on Chris's safety. But when they told me that they had not bothered to call him to his meal, or that he had not shown up, I was beside myself with worry.

On Thanksgiving Day, while my parents were busy in the kitchen and other family members chatted in the living room, I begged my husband to let me bring Chris home. I am sure that, if I had been my strong, healthy self, he would have questioned my sanity and turned a deaf ear to my pleas. But this time, miraculously, he relented.

The dinner table was already set when we sneaked out of the house with a kitty carrier. I hadn't seen Chris in over a week, and my heart was pounding as we neared the drive-in. Would he still be there? Would he come right away, as he usually did? When we pulled up next to the fence, I couldn't believe my eyes. Chris was curled up right next his bowls, as if he knew that we were on our way. He put up no resistance when I lifted him up and placed him in the carrier, and he chattered happily all the way home. That night, he slept soundly in the cozy bed that I prepared for him in the sunroom, and so did I, for the first time in weeks.

In the days that followed, I took Chris in for a checkup, and my worst suspicions were confirmed. Living out in the elements had taken a toll on his health: He had a respiratory infection and enlarged kidneys, which required a battery of tests. The vet's somber expression warned me that the news wasn't good. Chris was FIV-positive and had advanced kidney disease. The prognosis was grim: two weeks to four months, maximum.

"I know this is hard to take in . . ." the vet began.

I couldn't help laughing. "I am forty-three years old, and I have a rare tumor the size of a golf ball in my breast," I said. "You have no idea what I am capable of taking in."

With my immune system impaired by chemotherapy and disease, the veterinarian advised me to keep my distance from Chris. Soon, she said, I would have to make the ultimate decision to have him put down.

I walked out of the examination room and broke into sobs. My mother and aunt, who had accompanied me to the animal hospital, were adamant that I should opt for euthanasia with no further delay.

"Just look at him," my aunt snapped. "Why wait to put him out of his misery?"

With tears streaming down my face, I took a good look at Chris: the bald patches on his tail, the ragged ear, his sickly eyes so full of trust and affection. I took him out of his carrier and let him snuggle up under my chin, to my aunt's horror. As he purred away next to my heart, I felt the depth of our special kinship, and my commitment to him grew even stronger. We were united in our illness and misfortune, against all odds. No matter what the future held in store for each of us, I would never give up on him.

In the months that followed, as I fought for my own life, Chris fought for his. I got second opinions, tried new medications—ointments for his eyes, balms for his sores. He ate the best food money could buy and reveled in loads of TLC. At night, while he slept at the foot of my bed, I prayed for healing—for both of us. And, as my tumor kept shrinking with every round of chemotherapy until it became just a speck that the surgeon easily removed, so Chris thrived in his new, nurturing surroundings: His eyes cleared up, his tail filled out, and his kidneys returned to their normal size.

In the end, the cat who wasn't supposed to survive two months has been alive for more than two years. Today, he roams the house with the rest of the gang. And I am still here, too, celebrating another Thanksgiving with my family—and Chris—with double the gratitude for our second lease on life.

Silvia Baroni

Nurse Mima

When I was a small child, I spent months in the hospital with severe headaches for which the doctors could find no cause. It was finally determined that I suffered from migraines and would most likely be on medication for the rest of my life to control them.

In college, I was unfortunate enough to see a doctor who claimed that my headaches were all in my mind and took me off all my medications. The headaches I suffered during this time were debilitating, forcing me to remain in bed for days with the windows covered and the air conditioner on high. During these periods, I would be constantly nauseated and dizzy, unable to read or even type because my hands shook so badly.

After suffering through a particularly bad episode in which I lost partial vision in one eye, I was finally given a prescription for an injection to try when I had my next headache. I was returning from the drugstore after picking up the prescription when I first met Mima.

I heard a soft meow from under a nearby car and squatted down to see who was there. Lying under the oil pan was a wreck of a calico cat, crying piteously to anyone who would listen. Her fur was missing in patches all over her body, and she was covered with fleas, which I could see crawling across the bridge of her nose. At first, I thought her legs might be broken because they stuck out from her body at such sharp angles, but when I called to her, she pushed herself up on them and moved toward me. I realized they only appeared to stick out that way because of how emaciated she was.

Once she saw that I had no food, she darted back under the car and resumed meowing. Afraid of what might happen to her if I left her out there too long, I ran into the house and brought back the only thing I could find that she might eat. I broke the cheese into pieces and put it under the car for her, then got back into my car and drove straight to the pet store.

A name, a pet carrier and a trip to the vet later, I brought her into my house for the first time. Frightened and confused, she darted under my bed and was not seen for days. The only indication that she was all right was the rate at which the cat food was disappearing!

Those first weeks, Mima stayed as far away from my husband and me as she possibly could, slinking out from behind the toilet or between the cabinets when we came near them, and pressing herself flat on the ground when she couldn't get away fast enough. I decided after three weeks of failed attempts to simply stroke her head that she would probably never be an affectionate cat, but comforted myself with the knowledge that at least she wouldn't starve to death on the streets.

About a week after that, I was sitting on the couch, crocheting a blanket as a peace offering for Mima, when, suddenly, one of the worst headaches of my life came upon me. My hands shook so badly that I had to simply drop the yarn and hook on the floor as I stumbled toward the bathroom, my stomach churning. Mima was, as usual, behind the toilet and streaked past me as I entered the room.

Somehow, I managed to make it to the couch again, where I lay flat on my back with a cool, wet washcloth over my face. My head felt like it was going to explode, and I wished my husband were home from work. By this time, I was in so much pain that I couldn't remember his phone number and was having trouble even thinking. I found myself praying just to fall asleep.

All of a sudden, something poked me in the ribs tentatively. I opened one eye and saw Mima cautiously kneading her paws against my stomach, her face a mask of concentration. I reached out for her, and, as she rubbed her head under my palm, the only coherent thought I now remember having was that she was incredibly soft. With Mima's warmth in my arms, I fell asleep easily—and remained asleep for several hours.

When I woke up, Mima was lying on my chest, her chin resting on my neck as she dozed peacefully against me. One paw was outstretched and pressed on my cheek as if she had been stroking my face while I slept. Hoping that she wouldn't run away, I ran my hand down her back and was delighted to hear a small, rusty purr start in her throat.

As she opened one green eye, I realized that my headache was gone. I sat up quickly in surprise, and Mima slid onto my lap. She yowled at me, annoyed at having lost her place, and I cuddled her in my lap. For a moment, it looked like she was going to bolt away from me, but she changed her mind and set about making a nest on my legs.

Since that day on the couch, Mima knows when I am about to have a headache. She coaxes me onto the couch with her, then proceeds to crawl up onto my chest and lie down on me with her face just a few inches from mine. Before I know it, her purring has lulled me to sleep, and the pain soon fades away.

Over the years, Mima has proved to be better medicine than anything the doctors have prescribed, and our bond continues to deepen each day she is in my life. I feel very fortunate to have Nurse Mima to care for me, and, in return, will continue to repay her in the only way I know how: by making her life safe, happy and secure.

Natalie Suarez

Peace for Pickles

She just appeared one day, looking sad-eyed and mournful, peering in through the patio door. Her silky fur was jet-black, and her eyes were as big as saucers. I gazed at her and spoke the thought that was running through my head: "My, you are in quite a pickle." This beautiful, regal cat was definitely pregnant. Her stomach was bulging, and she appeared ready to give birth any day.

I was in a pickle, too. I had lost my father after caring for him through a long illness. My grief enveloped me like a black cloud. I sure didn't have the energy to take care of a cat. And a pregnant one at that. But I found myself pouring a bowl of milk and setting it outside. *She'll be gone by morning,* I thought. Pulling my bathrobe closer around me, I trudged back up the stairs.

The next day she reappeared. *What is she doing back here? I can barely take care of myself right now, let alone a needy cat.* But I couldn't turn away. I found an old basket and arranged a soft blanket inside. I walked outside, and she backed up about ten feet, watching me with wary eyes. I set down the basket and went back in the house.

Remembering my dad's kind and caring ways was the only comfort I had at the time. He loved animals and had a soft spot for all strays. When I was a little girl, our house was a revolving door for abandoned cats and dogs. I could at least *try* to take care of her. Dad would like that. But only until I found out where she lived.

I had seen a black cat in our neighborhood, so I assumed she was someone's pet. On one of my furtive runs out to the mailbox in my worn-out bathrobe and slippers, I saw my next-door neighbor.

"Hi, how are you?" he asked.

"Fine," I said as I ran my hand through my uncombed hair. "Can I ask you something? A black cat has been coming around my backyard. Do you know where she lives?"

"That cat has been around for years. Everybody feeds her, but as far as I know, she doesn't have a home."

"Thanks," and I shuffled back inside with the mail.

She must have had a hard life surviving on her own all those years.

"Okay, Dad, you must have guided her to my door. I'll take care of her," I spoke aloud.

I could almost hear him ask what I was going to call her.

"I'm going to name her Pickles."

I went upstairs to comb my hair. Looking in the mirror, I saw a wrinkled, creased face. *I wish somebody would take care of me.* Sadness etched the corners of my eyes, and my shoulders sloped with grief. The coolness of the water felt good as I ran a washcloth over my face. I changed out of my tired old bathrobe and put on jeans and a sweatshirt.

Over the next few days, Pickles came to drink the milk and eat the food I put out for her, but then would disappear. Each day, I eagerly searched the basket for some sign of the new life Pickles was carrying. One morning, I saw a tiny black kitten curled up inside. Then I heard the screech of brakes.

"Oh, no!" I cried out. There in the street was Pickles, running right in front of a car. She was carrying a solid gray kitten by the nape of its neck. Bounding across the yard, she deposited it in the basket and took off again. She made three more trips for a total of five kittens.

I made my way around the side of the house to get a closer look. I longed to hold Pickles and snuggle her close, but her years of living in the wild made her wary of human contact. I peered into the basket and watched as she licked and cleaned each kitten. *They're finally here!*

Since Dad had died, I had no one to take care of. Now, I couldn't wait to get up in the morning. The kittens needed me. I was showering, dressing and even making my bed. I began to say hello to the neighbors when I went out for the mail, wearing real clothes instead of pajamas and a robe.

And, when I looked out through the patio door, I sure didn't feel alone when six pairs of hungry eyes stared back at me. I sat with the kittens for hours. It was fun watching them roll around on top of each other and play hide-and-seek under the edges of the blanket. I even started to laugh again, surprising myself with that sweet, familiar sound. While Pickles watched from a distance, I stroked each furry little ball and soothingly crooned, "It's okay, Pickles. I won't hurt them. They're so cute, with their soft fur and big eyes just like yours. Look at this one with the black-and-white mask on her face. She looks like a little bandit. And this solid black one looks just like you."

Pickles seemed to understand my contact with the kittens was necessary, and it sure did my heart good. Sometimes, though, the sad tears would flow as I thought of how much I missed my dad. Then Pickles would look at me with those big eyes that seemed to say, *Everything's going to be all right. You take care of me, and I'll take care of you.*

When the kittens were old enough, I found homes for four of the five. The antics of every kitten endeared each one to me, but the solid gray one stood out among the rest. He was soft and cuddly, and I decided to keep him. When he stood up and stretched his paws against the door, he looked just like a bear, so that's what I called him.

I guessed Pickles was around nine years old and had obviously borne many litters. She was an excellent mother, but she looked exhausted after feeding, cleaning and tending to her offspring. Now that the rest of the kittens were in new homes, I knew there was one more thing I had to do. Pickles needed to be spayed, and Bear neutered, too, when he was old enough. Dad always told me how important that was.

I thought it would be easy to take her to the vet, but no matter what I tried—and I tried one thing after another for days—she wouldn't go into a plastic cat carrier. Unsure of what to do next, I sent up a silent plea to my dad. *Dad, I need your help. I want Pickles to live in peace. Please show me what to do.*

I picked up the phone and called the vet's office. After explaining my dilemma, they said they had a metal cage I could borrow, which had a trapdoor used most often to catch wild animals that needed medical care.

I retrieved the cage and then carried it out to the backyard as I talked to Pickles, who sat in the corner watching me. "Look at this one, Pickles. It's much bigger, and you can see through it. When you go inside, the door will shut behind you, but don't be afraid."

I placed a piece of chicken in the corner of the cage, with the metal door propped open. All Pickles had to do was approach the bait. What happened next seemed like a miracle. Although she had struggled and resisted my attempts to get her into the carrier for days, now, with a slow, steady gait, Pickles walked straight inside, almost as if guided by a loving hand. Her weight pressed down on the spring, and the door shut.

She sat inside, a calm emanating from her. I marveled at

her acceptance and surrender. *Is that what it takes?* I wondered. *Acceptance? Allowing others to help?* Maybe that's what had been lacking in my own life.

I brought her home from the vet the next day and let her out of the cage. She took a few steps, then turned and looked at me. Our eyes locked, and I saw the beginning of my own newfound serenity reflected in hers.

The gentle, guiding hand that showed Pickles the way to peace had shown me the way to acceptance—the first step in my journey back from grief.

B. J. Taylor

The Cloe Cure

"Why do I feel this way?" my daughter blurted out one day. "There's nothing really wrong with my life!"

I knew that depression often hounded young people, but it had been hard to accept that my bright, pretty teen was that unhappy. Corrie had been such a contented child. As an infant, a game of peek-a-boo would elicit baby belly-laughs. When she was a toddler, she stopped to hug every elderly lady at the mall. "Hug?" she would frequently ask me throughout the day, her small arms open to receive. As a young child, she was outgoing and friendly, but I began to notice a tendency toward worry, and, as she approached her teens, she became more and more cheerless.

My husband John and I weren't too worried about our daughter. After all, most teenagers occasionally feel morose and hopeless, and we were confident that we could help her through those instances. But, as time went by, Corrie's depression worsened. The day she questioned me about her dark moods, there was a vague suggestion of despair in her voice that started me thinking. My daughter slept whenever there was a lull in the activity of her day, dragged herself to school and back, and rarely smiled.

Daily headaches and a poor appetite plagued her as well. In the past, she had always been an above-average student, but now her marks were dropping steadily.

This was not something that a parent could reason away or kiss and "make better," so I took my daughter to the doctor's office. Corrie was diagnosed as suffering from a chemical imbalance, explained as a lack of serotonin, the brain's mood-lifting neurotransmitter. The doctor prescribed an anti-depressant, and I prayed.

Meanwhile, Corrie was approaching her seventeenth birthday. She wasn't excited by the prospect and couldn't even find enough enthusiasm to decide what she wanted us to give her. John and I knew that she had wanted a cat for years, but we had always said that one pet in the house was enough, and we already had Toby. However, the ten-year-old dog was a good-natured mutt, and John and I had hopes that a kitten would lift Corrie's spirits, if only slightly. At her birthday dinner in April, we gave Corrie a card with a picture of a kitten on it, and the "gift" she opened was a cat toy and a ceramic food dish decorated with playful cat-related drawings. I don't think Corrie was quite sure we meant it. She smiled faintly and asked, "You're giving me a cat?"

Even so, Corrie was eager to begin the search for her perfect companion, and she knew exactly what she was looking for. Corrie's Aunt Janet had a tortoiseshell cat, and Corrie had always admired Mieka's black, cream and caramel coloring. Toby had come from the local animal shelter, and I again wanted to give a neglected animal a home, but the kittens at the shelter were still too young to leave their mother, so I took Corrie to a local pet shop. I had no doubt that God had taken a hand in the matter when we got to the store. There in the window, romping and wrestling with her black and gray companions, was Corrie's heart's desire. The seven-week-old kitten was barely a handful of tortie fur, and, as Corrie held the docile little animal against her shoulder and smiled down into the large golden eyes topped by cream-colored "eyebrows," there was no doubt in my mind that this search would be short-lived. Soon, Corrie was seated in the car cradling a cardboard box emitting tiny questioning mews.

On the way home, Corrie began to think about a name for her kitten, but it would be two days before she finally settled on Cloe, which she selected from the same baby-name book from which I had picked her own name. (Corrie opted for the more unusual spelling—rather than the standard: Chloe.) She had rejected her father's suggestion of Marbles as too cutesy, insisting that it had to be a "real" name.

Cloe purred as she walked about exploring her new home, and we took that as an encouraging sign. We would often see her darting out from under a tablecloth, limbs splayed out like a flying squirrel, in preparation for tackling the unsuspecting dog as he napped on the floor nearby. Immediately following such an antic, I would hear my daughter laughing with delight. What a great sound! Someone once said that it's impossible not to smile in the presence of one or more kittens. They were right. Everything about Cloe enchanted Corrie, from the awkward little kitten walk to the way she wiggled her backside just before she pounced on a "victim." It comforted Corrie to have Cloe curl up next to her on the bed at night. One evening, the kitten jumped up on the bed and started purring and mewing until Corrie couldn't resist sitting up in bed to pet her. Before she knew what had happened, Cloe had taken possession of the pillow, and Corrie giggled as she realized that her kitten had tricked her. Cloe was sociable and easygoing, often adopting the dog's habit of following us from room to room or sauntering over to the door to greet whoever had just come in.

God gave John and me the miracle we were seeking in the form of a tiny multicolored ball of fur. Corrie no longer moaned, "I'm so depressed!" Instead, it was a joyful, "Mom, I love this kitty so much!" She slept less during the day, ate better, suffered fewer headaches, and her marks started to improve.

More than a year later, just the mention of her pet's name still puts a contented grin on our daughter's face. Corrie calls Cloe her "fuzzy angel," and it seems an apt description. Angels, after all, come to help heal our spirits, and Cloe has become a significant part of the remedy her young guardian needs. Sometimes, there's no medicine like the unconditional love of a trusting animal—no balm to the soul like the satisfied purr and silky coat of a little tortie cat resting against your shoulder.

Marlene Alexander

Angels Among Us

The large tabby tomcat simply moved onto their porch one stormy fall day and refused to leave. At first, Helen, a busy, hard-working single mother, felt she couldn't afford the time or luxury of a pet. But job success had required numerous relocations that left her eleven-year-old daughter, Amanda, with few friends. The young girl spent much of her time alone until the cat had appeared. It took some arguing—Helen was not an animal lover—but once she saw the joy the big cat brought her daughter, it was decided. The mangy, flea-bitten, old feline joined the clan.

Skylar, named after one of Amanda's favorite dolls, immediately visited the local veterinarian for routine tests, a comprehensive physical and neutering. During Skylar's tune-up, the vet noticed unusual color changes in his eyes, so, two days later, Skylar and his new family appeared at my veterinary ophthalmology office.

When I walked into the exam room, I found Amanda grinning from ear to ear as she grasped her feline pal around the middle. Skylar hung in her arms, long legs dangling, and looked up at me with a Cheshire-cat grin, obviously reveling in the attention of his captor. Over the years, I have noticed that tomcats who retire from a rough street life into the comfort of a cushy home often become the best patients and pets. There was little doubt Skylar was one of these cats.

"Hi." I smiled at Amanda and patted the rough head of the cat.

"Hello," she said. "This is my best friend Skylar."

I reached to take the cat. "He certainly seems to be a great fellow. Let's have a look at his eyes."

Once settled on the exam table, a rumble began deep in Skylar's throat until he vibrated with a full-blown purr. A sure way to shoot to the top of our favorite-kitty list is to purr through the rigors of my examination. Looking into Skylar's battered face, complete with a shriveled and drooping left ear, I too fell under the spell of this special cat.

Skylar sat motionless as I examined his eyes. Nor did he flinch when I administered eye drops or checked his intra-ocular pressure. My evaluation revealed a mild inflammation known as uveitis. He could see despite some irreversible scarring. Daily eye drops could control the condition, but I worried about the underlying cause, which could be serious.

When I received the faxed report of the blood-test results from Skylar's vet, my heart sank—he had tested positive for feline leukemia, the likely cause of the uveitis. The disease often proved fatal within a few years of diag-nosis, and nobody knew how long the cat had been infected. I gently delivered the unhappy news.

Helen shook her head and seemed to bite back anger as she watched her tearful daughter clutching her new best friend to her chest. Part of her—her protective instinct—had known better than to allow the cat into the family and open Amanda to this kind of hurt. Helen felt her daughter had already paid too big a price when Amanda's father abandoned her at the age of three. Since the damage had already been done, though, Helen couldn't bring herself to force an early separation. Skylar made Amanda happy now. Helen resolved to see the unhappy situation through to its inevitable conclusion.

Over the next two years, I enjoyed visits with Skylar, who became one of my favorite patients. He purred from the moment he entered the clinic. And Helen and the blossoming Amanda became part of our clinic's extended family, receiving holiday and birthday greetings.

Skylar's condition remained stable, and, over time, Helen became more optimistic and was more loving toward the chubby cat. He made a remarkable difference in Amanda's life. Helen watched as their mutual love pulled Amanda out of her quiet shell and transformed her into a beautiful, vibrant teenager, both popular and fun-loving. Amanda and I often talked of her desire to become a veterinarian. With her interest in medicine and the compassionate love and respect that she had for Skylar, I felt she had what it took to make that dream come true.

* * *

Now, I stood looking down at Skylar as I lovingly rubbed my weak, old friend behind his ear. Helen stood across from me, arms tightly clasped, weeping quietly.

The cat had not eaten for several days. Too weak to purr, nothing but skin and bones, my sweet patient barely remained aware of his surroundings. We had fought the fight, but now the time had come, and Helen knew it.

"I don't know if I can . . . put him to sleep," she said, and her eyes begged me to help.

Tears welled in my own eyes. I gently squeezed her arm and fought to keep my voice from breaking. "I can't even imagine how difficult this is for you." I paused, then said, "But we have to think of Skylar now. He has been a great gift to you and to Amanda, and this is how you can repay him for all his love. You can end his suffering and allow him to pass with dignity."

"But how do I know if it is the right time for him to go?" Helen leaned her head down to nuzzle the ailing cat.

"Helen, you love Skylar, and only you will know when you are both ready." I had counseled people on this decision for years, one of the most difficult in life to make—to end a beloved pet's suffering only to bring on one's own.

Helen straightened, a new strength drying her tears. She looked at me and nodded. "It's time. Amanda would have wanted this. I have to let him go so he can be with her. I'll be all right knowing that they are together again."

You see, eight months earlier, a drunk driver had hit and killed Amanda as she walked home from school.

Skylar's purring presence had pulled Helen through those black months after Amanda was killed. He had been a tiny piece of her daughter left on Earth, and, now, she was going to lose that. I steeled myself for one of the most difficult tasks of my life.

As I administered the injection, Skylar peacefully drifted off. I left Helen gently cradling Skylar, giving her time to say her final good-byes and compose herself. Later, after I gave her a consoling hug, I watched as this brave woman left our clinic to face the world alone.

That evening I thought about Skylar. I've heard many times about small, furry angels entering people's lives out of the blue, only to perform great deeds: the small stray dog found on a lonely widower's doorstep who brings a new lease on life, or the newly adopted cat who alerts young parents to their sleeping baby's distress. I was certain the miracle that was Skylar had been a divine gift to Amanda—and, especially, to Helen. I hoped that the friendly, old tabby was happily in Amanda's arms once again, and that another angel would soon appear to help a grieving Helen heal.

Vivian Jamieson, D.V.M.

The China Cat

I stuffed the small bag of ashes into the tiny china cat and carefully glued felt to the bottom. *How do I get myself into such strange situations?* I wondered. Sitting at my dining-room table, I stared at a bottle of glue, some scraps of felt, a pair of scissors and an elderly lady's china cat statue. I pondered over the sequence of events that had led me to this.

"Dr. Bryant, can you come over and talk Mrs. Painter into putting her cat, Callie, to sleep?" As a veterinarian, I often get strange requests, and this was one of the more unusual ones. The call came from Julie, a social worker at a retirement community close to where I worked. Callie was a patient of mine, whom I had diagnosed with failing kidneys a few months earlier. Julie explained herself: "Callie looks terrible. She won't eat, and she urinates outside her box. Mrs. Painter can't care for her properly. The staff is tired of cleaning up after the cat. Will you please come and talk to her?"

After work, I drove to the retirement community and met Julie. As she led me to Mrs. Painter's room, she said, "Sometimes, she has trouble understanding, but do your best to explain what's best." *Best? Best for whom?*

I gently knocked on Mrs. Painter's room, rehearsing silently what I was going to say. Julie asked me not to tell her that I was being "sent." Mrs. Painter opened her door.

"Hello, Mrs. Painter, it's Dr. Bryant, from the animal hospital. I was driving by and wondered how Callie was doing, so I thought I'd stop in."

Mrs. Painter recognized me. "Oh, hello, dear! How nice of you to come!"

She led me into her room. It was small, containing a hospital bed, a vanity, a tall dresser and a bathroom that looked like one you would find in a hospital. As I looked around at her few possessions, I wondered what it must be like to narrow down a lifetime of earthly belongings so they could all fit in one room.

Mrs. Painter and I sat opposite each other. Callie was sleeping on the bed. She petted the cat gently while she spoke. "Oh, she's fine. Such good company."

Trying to get a little information—or should I say "ammunition"—I asked about her appetite and drinking habits. Mrs. Painter assured me that she was urinating in her box and her drinking habits were normal. She claimed she wasn't vomiting, and even played with her a little every afternoon. A cat in end-stage kidney failure would not be playing and eating. I didn't know what to believe. Callie was painfully thin and looked dehydrated.

Mrs. Painter said that she and her husband had lived in the independent-living section of the facility until he died a year ago. She was then sent to assisted living. Nursing care inevitably would come next. As she told me that she wasn't feeling too well lately, I could almost hear her thoughts: *My cat is old; she is dying. I am old; I am dying.*

Mrs. Painter gently stroked her beloved cat and said, quite out of the blue, "She is the only friend I have in the world."

I will never forget that. *She is the only friend I have in the world.* Sitting in that darkened room that chilly winter afternoon, with an old lady and her old cat, I silently vowed that I was never going to discuss euthanizing Callie. Not today, not ever.

As I left, I told Mrs. Painter that if she felt that Callie was not doing well, the important thing was to not let her suffer. She seemed to understand exactly what I meant. Usually, the elderly consider their lives parallel to their elderly pets' lives.

It wasn't long before I heard from Mrs. Painter. She called the day after Christmas. She was very calm and matter-of-fact. "Dr. Bryant, it's time for Callie."

Once again, I found myself in Mrs. Painter's room. Callie looked even worse than she had the month before. Her skin was stretched over her bones, and her eyes were sunken. She was semi-conscious. I gave her the painless injection, and she silently slipped away. As I wiped away tears from my own eyes, Mrs. Painter just sat on the bed and watched, dry-eyed. She said nothing.

Afterward, I sat with Mrs. Painter; she seemed far away, lost in thought. She was just sitting on the edge of her little bed, fondling a small, ceramic calico cat. When she finally spoke, it was almost as if she were talking to herself. "My husband gave me this cat for our anniversary because it looked like Callie." She handed it to me. "I want Callie cremated, Dr. Bryant. I want you to place her ashes in here and give it back to me. Would you do that?"

I looked down at the ceramic cat, representing her husband, her cat, and a life silently slipping away.

So there I sat in my dining room that January evening, watching the glue dry thoroughly on the bottom of the china cat. When I delivered the cat statue to Mrs. Painter, the loneliness in that small dark room was hard to bear. I asked Julie if we could try to find a suitable cat for Mrs. Painter. She explained that Mrs. Painter was failing and didn't have the capability to take care of another cat.

A few weeks later, I asked Julie again. She again refused. As the months went by, my thoughts would occasionally go to Mrs. Painter, and a terrible sadness would descend upon me. I pictured her in that little room with her few possessions—joyless without a pet.

Months later, I decided to visit Mrs. Painter. As I stood in the lobby and waited for the elevator, a cat appeared and sat next to me, as if she were waiting, too. When the door opened with a loud *ding,* I got on, and so did the cat. She calmly sat down as the elevator ascended to the second floor. The doors opened, and she sauntered out. A nurse laughed at my bemused look. "I see you've met Pumpkin," she said.

As we spoke, Pumpkin made her way to Mrs. Painter's room. The door was slightly ajar, and she walked in. Not having special privileges like the cat, I knocked. Mrs. Painter opened the door. "Well! Two of my favorite girls in one visit!" she exclaimed. I marveled at her appearance: She seemed ten years younger.

After my visit, Julie told me Pumpkin's story. A nurse had found her in the parking lot as a kitten. Soon after, she became a "resident," too. Although she visited everyone in assisted living, Mrs. Painter was her favorite. Then Julie said something that made my heart sing: "Dr. Bryant, you were right about getting another cat. Pumpkin has made all the difference in Mrs. Painter's life here."

Veterinarians live to make a difference in people's lives through their beloved pets. This time, however, it was a cat who accomplished this. Pumpkin gave Mrs. Painter something to live for.

Mary Bryant, V.M.D.

4

CAT-EGORICALLY WONDERFUL

In ancient times, cats were worshipped as gods. They have not forgotten this.

Unknown

Catch of the Day

This is the story of the night my ten-year-old cat, Rudy, got his head stuck in the garbage disposal. I knew at the time that the experience would be funny if the cat survived, so let me tell you right up front that he's fine.

My husband Rich and I had just returned from a five-day spring-break vacation where I had been as sick as— well, as a dog—the whole time. We had arrived home at nine in the evening, later than we had planned because of airline problems. Exhausted and still suffering from illness-related vertigo, I sat down at my desk to prepare for teaching my morning English class.

At around ten o'clock, I heard Rich hollering something undecipherable from the kitchen. As I raced in to see what was wrong, I saw Rich frantically rooting around under the kitchen sink, and Rudy—or, rather, Rudy's headless body—scrambling around *in* the sink, his claws clicking in panic against the metal. Rich had just ground up the skin of some smoked salmon in the garbage disposal, and, when he left the room, Rudy (whom we always did call a pinhead) had gone in after it.

It is very disturbing to see the headless body of your cat in the sink. This is an animal that I have slept with nightly for ten years, who burrows under the covers and purrs against my side, and who now looked like a desperate, fur-covered turkey carcass set to defrost in the sink, still alive and kicking. It was also disturbing to see Rich, Mr. Calm-in-an-Emergency, at his wit's end, trying to soothe Rudy, trying to undo the garbage disposal, failing at both, and basically freaking out. Adding to the chaos was Rudy's twin brother Lowell, also upset, racing around in circles, jumping onto the kitchen counter and alternately licking Rudy's butt for comfort and biting it out of fear. Clearly, I had to do something.

First, we tried to ease Rudy out of the disposal by lubri-cating his head and neck. We tried Johnson's baby sham-poo and butter-flavored Crisco. Both failed, and a now-greasy Rudy kept struggling. Rich then decided to take apart the garbage disposal, which was a good idea, but he couldn't do it. Turns out, the thing is constructed like a metal onion: You peel off one layer, and another one appears, with Rudy's head still buried deep inside, stuck in a hard-plastic collar. When all our efforts failed, we sought professional help. I called our regular plumber, who actually called me back quickly, even at eleven o'clock at night, and talked Rich through further layers of disposal dismantling, but still we couldn't reach Rudy. I called the 800 number for Insinkerator (no response); a pest-removal service that advertises twenty-four-hour service (no response); an all-night emergency veterinary clinic (who had no experience in this matter, and, there-fore, no advice); and, finally, in desperation, 911. I could see that Rudy's paw pads, normally a healthy shade of pink, were turning blue. The fire department, I figured, got cats out of trees; maybe they could get one out of a garbage disposal.

The dispatcher had other ideas and offered to send over two policemen. The cops didn't arrive until close to midnight, but they were able to think rationally, which we were not. They were, of course, quite astonished by the situation: "I've never seen anything like this," Officer Mike kept saying. Officer Tom, who expressed immediate sympathy for our plight—"I've had cats all my life," he said, comfortingly—also had an idea.

Evidently, we needed a certain tool, a tiny, circular, rotating saw, which could cut through the heavy plastic flange encircling Rudy's neck without hurting Rudy. Officer Tom happened to own one. "I live just five minutes from here," he said. "I'll go get it." He soon returned, and the three of them—Rich and the two policemen—got under the sink together to cut through the garbage disposal. They finally managed to get the bottom off the disposal, so we could now see Rudy's face and knew he could breathe, but they couldn't cut the flange without risk of injuring the cat. Stumped.

Officer Tom had another idea. "You know," he said, "I think the reason we can't get him out is the angle of his head and body. If we could just get the sink out and lay it on its side, I'll bet we could slip him out." That sounded like a good idea—at this point, *anything* would have sounded like a good idea—and as it turned out, Officer Mike ran a plumbing business on weekends, so he knew how to take out the sink! Again, they went to work, three pairs of legs sticking out from under the sink surrounded by an ever-increasing pile of tools and sink parts. About an hour later—*voilà!*—the sink was lifted gently out of the countertop and laid on its side, but even at this more favorable angle, Rudy stayed stuck.

Officer Tom's radio beeped, calling him away on some kind of real police business. As he was leaving, though, he had another good idea: "You know," he said, "I don't think we can get him out while he's struggling so much. We need to get the cat sedated. If he were limp, we could slide him out." And off he went, regretfully—a cat lover still worried about Rudy.

The remaining three of us decided that getting Rudy sedated was a good idea. Rich and I knew that the overnight emergency veterinary clinic was only a few minutes away, but we didn't know how to get there. "I know where it is!" declared Officer Mike. "Follow me!"

So Mike got into his patrol car, Rich got into the driver's seat of our car, and I got into the back, carrying the kitchen sink, what was left of the garbage disposal, and Rudy. It was now about two in the morning.

We followed Officer Mike for a few blocks when I decided to put my hand into the garbage disposal to pet Rudy's face, hoping I could comfort him. Instead, my sweet, gentle bedfellow chomped down on my finger, hard—really hard—and wouldn't let go. My scream reflex kicked into gear, and I couldn't stop the noise. Rich slammed on the brakes, hollering, "What? What happened? Should I stop?" checking us out in the rearview mirror.

"No," I managed to get out between screams, "just keep driving. Rudy's biting me, but we've got to get to the vet. Just go!"

Rich turned his attention back to the road, where Officer Mike took a turn we hadn't expected, and we followed. After a few minutes Rudy let go, and, as I stopped screaming, I looked up to discover that we were wandering aimlessly through an industrial park, in and out of empty parking lots, past little streets that didn't look at all familiar.

"Where's he taking us?" I asked. "We should have been there ten minutes ago!"

Rich was as mystified as I was, but all we knew to do was follow the police car until, finally, he pulled into a church parking lot, and we pulled up next to him.

As Rich rolled down the window to ask, "Mike, where are we going?" the cop, who was not Mike, rolled down his window and asked, "Why are you following me?"

Once Rich and I recovered from our shock at having tailed the wrong cop car, the policeman led us quickly to the emergency vet, where Officer Mike greeted us by holding open the door, exclaiming, "Where *were* you guys?"

We brought in the kitchen sink containing Rudy and the garbage disposal containing his head. The clinic staff was ready. They took his temperature (which was ten degrees lower than normal) and checked his oxygen level (which was half of normal), then the vet declared: "This cat is in serious shock. We've got to sedate him and get him out of there immediately." When I asked if it was okay to sedate a cat in shock, the vet said grimly, "We don't have a choice." With that, he injected the cat, Rudy went limp, and the vet squeezed about half a tube of K-Y Jelly onto the cat's neck and pulled him free.

Then the whole team jumped into "code blue" mode. (I know this from watching a lot of *ER*.) They placed Rudy on a cart, where one person hooked up IV fluids, another put little socks on his paws ("You'd be amazed how much heat they lose through their pads," she said), one covered him with hot-water bottles and a blanket, and another took a blow-dryer to warm up Rudy's now very gunky head. The fur on his head had dried in stiff little spikes, making him look rather pathetically punk as he lay there, limp and motionless.

At this point they sent Rich, Officer Mike and me to sit in the waiting room while they tried to bring Rudy back to life. I told Mike that he didn't have to stay, but he just stood there, shaking his head. "I've never seen anything like this," he said again.

At about three, the vet came in to tell us that the prognosis was good for a full recovery. They needed to keep

Rudy overnight to rehydrate him and give him something for the brain swelling they assumed he had, but, if all went well, we could take him home the following night. Just in time to hear the good news, Officer Tom rushed in, finished with his real police work and concerned about Rudy.

Rich and I got back home at about three-thirty. "I need a vacation," I said, and called the office to leave a message canceling my early class.

I slept late, then badgered the vet until he said that Rudy could come home later that day. I was unpacking when the phone rang. "Hi, this is Steve from the *Times-Herald*," a voice told me. "Listen, I was just going through the police blotter from last night. Mostly it's the usual stuff—breaking and entering, petty theft—but there's this one item. Um, do you have a cat?"

So I told Steve the whole story, which interested him. A couple of hours later he called back to say that his editor was interested, too. Did I have a picture of Rudy? The next day, Rudy was front-page news, under the ridiculous headline, "Catch of the Day Lands Cat in Hot Water."

There were some noteworthy repercussions to the newspaper article. When I arrived at work, I was famous; people had been calling my secretary all morning to inquire about Rudy's health. When I called our regular vet to make a follow-up appointment for Rudy, the receptionist asked, "Is this the *famous* Rudy's mother?" When I brought my car in for routine maintenance a few days later, Dave, my mechanic, said, "We read about your cat. Is he okay?" When I called a tree surgeon about my dying red oak, he asked if I knew the person on that street whose cat had been in the garbage disposal. And, when I went to get my hair cut, the shampoo person told me the funny story her grandma had read in the paper about a cat who got stuck in the garbage disposal.

I don't know what the moral of this story is, but I do know that this "adventure" cost me $1,100 in emergency vet bills, follow-up vet care, a new sink, new plumbing, new electrical wiring and a new garbage disposal—one with a cover. Plus, the vet can no longer say he's seen everything but the kitchen sink. And Rudy, whom we originally got for free (or so we thought), still sleeps with me—under the covers on cold nights—and, unaccountably, he still sometimes prowls the sink, hoping for fish.

Patti Schroeder

The Cat Man

I sure love to fish. There is nothing more relaxing than being high up in the mountains and breathing in that fresh, cool air. My favorite fishing spot is a lake near a little four-building, one-gas-station town located high in the mountains of California, three hours from my home. Each year, as soon as the winter snow melts, I load my fishing gear into the station wagon and head out for a day of trout fishing.

Many years ago, during one of my trips, I crossed the small dam that had been built to create the beautiful mountain lake, pulled over to the side and began to unload my fishing poles. Suddenly, I heard a gunshot ring out, whistling as it flew over my head. I was quite surprised to hear someone shooting a firearm, as this was a restricted area: No hunting was permitted. Besides, in all my years fishing in the area, it was the very first time that I had ever come in contact with *anyone,* except for a few logging trucks that passed by.

I ducked down behind my automobile and carefully looked around, but I didn't see anyone.

Bam! Bam! Another two shots were fired.

Zing! rang the bullets as they hit against the large boulders. Still, I could see no one.

Then four young men came walking down the dirt road. One raised his rifle and fired off a shot. A cat ran across the road and into the bushes.

"Hey! What the heck are you doing?" I asked as they approached me. "This is not a hunting area."

"Just shooting at a darn cat," said the larger boy.

Slowly, another one of the boys raised his rifle and fired another shot at the cat, who was still hidden behind the large rock.

"Come on, guys. Why kill something for no reason?" I asked.

"What's the cat worth to you?" asked one of the boys.

"How about ten dollars?" I said.

Bam! Another shot in the cat's direction.

"How about a hundred dollars? That's what it's going to take," said the largest of the four boys, taking another shot in the cat's direction.

For weeks, I had been saving money to buy some type of used boat and motor so that I would not have to fish from the bank. I had about $110 in my wallet and maybe another twenty in my pocket.

"Okay, I'll give you a hundred dollars for the cat. Just don't kill it. Please," I said.

I pulled out my wallet, took the money out of the secret compartment and put it on the hood of my brown station wagon. The four boys walked closer and stood looking at the money.

A very serious look came over their faces. The biggest boy reached down and picked up the money and put it into his pocket. As the four boys disappeared around the bend of the road, I began to look for the cat. Several minutes later, the boys, in an old pickup truck, drove past me, heading back up the mountain toward town.

It took me more than an hour to get the cat to trust me enough to let me catch her. I petted her for five minutes or so, then put her into my vehicle, along with my fishing gear, and drove back up the mountain to the little store.

I asked the owner if he knew if anyone in the area had lost a cat. He walked out to my vehicle and looked at the cat. He told me that the old man who lived next-door had lost his cat about a week ago. The old man was very upset because it was his wife's cat. His wife had died several months before, and the cat was all that he had left.

The owner of the small store went to the telephone and made a call. When he returned, he poured a hot cup of coffee for each of us, and we talked for about ten minutes. I heard the door open behind me, and I turned around. A gray-haired man, all hunched over, who looked to be at least a hundred years old, slowly made his way to the corner. He sat down in a rocking chair, but didn't say a word.

"It's his cat," the owner told me.

The old man tapped his walking cane three times on the floor. The owner came from behind the counter and walked over to where the old man sat. The old man whispered something to the owner, then handed him a piece of paper. The owner took the old man by the arm, helped him up, and the two of them walked outside to my station wagon.

I watched through the window as the old man reached in, picked up the cat and hugged her to his chest. Then the two men walked to a mobile home next-door and went inside.

Several minutes later, the storeowner came back.

"I had best be hitting the road," I told him.

"There's a reward for finding the cat," he said.

"I don't want a reward," I replied, but the man held out a piece of paper, and I took it from him. I opened the folded paper and saw that it was a personal check made out to "cash" in the amount of $2,500. I raised my eyebrows in surprise.

"Don't worry, that check's no good. Old man's been off his rocker since his wife died," said the owner of the store.

I folded the check again and threw it onto the counter so that he could throw it away. Then something inside me told me to keep the check. Retrieving it, I tucked it into my shirt pocket.

"I guess only an idiot would think that a cat is worth paying that kind of money for," he said, laughing out loud.

"Yeah! Only an idiot would think that," I said, laughing, too.

I walked out the door, got into my station wagon and drove home. The boys and their guns had made me decide to postpone my fishing trip.

When I arrived home, my wife handed me a note from a friend of mine. It said that he knew a man who would sell me his boat on a monthly payment plan. I telephoned the man with the boat. After discussing the boat, I asked him how much he wanted for it.

"Twenty-five hundred dollars. Three thousand if I have to finance it for you," he replied.

I told him that I would call him back in about an hour.

Taking the check out of my pocket, I telephoned my bank. I told them the story and asked if there was any way to find out if the check that the old man had given me was good. I gave them the numbers from the check, then waited for them to call me back. Ten minutes later the phone rang.

"Mr. Kiser, the check is good," said the woman at the bank, laughing.

"What's so funny?" I asked her.

"Well, when I called the other bank to ask if the check would clear, the gentleman there laughed. He told me that the old man who gave you the check is extremely wealthy. He owns most of the logging companies that operate in that area of California."

And that wasn't the only surprise.

That evening, I drove over to see the boat, motor and trailer that were for sale. When the tarp was removed, the boat was like new. It was a great deal; I knew I wanted it. But, when I saw the boat's name, I decided—right there and then—that it was meant to be. Painted on the back of the boat were the words: "The Cat Man."

Roger Dean Kiser

Serendipity

There is no more intrepid explorer than a kitten.

Jules Champfleury

"Thank goodness you answered the phone! I've tried to fax you for three days. This line's been busy, too."

I didn't know what to say. I checked the machine, and, sure enough, it was off. Again.

"Sorry for the inconvenience," I told my very-most-important-client-in-the-world. "I just turned it back on, so please fax the material now. I'll wait." I glanced at the kitten sleeping on "her" chair across the room and added, "I've been having trouble with office gremlins."

The "office gremlin" in question opened blue-jean-colored eyes, yawned, then came fully awake when the fax squawked back to life. "You nearly cost me a client," I muttered.

The kitten hopped off the chair and raced to her toy *du jour*. But I stood firm, between Seren(dipity) and her target, poised to collect the fax before the Siamese-wannabe could hole-punch the pages with her baby teeth.

"You've been playing the fax buttons again, haven't you?"

"Mew-mewoy."

"No excuses. I don't care if the fax looked at you funny. . . ."

"Meerowing-ing-ing!"

"Seren, fax machines do not talk dirty!"

"Phttt-ptuii. Merro-wumff."

The five-month-old juvenile delinquent grabbed my ankle as if to punctuate her remarks, executed a thirty-second feline headstand while bunny-kicking my calves, then dashed out the door. I could hear her playing trampoline on the bed in the next room as the fax stuttered to a stop.

Weeks before, a friend discovered the dumped kitten napping in an empty flowerpot on her back porch and called me, her pet-writer buddy, for help. I had been pet-less for longer than I cared to admit. E-mail, phone and fax lines kept me connected to my clients, but I figured the kitten would brighten my long, sometimes lonely workdays. So it was Amy-to-the-rescue, and love at first sight.

I convinced my husband that a sweet, lap-cuddling kitten would be no trouble at all. Less than a month later, though, I realized the cat-gods have a wicked sense of humor.

Seren had no off-switch. She wanted a job—and told me so in long, meow-punctuated conversations, in which she always got the last word.

She emptied my sock drawer. She played patty-cake in the toilet. Sparkle balls (first soaked in the water bowl) sabotaged our shoes. Vital Post-it Note messages were stalked, stolen and killed. Coffee cups invited paw-dipping (and shaking) to create feline splatter art on computer monitors, reference books and pristine manuscripts.

But Seren really pushed my buttons—literally—by tap dancing across the fax machine. The ringing was a kitty dare; emerging paper, a cat temptation; the musical push-button tones, glorious fun. I have no idea how many faxes I missed due to a furry butt-perch taking the machine off-line.

Instead of corporeal punishment—which won't work—I practiced tough love, kitten-style, in the form of squirt-gun interruptions.

Seren decided she liked being squirted.

Dang!

She rattled the wooden blinds, pulled books off shelves, and played "gravity experiments" paw-patting breakables off the mantel—all to invite games of squirt-gun tag.

I figured water on a fax machine probably invalidated the warranty, so I got a cardboard box and jammed it upside down over the top of the fax machine.

Seren vaulted to the box-covered fax. *"Mew-mewoy."* She thumped a kitty jig, but the shielded buttons remained mute.

"Ha!" I told her. "Foiled at last!"

"Meerowing-ing-ing!"

"Seren, find something else to play with."

"Phttt-ptuii. Merro-wumff."

And she did.

When engrossed in a writing project, I can lose track of time and of my surroundings. I didn't realize Seren had managed a great escape until I heard the repeated thumps behind me, followed by an ominous silence.

I'd hung a delicate crocheted Christmas ornament on the handle of my office door. The ornament lay on the floor. The door stood ajar. The cat was gone.

The ornament caught the kitty's eye for trouble, so she'd tried to paw-catch the new toy *du jour*. Hooking claws into the toy, she'd pulled the lever-shaped door handle just enough to unlatch the door—and let freedom ring! I could hear her galumphing up and down the staircase.

I hid the ornament. That didn't stop genius-cat. She remembered every single success.

She leaped for the handle again and again. Every second or third attempt, she managed to hook a paw over the handle. But without the added purchase of crocheted material to claw-clutch, Seren's paws slid off the handle before the door could unlatch.

Thud-slide, claw-scrabble. Leap. *"Mew-mewoy."* Thud-slide, claw-scrabble.

"At last!" I told her. "Gotcha this time."

"Meerowing-ing-ing!"

"Seren, can't you find something productive to do with your energy?"

"Phttt-ptuii. Merro-wumff."

I wondered what sort of curse she'd hurled at me. "Such language—don't make me wash your mouth out with dog biscuits, little missy."

At last, with the fax protected by its cardboard canopy, and the door-handle exploits thwarted, I felt comfortable leaving the kitten safely sequestered in my office while I ran errands. The first time, I was gone maybe twenty minutes. And, when I returned, I congratulated myself that my office looked the same—and Seren, that angelic purr-kitten, must have slept the whole time.

"How's my Seren-kitty?"

"Mew-mewoy. Purrrrrrrrrrrrrrrrrr."

"Took a nap? What a good kitty!"

"Meerowing-ing-ing!" She head-butted my cheek.

All was calm.

It was about a week before I noticed anything wrong. The first e-mail message sounded cordial, but others got increasingly testy. I remembered that my very-most-important-client-in-the-world also had complained about the office phone's busy signal and being unable to reach me. I keep a log of all calls made and realized the phone bill didn't match my records. It listed several long-distance charges to unfamiliar numbers. Wouldn't I remember dialing the Yukon territories or Fink, Texas?

Two days later, I caught the office gremlin in action.

The phone was ringing as I walked into the office. I saw Seren race to my desk, hook one paw under the receiver and tip it off the hook.

"Mew-mewoy?"

She paused (or should I say "paw-sed"), then added, *"Meerowing-ing-ing! Phttt-ptuii. Merro-wumff."*

I hurried to intercept the call, praying it wasn't from my very-most-important-client-in-the-world. Damage-control time. Maybe the client didn't understand cat curses . . .

"Hello? This is Amy. How may I help you?" But only a dial tone hummed in my ear.

Seren glared at me, and before I could hang up the receiver, she began paw-playing the buttons on the phone. Probably redialing the Sardine House Take-Out in Moose Run, Arkansas.

I looked at the phone bill again, then at my feline Einstein. She grinned, then dashed out the door to find a new pastime.

I couldn't help smiling and consoled myself, "Just the cost of doing business with a furry muse. At least phone calls are tax deductible."

Amy D. Shojai

Panther and the Pigeons

Panther wasn't the kind of cat who would cuddle up in your lap and purr; she was feral. Her name suited her. A beautiful black cat with piercing green eyes, she roamed—and, in her own way, ruled—the neighborhood. Shunning people, she strutted as if she owned the block.

Other cats gave her room. Panther showed no mercy to birds or mice, and didn't run from dogs, either. She had been known to fly out of nowhere at unsuspecting dogs, then take off in a black flash. She had everything under control in her territory—except for Artie's backyard.

In Artie's yard, there was a pigeon coop that stymied her. Panther's pride could not allow this. She eyed the coop up and down, but hadn't been able to enter it. Panther's big obstacle was Artie. He secured the coop with two latches and was always on the lookout, thwarting her plans. Sometimes, he would chase her out of the yard, but he couldn't keep her away. Panther would wait until he was gone, then slink back to circle the coop, again and again. At the first sight of Artie, though, she took off.

One morning, as Artie walked across the yard, Panther darted by in her usual flash of black, then disappeared. Only this time, he saw that she had darted from *inside* the coop, exiting through a small hole in the mesh. Artie was afraid to look. How many birds had she killed or maimed? Cursing the cat, he slowly looked inside the coop.

The birds were all there, alive and unhurt. They weren't even in the state of frenzy he had expected; they seemed unusually calm. Artie was puzzled. *Well,* he thought, *perhaps he had gotten there just in time—before Panther had a chance to attack.* Then something caught his eye. Over in the far corner he found three newborn kittens. Panther had chosen the coop as the safest place to deliver her litter.

Now, Artie was in a quandary. Should he move the kittens? She hadn't touched his birds, but would she in the future? He decided to wait out of sight and watch what Panther did when she returned.

Sure enough, when the cat came back, she entered the coop. He listened, but heard nothing. As quietly as possible, he crept toward the coop. When he got close, he caught her by surprise. She was only nursing her kittens and gave him a frightened look. He felt the appeal in her eyes.

So Artie made a deal with Panther. She could stay there, and he would even feed her while she was nursing, but under no circumstances was she ever to touch his birds, not now or anytime in the future. A breach of contract would not be tolerated. Somehow, it seemed as if she understood and accepted his offer.

The birds did not like the idea at first. They fluttered a little uncomfortably whenever Panther entered the coop. However, in time, they got used to the new living arrangement.

Then, on one particularly cold and nasty day, Artie walked over to the coop and looked in. Incredulous, he blinked his eyes to make sure that the scene in front of him was real. Panther wasn't there. Instead, one of the pigeons was actually sitting on the kittens to keep them warm.

Motherhood didn't calm Panther down. After the kittens were weaned and gone, she continued to terrorize the neighborhood, with one exception: She purred for Artie, and never, ever touched his pigeons.

Barbara Vitale

The Cat's Bill of Rights

Cats are animals [who] know what their rights are.

Eli Khamorov

I am the cat, and I have certain inalienable rights:

I have the right to walk over your face anytime I wish, day or night.

I have the right to observe and comment on any and all bathroom behavior. Further, I have the right to be highly offended by any closed door.

I have the right to smell your shoes to determine if you have been fraternizing or cavorting or frolicking with any highly questionable animals.

I have the right to assist in any food preparation, cooking, cleaning or eating event that may occur in the home.

I have the right to wake you at three in the morning if I find my food dish is not to my satisfaction.

I have the right to tip over any water container I deem unsuitable for consumption.

I have the right to curse at squirrels and birds that may dare to pass my windows.

I have the right to inspect any grocery items that come into the home. Further, I have the right to inhabit any paper bag or cardboard box that you bring home for as long as I wish.

I have the right to nap at any time and place I darn well please, without the distraction of being called or moved just because you want to sit down, wash your hands or use your computer keyboard.

I have the right to sleep on top of any appliance that is warm.

I have the right to assist in any changing of bed linens and to chase the phantom creatures that hide beneath the sheets.

I have the right to look aloof when scolded for mistaking your toes for one of those pesky phantom creatures that hide beneath the sheets.

I have the right to kill paper-towel rolls that otherwise might sneak up on you at night.

I have the right to your complete attention anytime you sit down to read or work.

And, finally, I have the right to be loved, petted, pampered and entertained, for, as you know, the best things in life . . . purr.

And, should you err in your ways, I will graciously forgive. After all, you are only human, but I love you anyway.

Signed,
The Cat

Michael Ruemmler

The Ins and Outs of Cats

The cats are in, and they want out,
So they begin to dance about.
They stroke my chin and then they pout
Because they're in, and they want out.

They purr and mew and tantalize
and kiss me, too, and vocalize.
What can I do but theorize
That I am duped by their sweet eyes?

So out they go, I hold the door.
I hope they know they must endure
the rain and cold. But they are sure;
So out they go. I hold the door.

Yet very soon, I hear their cries.
(I will presume they caught no mice!)
Here's one, now two, back to entice.
It is their due, and I'm so nice.

The cats are out, and they want in.
They start to shout; no discipline.
But have no doubts, 'twould be a sin
To keep them out when they want in.

So open door, and in they come.
They're coy, demure—I'm overcome.
I'm never bored and never glum;
I can't be poor with cats for chums.

And so it goes, the cats are in.
They want to go where they have been.
And so it goes, the cats want out
'Cause that's what cats are all about.

Betsy Stowe

One Smart Cat

There is no snooze button on a cat who wants breakfast.

Unknown

Nicole and I sat on the futon watching a TV movie in the house we shared with three other college students. The music's crescendo, the beating drums, the danger lurking behind the corner on the glowing screen gripped us completely. If there was a world outside the television, we did not know it. Then a sound from upstairs momentarily overrode the pounding drums. *Thump, ting!* In the back of my mind, I wondered, *What is that cat doing?* I decided to ignore the sound. What harm could a cat do in the space of a few minutes?

Ting, thump. Then came a strange grating noise, slow and deep at first. "What *is* that?" I asked Nicole.

"Huh? Probably Nermal," she answered, her eyes fixed on the flickering screen. I was about to dismiss the repeated thumping when it stopped, and, as if on cue, the cat appeared. She hung from the metal banister like an adolescent boy struggling to do chin-ups—forearms extended up, body dangling below like a wet towel. Nermal slid down, gaining speed. She reached the end of the banister and went flying—her journey ending when she landed a few feet from where we sat. It was a spectacular entrance, one never performed before or since.

Nermal looked at us, eyes wide. We stared back at her. The room was still; the booming noise from the television had suddenly gone silent. The stillness was broken only when I started to laugh. Nicole joined in. Nermal licked her paw, as though nothing had occurred. She held our attention, and that was all she had wanted to do.

Nermal does not tolerate inattentiveness. A quiet human with eyes drawn elsewhere is a no-fail formula for mischief. She was given to me when she was no bigger than my palm, and, even as a kitten, she was deceptively innocent, with large green eyes and ears that were too big for her small head. In snapshots taken when she was four months old, she appears to be the epitome of sweetness and serenity, with tigerlike stripes adorning her black-velvet body and green eyes glowing like heated emeralds. Little did I know those eyes were not only marking each passing moment and calculating her plans, but also waiting for the next opportunity to pounce on a sleeping face or a moving foot beneath the comforter.

As an adult cat, she has become amazingly creative and persistent at getting what she wants. When I tell my friends and family about her exploits, no one believes me.

One night recently, I discovered yet another of Nermal's uncanny skills, one that I could hardly believe myself. I lay huddled under my duvet, waiting to fall asleep, Nermal curled into a ball at my feet. She fell asleep before I did, and, as I listened to her snore, I sighed. I knew that, by four o'clock, she would be screaming to be let out into the hallway. It's the same routine every night: She awakens at four, stretches, hops off the bed, and begins to scratch and meow impatiently at the door. This continues until, groggy and slow, I finally shuffle across the floor of my room and let her out. Some mornings (especially those that follow late nights), I find it more convenient to ignore the scratching and meowing until it is *my* time to get up, announced by the blaring noise of the country-music station coming from my small clock radio. She doesn't like the delay, but, as she can't open the door herself, she has to wait.

That night, as the minutes continued to pass without sleep, I knew that I would have to ignore her early call if I was to get enough rest. Finally, I fell asleep.

One moment, I was sleeping. The next, the twangy voice of Tim McGraw jarred me from my dreams. It was still dark outside, and, confused, I checked the digital display: 4:11 A.M. Why had the alarm gone off? Had there been a power failure? A single triumphant meow came from beside the bed. It was time for the cat to be let out. Puzzled, I got up and opened the door. The cat gleefully bounded out the door, the bell on her collar announcing her joyous exodus. I shook my head. *Fluke,* I thought. *Cats don't use alarm clocks to wake their humans.* And I would have left it at that, too. But the next morning, it happened again. And then again. Until finally, three days later, I caught her in action.

It was one of those nights when more thinking about sleep is done than actual sleeping. No amount of pillow fluffing, rolling over or augmenting blanket layers could remedy my sleepless state. Then, as I stared at the shadow-covered ceiling, I spied a stealthy feline figure slip from bed to nightstand. She stepped lightly, paws making a soundless transition from soft mattress to wooden nightstand. First one forepaw, then the other, both of them followed by two hind feet as she silently stepped up onto the alarm clock. The soft pad on the bottom of one paw pressed the sleep button. Country music began to play: Time to get up! She wanted out.

I couldn't believe it! Nermal must have noticed a correlation between my waking and the alarm going off. I couldn't bring myself to get mad at her. I realized that I was actually proud of her intelligence. I mean, how many cats use alarm clocks to wake up their people? Not that four in the morning is appealing, but, nonetheless, she is one smart cat.

Nermal—for better or worse—has become a fixture in my life, an irreplaceable presence who keeps me on my toes. When I return home after a long day, I call out her name at the foot of the stairs; the faint jingle of her bell always answers my appeal. Following the sound into the living room, I find her perched on top of the covered fish tank. *"Ik-ik-ik-eow!"* she says. *"You're home."*

I pick up her soft body and carry her to my rocking chair. She first sits, then stretches out, finally curling up into position on my lap, then a deep purr emerges from her depths. I can feel the vibrations filling my legs, persuading me to relax. I take comfort in her company as she takes comfort in mine.

Her eyelids become heavy, yet before she succumbs to slumber, she looks up at me expectantly. I imagine she's asking me, in that way she has, if I am okay. I smile and caress her soft, warm body until she is convinced she can sleep. And, as she gently snores and drifts into the realm of dreams, I feel immensely lucky, despite the fact that, with Nermal at my side, I know tomorrow will be a very early morning.

Rebecca A. Eckland

Jaws, the Terror

I've never met another cat like Jaws, my sister Susan's eccentric, eighteen-pound, black-and-white feline. His Batman mask and the black heart on his chest are unusual, but it's his off-kilter personality that definitely makes him stand out.

When I visit Susan, I usually sleep on the couch. One morning, I woke up to Jaws stomping up my chest. Then he socked me on the chin.

Later, over breakfast, I said, "Susan, I don't think your cat likes me. He just socked me on the chin."

Susan laughed. "Oops, I forgot to tell you! That's his way of telling you that he's hungry. He only does that on mornings that he hasn't already helped himself to the food in the refrigerator in the middle of the night. I blamed my poor husband for years," sighed Susan. "Hard-boiled eggs disappeared, shells and all; food scattered everywhere."

Susan said she discovered the true culprit when she stayed up one evening until midnight baking brownies for her daughter's school program. The next morning, the refrigerator door hung open, and the brownie pan lay on the floor, with the foil cover chewed open from the middle and brownies all over the floor. Jaws sat up like a prairie dog, looking back over his shoulder at her. "Talk about looking like the 'cat who ate the canary,'" Susan laughed.

Jaws also adores bubbles. If anyone leaves a glass of soda unguarded, Jaws sticks his paw in to feel the fizz, leaving the drinker with a hairy soda. Toilet paper is another favorite. If left alone, Jaws can decorate an entire house with an unbroken roll.

But back to the bubbles. One evening, I decided to soak in a nice, hot bubble bath. I went into the bathroom and closed the door. Big mistake. To Jaws, a closed door means: "Challenge!" He slipped his paws underneath the bathroom door and rattled it until he drove me nuts and I let him in. I finished running the bath and got in while Jaws hung his paws over the side of the tub, stirring the bubbles. My long, soothing bath became a battle of wills between Mr. Blackheart and me. He wanted to slap at all the bubbles. I wanted to finish my bath without him falling in.

The next day, I figured I'd solve the problem by taking a shower. Even if I had to let Jaws in, there would be no bubbles. Jaws wasn't happy about this, and he let me know it. I lathered up my hair with shampoo as the warm, relaxing water flowed over my body. *Flush!* went the toilet. I quickly moved to the side and readied myself for the inevitable. The next thing I knew, my nice warm shower had turned into a scalding stream. *What's the matter with those kids?* I asked myself. *Can't they see someone's in here?*

Avoiding the hot water, I hurried to wash the soap out of my eyes. But it was too late. *Flush! Flush!* And *flush* again! Teeth gritted, I leaped out of the shower. And, there, balancing on the edge of the commode, was Jaws. He almost grinned at me as he continued to flush—in apparent protest of the lack of bubbles. As an extra bonus, he gleefully watched the water swirl around as it went down.

In spite of everything, I had to laugh. Of all Susan's cats, Jaws will always be my favorite. After all, who can resist a cat that smart?

Carol Shenold

The Cat Who Brought Us a Bottle of Wine . . . from the Popes' Private Reserve

When he came to live with my mother, he was a bundle of fur the color, size and shape of an orange, with the appetite of a small horse. Before long, he gained the name Wolfgang. Before too much longer, he had grown to twenty-seven pounds—about the weight of a typical cocker spaniel. Wolfie was a Maine Coon cat, with a keen sense of his own power and presence, and resembled Garfield in both color and disposition.

When he became too much for my mother, he moved south to live with us. We cut his hair short for summers, leaving it full only on the head and tail, so he resembled a miniature lion. That perfectly suited his nature. Just as his feline relations were known as "king of the jungle," so Wolfie quickly became "king of the neighborhood." Dogs kept their distance, and humans competed to gain his favor.

Cats may have nine lives, but, sadly, each of those lives comes to an end, sooner or later. By the time he passed on at the age of seventeen, Wolfie had shrunk all the way down to eighteen pounds. We buried him under a row of balsams at the edge of our property.

About a week or so afterward, I happened to look out the window before going to bed. On the grass in front of Wolfie's grave sat a pure-white cat who looked uncannily like him, save for the color. Through the open window, I said hello, but she bolted and jumped the fence. (That same week, our next-door neighbor saw the snow-white cat and wondered whether she was seeing Wolfie's ghost.)

During the three months that followed, a sort of courtship developed, with "Nervous Nellie" gradually coming closer and closer. Oddly, whenever Nellie appeared, it was from the trees at Wolfie's grave. Sometimes, we'd look out into the night and see her white shape glowing there in the dark as she stared at our house.

As the temperature dropped through the early fall, Nellie's reserve gradually thawed, until in the span of about two minutes on a crisp October Sunday, she came up onto the porch, let my wife Susan pet her, and made it clear that now she was ready to move in.

A few months after Nellie arrived, we began to see a gaunt, scruffy gray-and-white cat passing in front of the house nearly every day. He was bigger and clumsier than Nellie, and obviously male. His footprints in the snow led back along that path to the trees at Wolfie's grave, and, again, we joked that Wolfie had sent him to this house so he could partake of the good life here.

As we had with Nellie, we checked old lost-and-found ads and learned that a cat named Al had been advertised lost in December, but when we called, they were no longer interested in him. His paws were big and round like boxing gloves, and even had thumbs, so we called him Albert McThumbs.

Each day, when Al dropped by for his daily handout, quiet little Nellie became transformed, launching herself at the window, screeching and hissing and pounding the glass with her tiny, de-clawed paws to scare him off. He didn't take the hint, but it was equally clear that he couldn't last outside much longer in winter.

Al solved the problem for himself by getting locked in our garage the night of a ten-inch snowfall when the temperature dropped into the teens. After that first night, we rigged him a home out of a cardboard carton and a blanket. From there, he progressed to the basement, which was warmer, then eventually got a spot upstairs.

Over the next few months, Nellie's hostility turned to fascination, and, now, she constantly comes up to him to snuggle or lick his ears until he's had enough and walks away. We found that Al, like Nellie, had been de-clawed before coming to us.

We began to refer to our departed cat as St. Wolfie, Patron Saint of Homeless Cats, and to the rescue of Al as his Second Miracle. In the Catholic process of sainthood, it takes three miracles before the canonization process begins, and I joked that I'd call the Pope if Wolfie worked another miracle for a homeless cat.

On Christmas Day, I looked out the window and saw a small black-and-white cat sitting on the roof of the car, staring in at us. We'd seen her around the area since the summer, but she always ran away when we called. This time, when Susan opened the door, the cat ran only a few steps before coming up onto the porch to rub against her hand.

Nellie and Al stood on their hind legs at the window, watching this visitor with quiet interest. Were they ready to welcome another orphan?

Buried in the visitor's shaggy fur was a nametag. This was Elsie, and her humans were Jeanne and Nick Pope. Ironically, we had known Nick and Jeanne for several years before they moved farther out into the country. We phoned the Popes immediately with the news of their Christmas surprise. Elsie, they told us, had disappeared in

July while visiting Jeanne's mother, who lived about three miles from our home. They had almost given up hope that Elsie, who had lived with them for seven years, would ever come home. Almost, but not quite: Jeanne decided to hang Elsie's Christmas stocking one more time . . . just in case.

I remembered the joke I'd made: "The next time Wolfie sends a homeless cat to us, I'm going to call the Pope and recommend him for sainthood." Well, a homeless cat *had* appeared, and, as it happened, I *had* called, not *the* Pope, but the Popes, to inform them of this miracle!

That Christmas night, Elsie slept snuggled up next to Jeanne's mother on her bed. The following day, Nick and Jeanne came to bring her home. On the way, they stopped by to drop off a gift box to us. Susan and I were both down with stomach flu and in no mood to open it then.

The day after, we opened the gift box, and—dare I call it Wolfie's Fourth Miracle?—found a bottle of wine with the label, "From the Private Reserve of Nick and Jeanne Pope."

And *that* is the true story of how St. Wolfie saved three homeless cats and got us a bottle of wine from the Popes' Private Reserve.

Michael McGaulley

In-Flight Movings

I was settled into my seat for the flight to San Francisco, and, like the rest of the passengers on the sparsely populated airliner, I was prepared for a few hours of suspended numbness. With me, I had a list of things to do on this trip, a good book, and my Bengal cat, Callie Mooner, tucked into her carrier underneath the seat in front of me. It was a morning flight, and all the indications were that it would be a quiet, uneventful journey to the Bay Area.

Callie had expended most of her vocal energy in protest during the short taxi ride to the airport; now, she was resting in preparation for a renewed assault at the rental-car counter upon our arrival in San Francisco. I assumed that, after takeoff, she would curl up and simply go to sleep as she usually did when I took her along on a flight. She would be lost in slumber for the majority of the flight, only to complain with a raspy meow when awakened after we landed. Callie is not a volunteer on these flying forays, and she generally picks opportune times to remind me of this.

About an hour into the flight, I looked up from my book, startled by a flight attendant's very concerned look.

"I believe that may be your cat up in the front cabin," she said in a confidential tone.

Uh-oh.

I glanced down at my feet to see a very still carrier with a suspiciously open zipper. Obviously, a feline escape had indeed taken place, and that feline did appear to be mine.

I bolted down the aisle. Callie had worked the zipper open just enough to allow her to emerge and explore one of Boeing's finest. Apparently, she had made a determined beeline to the first-class cabin, where she encamped in a window seat and requested a Bloody Mary and a smaller-sized headset. Unfortunately, making her way to the window seat entailed climbing over the passenger in the aisle seat, as well as his open laptop computer. The gentleman's computer screen was filled with all sorts of backslashes, meaningless keystrokes and blank lines, testimony to Callie's poor typing skills and careless grammar. The passengers in first class had only recently been served a morning shrimp cocktail, a part of which Callie had appropriated from her new seatmate, as evidenced by a shrimp tail protruding from her tight little jaws.

Indeed, that was how I found her. As soon as she saw me, her face registered that she knew the jig was up.

"Callie, honey," I said in my best mother-kitty voice, "we don't have enough miles for an upgrade!" With that, I reached across the previously violated laptop computer and scooped up my cat. I apologized profusely to the extremely startled gentleman, whose journey my cat no doubt had enlivened. As I pulled the shrimp out of Callie's mouth, I offered it back to him in a gesture of goodwill. Graciously, he demurred. I inserted the shrimp back into Callie's mouth, and, since it was now "captured," she figured she would simply growl all the way back to our seat.

It was a terribly long, quiet walk—except for the growling—back to seat 34E, as all the other passengers watched our procession—a red-faced human carrying a cat with a shrimp tail sticking out of her mouth—back to our assigned seat.

To prevent a recurrence of such an "event," I've outfit-
ted the cat carrier with multiple Velcro straps securing the
zipper tabs. But, just to be on the safe side, I now travel
with my own supply of shrimp.

Lisa-Maria Padilla

Comedy Pet Theater

Imagine a theater production featuring performing kitty cats. Sound crazy? Let me tell you how it happened.

I was born in what is now called Russia, the fourth generation of a circus family. My parents were dog trainers. Although I loved animals and learned from my parents how to work with them, I wanted to be a juggler. I started my training as a juggler when I was six years old, trained for the next six years, then began performing with a circus when I was twelve. At sixteen, I was asked to join the Moscow Circus—a dream come true for any circus performer—and toured with them for four years, even traveling to America. After winning many awards for my performances, including World's Best Juggler, I felt that I had progressed as far as I could as a straight juggler and decided to train as a clown. Not long after that, I returned to America and was hired by Ringling Brothers, eventually performing in a Las Vegas act.

By this time, I had brought my wife and daughter to America. We wanted to complete our family with a pet, so I went to a pet store to buy a cat. I was shocked by the price they were charging for a cat. I couldn't afford it. Then a friend told me to go to the animal shelter to adopt a cat.

Adopt a cat? What did that mean? And what was an animal *shelter*? In Russia, I hadn't been aware that there were animal shelters. It seemed like such an American concept: to have pet stores where people bought cats and dogs, as well as shelters for the animals when the same people no longer wanted them. Still, I went to the shelter and found a beautiful, white longhair kitten to adopt. We named her Sugar.

Like all kittens, Sugar was endlessly entertaining. She pounced on everything and seemed to especially like chasing her own tail. We were constantly laughing at her behavior. I suppose that is what gave me the idea to include her in my clown act.

As a novice clown, I was not as confident as I was with my juggling skills. I felt I should have a back-up joke, in case any part of the clown act was a flop. After watching Sugar, I came up with an idea for a back-up routine: I would reach for a bag on the stage, and, when I opened it, Sugar would jump out. I would clutch my head over the mistake of the wrong bag while Sugar entertained everyone with her cute cat antics!

When I tried it, it worked! In fact, it was wildly successful—audiences loved seeing Sugar onstage. And Sugar seemed completely comfortable with her role as chief tail-chaser. The audience and stage lights didn't seem to faze her.

And, so, my Comedy Pet Theater was born. I saw that audiences were very excited to see performing cats. Although dogs are more commonly trained, I knew cats could definitely be trained as well; they just needed a different approach.

To start, I found out what the cat liked to do naturally, then incorporated some show business into that activity. For instance, some cats love to climb, others love to jump and still others like to chase things. With the appropriate props and staging, the cat's natural behavior took a fascinating turn. The other secret was to have lots of cats onstage, because not every cat wants to perform every time. Onstage, if I walked up to a cat, looked into the cat's eyes and got no connection, I knew to move on to another cat. When I got that connection, the magic and fun would happen. I could tell that the cat was up for doing the special thing that cat loved to do anyway.

My reputation grew, and I began receiving phone calls from other places asking me to perform. A man called me from Los Angeles and offered a large fee. He asked me about my dog act—I had added a few trained dogs to the Comedy Pet Theater by that time—and then he asked if I performed with cats, too. I said yes. He replied, "Great! How many?" I told him six cats, and then he sent me a contract to sign.

The day before I was to leave for L.A., the same man called and asked me about my transportation—how was I getting the cats to L.A.? I told him I was driving my Ford Escort with the cats in the back in their carriers.

There was a moment of puzzled silence, then he said, "How are you going to fit six big cats in a Ford Escort?"

Then it hit me. He thought I was a big "jungle cat" act. "These are house cats," I told him.

At first, he hit the roof! He had advertised a circus act with trained dogs, juggling, a clown and big cats. Then we decided that, of course, the show must go on, and we would use the audience's expectation to comic advantage.

When the cat act was announced, we made a big fuss about how unprecedented the stage setup was: no nets, no cages, no audience protection at all. We really built the tension, so that, when the "cats" came out onstage, the audience went wild. It was a huge success—to everyone's relief.

Since then, many new animal performers have joined

my Comedy Pet Theater. In America, all animal acts must be regulated by the local humane society to make sure that there is no cruelty, abuse or neglect occurring. I have become good friends with the local representatives of the humane society because, not only do I treat my cats, dogs, birds and rats as the family pets that they are, but I always add to my act by adopting from the shelter! I even like to plug adopting pets from shelters in all my shows.

Today, we divide our time between Las Vegas; Branson, Missouri; and touring. Each of my animal performers is a beloved pet. We travel together, perform together, and eat, drink and rest together. It is a true "family circus"!

Gregory Popovich

Ringo, the Hero Cat

We adopted our red tabby Manx, Ringo, from a litter of kittens found in a shed outside my mother's nursing home. His mother, who had half a tail, was feral. We fell in love with Ringo when he was only ten days old. He had brilliant red fur, a tiny stump of a tail, bright-blue eyes and a high-pitched, squeaky mew. How could we resist? At the time, we already had three cats and had made up our minds not to get another.

Had we stuck to our promise, we would not be alive today.

Ringo was special from the beginning. He had a wonderful personality and loved nearly everyone who came to visit. An expressive cat, he could move his little bunny puff of a tail in any direction he wanted, depending on how he felt. That red pom-pom tail could speak a thousand words. He was a delight to live with—and, as we were about to discover, a hero, to boot.

Throughout the late spring and summer of 1995, my husband Ray and I developed troubling symptoms, including dizziness, headaches, high blood pressure and oversleeping. Ray was recovering from heart surgery, and I was laid up with a cast on my leg. Naturally, we thought these symptoms were part of our illnesses. We were wrong.

One hot August afternoon, we had the air conditioning going full blast, and the doors and windows shut tight. Ringo, who was inside with us, started slamming his body against the front door of our house and wouldn't stop. In addition, he meowed loudly, over and over. I had never seen him act this way before. Finally, I hobbled over and let him out.

Once outside, he continued his loud meowing, acting as though he wanted to come back in. Again, I had never seen him act this way. His unusual behavior let me know that I was to follow him. I thought he was going to take me to one of his favorite spots; instead, he led me to the south side of our house, a place on our property that we don't visit too often. Only our air conditioner and gas and water meters are there, hidden behind large bushes. Ringo began to dig in the jagged lava-rock landscaping, about three feet in front of the gas meter. Normally, a cat wouldn't dig among these sharp stones as the edges could easily hurt a paw. Then he lifted his head, opened his mouth and wrinkled his nose to let me know that something smelled awful. When I leaned down next to Ringo, the smell of natural gas nearly bowled me over.

I called the gas company immediately. They sent out an emergency crew, who told us that we were at explosive levels around our foundation. A pilot light or a spark outdoors was all that stood between us and oblivion. In addition, the gas had permeated the walls of our home and traveled up into our bedroom. Our doctor said that if we escaped being killed by a deadly explosion, we would still have succumbed to methane poisoning.

When the plumbers came, they found the leak about three feet in front of the gas meter—right where Ringo had dug. An old steel coupler had split open, and the crack was growing larger as a result of rust and corrosion. Ringo had smelled the escaping gas four feet beneath our landscaping. He led us to the gas leak that we couldn't smell—and the meter didn't register. What a nose for trouble!

After we aired out the house, our health improved rapidly. For his outstanding heroism, Ringo received the American Humane Association's Stillman Award. Only ten cats in nearly a hundred years have received this honor. While many pets have saved their families by insisting that they leave a hazardous situation—saving the pet's own life in the process—it is highly unusual for any animal to lead his family outdoors to alert them to the source of a lethal problem. Ringo, our guardian angel, is gone now, but his extraordinary love and heroic actions will remain with us always.

Carol Steiner

5

CATS AS TEACHERS

There is, indeed, no single quality of the cat that man could not emulate to his advantage.

Carl Van Vechten

Clueless About Cats

In 1997, I had been working with the local no-kill animal shelter for a year. Mostly, I walked dogs and cleaned out the runs. It wasn't glamorous work, but I found it satisfying. I rejoiced when a shelter dog found a loving home, and consoled the pooches left behind with hugs and treats. I didn't spend time with the cats—a confirmed "dog person," I focused my energies on the canine aspects of rescue work.

Around that time, the shelter began to tape a local cable-television pet-adoption show. For the first show, I, as chief dog volunteer, selected a few dogs to showcase. My friend and cat volunteer, Diane, picked out two or three cats. At the start of the program, Diane and I stood together in front of the camera and talked about the shelter. Then we had helpers hand us the leashes of dogs being held off-camera, and we introduced each dog, extolling his or her particular virtues. Once the dogs were done and led away, we had the helpers open up the cat carriers and bring us the cats.

Unaccustomed to holding kitties, I marveled at their warm, compact bulk, their hypnotically beautiful eyes and their soft, fine fur. When a cat I was holding began purring in my arms, I thought I would melt with the pleasure of the sensation. Cats, I realized, were marvelous.

Unfortunately, my newfound love of cats was doomed to remain "admiration from afar," since I was (and still am) happily married to a wonderful man who is deathly allergic to cats. I resigned myself to getting my "kitty fixes" at the shelter and doing my part to find these cat-orphans loving permanent homes through the cable-television adoption show.

Soon, it was time for the second show. All was going well. The dog segment was finished, and we were in the process of bringing on the cats. Diane handed me a large orange tabby named Julius, then, because we were short on helpers that day, she walked off-camera to get the next cat.

I held Julius tightly, stroking his back while I chatted to the camera—and our viewers—about how great it was to adopt a pet from a shelter. Julius began to squirm; I held on tighter to make sure he didn't get away and ruin the show. His ears tilted back, and he began making a strange low noise, something between a moan and a howl. Out of the corner of my eye, I noticed his tail was twitching from side to side. *Hey,* I thought, *I didn't know cats wagged their tails.* I quickly returned my attention to the camera and focused on keeping my cheerful stream of patter going. Suddenly, Julius made a loud yowling noise, and, before I could even get out the words to ask what was wrong, he turned and bit me on the cheek. I screamed and dropped him.

Diane came running. She found Julius sitting calmly on the floor and me holding my cheek and looking dazed. I was bleeding a little, but mostly just surprised.

We stopped taping—luckily, it wasn't a live program! My tetanus shots were current, and there was no real harm done, but how embarrassing! Anyone with even a little knowledge of cat behavior could have avoided the whole situation easily. Julius was clearly saying, "Unhand me, you knave," if I had only understood. That day marked the beginning of my "cat education." I applied myself diligently, taking every opportunity to learn more about all things feline.

A year later, when I was on a book tour promoting *Chicken Soup for the Pet Lover's Soul,* I had occasion to remember Julius's lesson when I made an appearance on a morning news program. The newscaster had arranged for the local humane society to bring a cat for me to hold during the interview. The cat, a delicate-looking, white short-hair—a real beauty—sat perched upright on my lap, looking around nervously. I held her gingerly, just tightly enough to keep her from running off.

As the interview progressed, I felt her start to squirm, ever so slightly. I waited a moment to see what she would do next. Sure enough, she became more restless, and her tail started moving back and forth. It took a nanosecond for me to shift my hold on her and let her change positions. She settled down nicely, folding her paws under her body, and, a few moments later, even began to purr.

I breathed a quiet sigh of relief. My experience with Julius had most likely saved me from making a fool of myself on a live television broadcast. But, even more important, I felt I had officially graduated, ending that initial, painful, clueless-about-cats stage through which every cat lover must pass.

The newscaster said jovially, "Gee, that cat seems really happy. You certainly have a way with cats!"

Smiling modestly, I sent a silent thank-you to Julius.

Carol Kline

For Every Cat, There Is a Reason

These were the worst kinds of calls, the ones I had come to dread. As the animal-control officer of a small city, hearing the police dispatcher say the words "animal" and "car" over the radio in the same sentence was never good news. Sighing, I drove to the address I'd been given. Pulling up to the scene, I saw several people out in front of the apartment building huddled over her. She had been a beautiful cat, gray stripes with white paws. She was already gone, which gave me some relief as it broke my heart to see them suffer. I wrapped her in a blanket that I kept in the car for this purpose and gently laid her down in the back of the wagon. Grabbing my clipboard to write the report, I walked back to the small crowd that had gathered. The building superintendent had his arms folded across his chest, rocking back and forth, and shifting his weight from one foot to the other. He looked like a man who had many things to do, and taking the time to answer questions for my report wasn't one of them.

"There's no pets allowed in this building . . . no dogs or cats, so's I have no idea why this one was around." He looked pointedly from me to the elderly lady who was standing to the other side of me. Her eyes widened, and she quickly looked down at her feet.

"He's right. No pets in this building," she said in a low voice.

I put the clipboard under my arm and said, "I can write the rest of this myself." I wasn't in the mood to deal with yet another person who just didn't care. The super walked off in the opposite direction, obviously glad that this disruption to his schedule was over. As I walked to the car, pulling my pen out of my pocket, I felt a hand on my shoulder. "Please wait," the voice said, "I want to show you something."

It was the lady who had been standing with the super.

I looked at my watch. I was already twenty minutes late to my next call.

"I had to wait until he was gone," she said. She looked in the direction of the departing super. I was beginning to understand.

I walked with her around the back of the building and into the laundry room. The woman crouched down next to a dryer. "I knew the cat who died. I called her Misty because of her gray color, even though she would never come too close to me. I think she was one of those—I think they're called feral cats. She didn't trust people, but I left her a can of food and fresh water every day."

When she paused, I heard a tiny mewing sound coming from the back of the dryer. Reaching my hand in under the machine, I felt a warm, fuzzy lump of fur. I carefully pulled the lump out to find a tiny gray-and-white, spitting, growling, mewing kitten, no more than a week old. She was looking at me with one eye, the other one not yet opened, as is the way with newborn kittens sometimes. She seemed very frightened, although she was actively trying out all the new sounds she was capable of making.

"I couldn't say anything in front of the super," the lady

continued. "I've looked all around the building, and this is the only kitten. I couldn't tell she was expecting. Like I said, I could never get that close." The lady struggled to stand up, gripping the dryer for help. She asked, "What's going to happen to her without her mother?"

I understood her concern. Kittens less than five weeks old need a lot of care. Nursing every few hours round-the-clock is only part of the challenge. The local animal shelter didn't have the manpower necessary to care for a kitten so young, but would take her at six weeks when she could eat solid food—which didn't help right now. I knew that the best place for this kitten would be with a mother cat who could nurse and clean her. Now, where could I find one who would accept this little orphan as her own? "I'll figure something out," I said, tucking the tiny kitten inside my coat. The day had started out with a tragedy, but I was determined not to let it end with another one.

It was easy enough to find the necessary equipment, tiny bottles and kitten formula, and even easier finding the time to stop and care for her during the day, given the nature of my job. It was a common sight to see me at my desk with a cat or a dog on my lap while I filed reports. In the hectic atmosphere of the police station, no one seemed to care or even notice.

At night, I brought the kitten home with me, setting the alarm every three hours for feedings. Unfortunately, the kitten wanted to be fed every two, and, soon, the lack of sleep began taking its toll. I was also starting to worry that the tiny gray kitten didn't seem as strong or to be growing as fast as I would have liked. I felt very alone— solely responsible for her survival and at a loss as to what to do next. To make matters worse, my landlord approached me as I came home one evening and said he'd reached his limit regarding my pets. The kitten needed a home—and fast.

The next morning, the dispatcher told me to "10-33 the lieutenant." This meant that I had to return to head-quarters and speak with Lieutenant Harris. He had been with the department longer than anyone else, and even the mention of his name made you stand up straighter. He commanded respect, and even a little fear. Being summoned to his office was probably something very serious, as he rarely had contact with the civilian employees. I left the kitten in a carrier in my car and went inside to face my fate.

I knocked quietly on his door. "Come in," he barked from behind the door. Slowly, I entered his office and stood in front of his desk. Lieutenant Harris didn't look up. I stood there awkwardly, scanning the numerous framed awards and commendations on the wall. He was writing busily on a legal pad.

"You can sit down now," he said, still not looking up.

I sat. The lieutenant put his pen down, sighed, clasped his hands in front of him and looked up at me for the first time, his eyes flinty.

"So, I understand that you have in your custody a very young kitten. Is this so?"

My heart sunk. Now I was in for it! Flustered, I opened my mouth to tell him that, yes, I did have this tiny kitten with me all the time, but I hadn't let it interfere with my job. That I couldn't bring this kitten to the shelter because she was too young to survive there. That I was worried that she wouldn't make it. That I was exhausted because I hadn't slept more than two hours at a time for a week, and I felt like I was going to cry. I was going to say all of these things, but the only words that came out of my mouth were, "Yes, sir," spoken in a hoarse whisper.

He looked at me sternly, then his face broke into smile, and he said, "Can I see it?"

Surprised relief coursed through me, and, eager to

comply, I rushed outside and brought in the carrier, a bottle and some formula. "Close the door," the lieutenant said, gesturing for me to give him the kitten.

"She has some longhaired breed in her," Lieutenant Harris said as he carefully scratched behind her ears. I handed him the bottle, and he started to feed the kitten. He looked happier than I had ever imagined he could look. I told him the story of how I had come to have the kitten.

When I finished, he said, "There's something very special about this little cat, surviving like that when the odds were against her. Yes, there's definitely a special reason for this little girl here. Hey, that might be a good name for her: Reason!" He smiled at me and said, "Now let's put our heads together and figure out how we can help her."

By the end of the day, a plan was in place. It seemed as though everyone stopped what they were doing to consider how they could help. The assistant district attorney spoke to the youth officer, who had a friend who bred Persian cats. The youth officer called her friend and learned that one of the Persians had just had a new litter and was nursing. The breeder said I could come over to her apartment to see if her cat would accept Reason and let her nurse with her own kittens.

When we got there, I put Reason down close to the mother cat and the other kittens. The youth officer and I stood there, waiting to see what would happen. The tiny kitten padded over to the others and nosed her way into the crowd. As I stood there, holding my breath, the mother cat stretched out her paw and drew Reason to her. She started bathing her, licking her all over her head, as if she were saying, "Just *where* have you been? You're filthy!" The gray-and-white kitten then took her place among the five cream-colored Persian kittens to nurse.

Six weeks later, when she was weaned, Reason was adopted by a young woman who, initially, had come to

purchase a Persian kitten, but decided that she wanted
Reason instead. Reason would be pampered and loved for
the rest of her life.

I think the lieutenant was right. Reason *was* special—
surviving against all odds and inspiring a whole police
station to rally around her. Too often, in my line of work,
situations like these do not end well. For a period of time,
a tiny homeless kitten gave all of us who were touched by
her plight the opportunity to make this ending a happy
one. Reason gave *me* a reason to believe in others again,
and taught me that sometimes all you really have to do
when you need help is to ask.

Lisa Duffy-Korpics

Warm Rocks and Hard Lessons

I have studied many philosophers and many cats. The wisdom of cats is infinitely superior.

Hippolyte Taine

For weeks, I had noticed the small but wiry gray tomcat, with the split ears and the fighting spirit of a tiger, hanging around our yard. Since we lived in the country, far from any neighborhoods, I wondered how he had found his way to our house. Of course, we'd broken our don't-ever-feed-strays rule when we saw that he was hungry.

"Maybe we should take him to the animal shelter," my husband suggested. But the cat was wily, eluding our best efforts to catch him.

One day, I found the tomcat high in a box in the storage shed. This time, he didn't slink away when I approached. I climbed up to see four kittens sucking greedily, kneading their mother's stomach with tiny paws. Our "tom" was a "thomasina"!

"Well, it looks as if we have a new cat," I told the family. "Now, all we need to do is to find a feminine name for her."

Our two teenagers rose to the occasion. "Louella," they said, and it stuck.

Lou was a good mother. I moved her kittens into a more comfortable box in our garage. When she wanted some time away from her family, she would query me earnestly about my appropriateness as a kitten-sitter, all the while anxiously eyeing her babies. After I reassured her that I would baby-sit, she would go off on her own for an hour or so, looking refreshed when she returned.

The kids begged me to keep the kittens. They named one, a striped gray like his mother, Reuben Caine, after a Joan Baez ballad. Reuben's sister, who looked nothing like the rest of her family—a blue-eyed beauty who could have passed for a full-blooded Siamese—the kids named Lotus. I relented, saying we could keep those two, but I drew the line at the third and fourth kittens. These were placed in the arms of a gentle mother and kids who saw our ad in the paper.

Kittens grow up quickly, and, soon, we had both of them altered. Lotus enjoyed going off on her own in the pastures and farmlands that surrounded our acreage, but Reuben gloried in being the only son, clinging to his mother in a shameless show of dependency. Having grown to a great length, far exceeding his diminutive mother, he had a habit of stretching himself out on the hood of our car and allowing Lou to bathe him from head to toe.

Our kids were growing up, too, making noises about launching their own lives, considering schools and jobs. I hovered in the background, asking vague questions about appropriate apartments, laundry facilities, security and all the other things mothers worry about. In truth, I was scared to death at the thought of them on their own. *How will they ever set their alarm clocks and get up in time for class or for work when I have to call them at least four times every morning? And who will turn off their radios at three in the morning when they finally fall asleep?*

One day in late summer, I was watching Lou groom the heir apparent, now an enormous creature whose body dangled off the front of the car. Reuben Caine was in his usual ecstatic pose, eyes closed in bliss, legs stretched out so Mama could properly bathe every inch of him. *What a ridiculous sight,* I thought.

And, as if she heard me, Lou stopped her vigorous licking and regarded Reuben. Was she having an epiphany? Her One and Only opened his eyes in amazement. What had interrupted the ablution? Then, the kind little mother cat did an amazing thing. With one swoop of her paw, she knocked her enormous son off the car. *Thud!* Dazed, he looked up at Louella. *It must be a mistake,* you could see him thinking. But the usual adoring expression on his mother's face was replaced by a snarl. Reuben slunk off and hid. After that, Louella treated her son as she would any other adult feline. She was polite, unless he tried to invade her space. I made a mental note.

When autumn came, I watched my kids pack. "I can't find my new Rolling Stones tape," my son complained.

"My luggage won't fit into my car," my daughter said, with just the right amount of pathos in her voice. "Do you think Dad could make a rack or something?"

"Dunno," I said lightly, as I went downstairs and resurrected my easel from the storage room. I had a few days until my teaching duties called me back to work. Striking matches, I heated the caps on the tubes of oil paints that had been stuck for years. Rose madder. Yellow ochre. Burnt sienna. Titian red. The names of the colors seduced me, and the scent of the linseed oil and turpentine took me back to studio classes in college when I had finally learned to shut out everything but the brush, the paint and the blank canvas before me. Now, I stopped listening to the house noises, stopped thinking about how much they would soon change when the kids were gone.

Instead, I tuned my ear to the distant fields. A crow called, his voice accentuating the silence. Dipping my brush into the paints, I gazed at the landscape outside my window and started to paint. I don't know how the cat crept into the painting, but there was Lou, sitting among the gold grass of autumn, the picture of feline grace and serenity. I couldn't help but wonder if she was grateful that we, with the help of our veterinarian, had arranged for her mothering days to end.

*   *   *

Our children left home, made a few mistakes, called home and didn't call home.

And the world did not end.

And Louella, freed from motherly duties, found time to luxuriate on the sun-warmed rocks in front of our house. She also had a habit of wandering alone each evening to the western slope of our acreage and sitting there until dark. "Lou's watching the sunset again," my husband would remark as he came home from work. And I, needing a break from grading stacks of papers, would pause for a moment, rub my eyes, and join Lou to watch the landscape give up its color and turn into a serene study of twilight—mothers enjoying the peace that comes when one phase of life ends and a new one begins.

Joan Shaddox Isom

Beginning Again

*One small cat changes coming home to an
empty house to coming home.*

Pam Brown

New beginnings are like getting ready for an exciting
trip to a place you've never been before. Or like falling in
love without a parachute. There is always the promise of
adventure and none of the security of knowing the
outcome.

When my twelve-year-old cat had a stroke and died, my
grown children suggested that I get a kitten. I was uncer-
tain whether I was ready for this new beginning. No matter how tempting the journey, for the first time in all my
years of loving pets, I wasn't certain that I should continue
bringing animals into my life. Although I still had my five-
year-old dog, another twelve-year-old cat and a parakeet, I
felt that perhaps I was being selfish at my age, adding
another animal to my family. When, in my thirties, I adopted
a pet, I was confident that I would outlive him. But now, at
more than twice that age, my sense of certainty had disappeared. Chances were, the animal might outlive me. And

then what? I had never thought of the future in these terms before and did not enjoy thinking about it this way now.

There were other reasons for not introducing a new pet into the house. I told myself, *Be reasonable. Be practical. There are benefits. Less work emptying kitty litter. Less money spent for pet food. Fewer trips to the veterinarian. When the one cat remaining is gone, that will be the end of it. No more cats. Eventually, no more pets. And then I will have more freedom.*

But the house took on shadows I never noticed before and a stillness that seemed ominous. I had always had two—sometimes, three or four—inside cats. Now, the one remaining cat, who had daily groomed the other, slept with her paws wrapped around a stuffed animal. Something was missing from her life, and she knew it. The dog, who had been a loving companion to his deceased cat friend, appeared listless. Bored. His nap times increased, and so did mine.

Yes, it was easier now. Too easy. I lay in bed one day, persuading myself to remain there another hour, then another. In fact, when I piled up all the sad stories I could think of and all the pets I had bid good-bye, I thought it would be quite easy to remain in bed for the entire day. After all, what did the outside world offer? Trouble, that's what. If I didn't go out, why even bother to get dressed? Who would know anyway, if I walked the dog in my long coat?

"You need a kitten," my daughter told me one day as she frowned in my direction, sensing my mood. "This place needs some excitement."

That's how Sunny came to live with me. A tiny thing rescued from the woods, he arrived in my daughter's arms, rehabilitated, cleaned, de-fleaed and inoculated. "He's perfect for you," she said. I had not yet reached that conclusion. Neither had Sunny.

It took only a second for him to step onto the living-room rug, but, in that moment, silence rushed from my

home—exiting through the front door—and chaos
entered without warning. The dog ran after the kitten. The
older cat hissed and spat. The two ganged up on the new
kid in town. *What ingratitude,* I thought. Here I had been
concerned that they were lonely, in deep depression, and
they were rejecting my solution.

"I'm too old for this," I said at one point during that first
evening, as I tried to catch the kitten, who had hidden in
the basement.

"I'm too old for this," I repeated after four trips to the
basement, two stiff knees kneeling on the kitchen floor,
two attempts to scramble beneath the bed to retrieve
Sunny, frightened into hiding by the dog, who was on
guard duty.

Exhausted and certain I had made a mistake, I pleaded,
"Take him back. I'm too old for this," as soon as my daughter entered the house the next day. At that moment, I
meant it; I *believed* it.

I stood in the kitchen, tears in my eyes. I was crying not
only for the cat, who in my mind was already gone, but
for the part of me that had vanished also. My enthusiasm
to try something new. The belief that I could. The energy
to do it.

I wanted everyone who told me I *was* young enough to
be here, running after this kitten. I wanted them to be with
me at five in the morning when Sunny arose and decided
to attack my feet beneath the covers, then wake up all the
other animals in the house. I wanted them here when he
explored the lampshade until he knocked over the lamp,
or decided everything on the kitchen table needed reor-
ganizing, removing all napkins, spoons, glasses filled with
water, and, of course, any tempting food on the plates that
begged to be shared. But I knew that I could not blame it
all on Sunny. It was just too difficult to begin again. To
love again. To take on the responsibility again. I was

frightened because I did not know if I had it in me. And I didn't want to find out.

While I agonized over his future, Sunny had settled in a basket and was enjoying a nap. The sun settled on his beige fur. The old cat had left her stuffed animals to sit by the basket, suddenly interested in the new member of our family. The dog, exhausted from kitten guard duty, had settled in the same sunny spot, sharing it. It was as if they understood things had changed. Nothing would ever be the same. Something had left, and something else had entered. Now, they would have to adjust. I understood the message in their eyes. We could do it together, accept the change, and perhaps even enjoy the challenge of beginning again—but only if I let myself.

The next morning, Sunny investigated the kitchen with renewed interest. Something was different, and he noticed it immediately: It was raining for the first time since he had come to live with me. The raindrops splattered on the roof, making tantalizing sounds. He looked up as he explored each room, as if he expected whatever he heard to eventually come down and introduce itself. They were just raindrops falling, but their sound was new to him. And, suddenly, through his eyes, the falling rain became refreshingly wondrous for me, too.

I hurried to get dressed. Sunny started his adventures early, and I didn't want to miss any of them.

Harriet May Savitz

Solomon's Smile

All right, I admit it. I was a self-confessed doorknob polisher. You know the type. Every can in the cupboard lined up military-style with its label facing forward. No can upside down, no dents or dimples on the tin (the risk of botulism!), and the labels pristine, never ragged or torn. Classification was as important as appearance. Vegetables were stored with vegetables, fruits with fruits. Still, peas were not stored beside corn. I had good reasons. Obviously, color: Peas are green, and corn is yellow. Besides, everyone knows peas are legumes. Thus, peas and corn couldn't be allowed to indiscriminately mingle on a single shelf.

Elsewhere in the house, a crooked picture made me twitch. An open drawer with an inch of sweat sock hanging out had me searching for the nearest bottle of Zoloft. I don't need to tell you that a dust-bunny didn't stand a chance around my house. Not only could you eat off my floors, you could perform open-heart surgery on them.

Until I got the cat.

As you've probably observed, cats remain notoriously indifferent to others' wishes. It's not that they mean to be disdainful, but, elegant and aristocratic, they can genuinely claim royal lineage and display the very epitome of majestic attitude. Their unwavering stare is nothing less than regal. Then witness their incredible gymnastic ability and talent for catapulting themselves to places thought unreachable, and you understand the depth of their complete lack of respect.

Not only that—they have fur.

Fur that comes out all over the place, fur that layers sofa cushions and area rugs, fur that winds up in your toothpaste and on your little black cocktail dress. Fur even winds up in an obscure corner of the La-Z-Boy—looking like a repulsive version of a Tootsie Roll-shaped nut bar—as a hairball.

So you can imagine how far in the loosening-up department I've had to go. Flexibility is not my strong suit. It never was. I think it's a genetic thing.

As a kid, I had foisted upon me a series of cold-blooded creatures that were purchased as substitutes for cuddly, high-maintenance pets. No puppies or kittens for me! My folks, both working parents, persuaded me that a goldfish or a turtle could be just as fulfilling as something warm and furry. A bribe in the form of a Caravan Bar (remember those?) and a bottle of Jersey Cream Soda always made the alternatives to "warm and furry" seem much more appealing. I think that I would have gone for a baked potato at the bottom of a fish tank had I been plied with enough sugar.

At any rate, after more than fifty years of pet deprivation, at last I resolved to get the animal-child I had always wanted. Thanks to a desperate plea by his owner in the pet-giveaways section buried deep within the classifieds, a ragdoll cat (Siamese mixed with Persian) came to live with me. Solomon, my gentle, fearful Buddha-cat with the Mona Lisa smile, also proved to be the instrument of an amazing, life-changing transformation.

For one thing, I stopped wearing black. I even tossed the charming little black cocktail dress. And I *really* like black. It's dramatic. In fact, I stopped wearing dark-colored clothing altogether. I just couldn't be bothered. The upholstery and the carpeting were more complicated. How many hours of the day did I really want to vacuum? I decided that I couldn't be bothered.

I overlooked long white hairs the consistency of fishing line. I squinted myopically at my houseplants when I watered them; the sweater of white cat-fluff that coated the leaves actually made them look fuller. I ignored the dusty paw prints dotting my countertops, appliances and the glass doors of my china cabinet. They could be brushed away with a careless swipe of my sleeve. Did I really want to obsessively follow my cat around with a cloth and bottle of Windex? No way; I couldn't be bothered.

I couldn't believe it! Had I actually said, *I couldn't be bothered?*

I'm not sure when the epiphany came, but the moment of insight slammed into me like a tractor-trailer loaded with perishable food late for a delivery. I had actually let go, chilled out. I found myself on the road to change, saying good-bye to my anal-retentive ways. Without even realizing it, I had made a life-altering choice. I had opted for a fur-covered existence, a permanently fluffy ambience, a softer world with a little less shine.

Now don't get me wrong. I'm not saying I turned into Oscar Madison. I'm not wiping my jam-covered hands on the drapes yet. But what I have done is cut myself, and the others I live with, some significant slack. Peas and corn amicably dwell on the same shelf in the cupboard, a crooked picture goes unnoticed for days, and sweat socks can hang out until the next time the laundry gets done. I'm saving a fortune on prescriptions.

Truth is, I'm pretty proud of myself. When friends

express wonder at what's happened to me (in a good way), I know what they mean. I hardly know myself. No more worrying about little things that don't matter—let me tell you, it feels great! I do have one question, though: Is anal-retentive spelled with, or without, a hyphen?

Sharon Melnicer

What Willa Knew

"Willa Cather sat under the tree all morning again," Alan said.

I didn't have to ask what Willa was doing under the hundred-foot pine that dominated our backyard. She crouched under the branches day after day, hoping a bird would fall out of its nest.

Willa, who resembled an overstuffed penguin, was the least athletic of our four cats. When young, she'd never taken to hunting the way her siblings had. She preferred canned food, served twice daily. Now old and heavy, Willa showed even less inclination to hunt. She'd taken to hunkering under the tree, head tilted upward, gaze fixed. Willa knew that birds have nests. She must have figured that, eventually, her luck would change.

Next morning, fat Willa claimed her usual spot, whiskers aquiver.

"Won't work," I called to her. "Birds hardly ever fall out of trees. Get real."

Willa ignored my advice and sat under the tree all spring.

One day, Willa didn't show up in her usual spot.

Good. She'd finally learned. But I was mistaken. Willa had apparently realized her current scheme was unworkable, and, by early summer, she'd refined her plan.

"Who dragged in the mouse?" I asked one June evening.

"I'll take care of it," Alan said. "Must have been Thackeray or Dickens."

I said nothing, but I had reason to believe it wasn't either of our boys. Thackeray had napped all afternoon, and Dickens never hunted mice. That left Charlotte Brontë or . . . nah, impossible.

Dead mice continued to appear. Our puzzlement grew to amazement when we concluded that Willa, and only Willa, could be catching the mice. Still, we couldn't quite believe it.

"How does she *do* it? She's too fat, too old to hunt."

Next day, I tracked her. "She's not going far," I reported. "There's a pack of mice under the woodpile."

Toward summer's end, I followed Willa into the backyard. I brought a chair and a large cup of coffee, expecting a long wait. Mousing with Willa is not a sport for the impatient. I waited and watched.

Willa's plan was ingenious. She climbed the woodpile and crouched above the den opening. She perched, motionless, until her prey grew complacent. When a mouse ventured out, Willa's black paw slammed him down.

That summer, Willa did in the entire rodent pack. One after another, they fell to her patient paw.

* * *

Willa stretches out on my lap. She turned sixteen not long ago, but, tomorrow, we have an appointment with her vet. Willa has cancer. There's nothing else we can do.

I ruffle Willa's fur and realize how lucky I am to know her. Smart cat. She taught me an advantage of growing older: knowing where to position yourself so what you seek comes to you.

Willa looks up.

I swear she's smiling.

Kate Reynolds

Learning with Roscoe

Roscoe is one smart little boy-cat. Formerly feral, he was smart enough to dash into our house, three years ago, scrambling in ahead of my husband, Roy, who was holding the door ajar while picking up the empty food dish.

Weeks earlier, Roscoe had perhaps peered in and seen April (formerly feral, herself) curled peacefully atop her fleecy bed. Or, perhaps, he liked the gentle petting that Roy had dared to give, two days earlier, at kibble-time. Roy was following a plan to get closer to Roscoe each successive day, and he swore he saw a light bulb go on over Roscoe's head the day the petting began. *How long has* this *been going on?* Roscoe thought. Roy is smart enough to know almost everything that Roscoe thinks. (It goes the other way, too, says Roy, "Roscoe reads my mind.")

The name Roscoe was given to him by a joyful Roy, who hadn't had a male cat since before we married. Something lively about Roscoe, something rambunctious, something curious and eager to learn sounded like a "Roscoe" to Roy. We were soon to learn exactly how smart Roscoe is. He's also beautiful—mostly black, with white paws, white bib, white whiskers and one lovely white eyebrow (on the right side).

More about his smarts. He learned the litter pan in a

day. Nothing special about that. So did our several other formerly feral cats. He learned instantly that food comes from the kitchen. Again, nothing special. He never begs at the table, never intrudes upon our preparation of food. That doesn't mean he knows to stay off the counter. But he learned, early on, to stay off the counter *when we were around.* And we learned to remove any serving dishes when *he* was around. Like the other formerly feral cats we have lived with, he is no longer interested in going outside. "He's *been* out," says Roy.

He's also curious beyond anything we've ever seen in a cat. When the repairman was sprawled on the floor fixing the innermost parts of the dishwasher, Roscoe almost entered the machine with him. When the man who cleans the furnace was standing in the kitchen with us, explaining the intricacies of his visit, Roscoe climbed onto the back of the nearest chair to be part of the conversation. Our vet, observing Roscoe examine the examining room, proclaimed Roscoe the most confident cat he'd ever seen.

At night, this smart little cat has learned that lying briefly on Roy's chest is pure pleasure—for them both. Roscoe rests his head only inches from Roy's face, tucks in his paws and gives a deep sigh that elicits from Roy the same sigh of contentment. With me at night, he nestles his head into my armpit to munch briefly on my nightgown. He has never deposited his whole body on my chest. Until recently, one memorable day.

Up to that point, I'd thought of Roscoe mostly as a little boy who needed to be taught rules for managing his new environment and housemates. I'd also thought of him primarily as Roy's little buddy. On that day, though, I learned that he is also my sweet friend, able to give greatly of his comfort and his love. We'd just had a phone call from my dear cousin Joan, one of my truest friends over many years. Her message was brief: lung cancer. Metastasis to the brain. Prognosis poor. Roy and I hugged each other for a long time after the call, exchanging loving words. I went upstairs to lie down, unable to do anything except wince at the news and stare at the ceiling. Suddenly, I was joined by Roscoe, who—wonder of wonders—had climbed gently onto my chest. What had he understood? We lay there for an hour or more, listening to each other's breathing. He sighed occasionally, and I did the same as I thought about the sadness of life. But I also thought about the beauty of life—its magnificence, its richness—as I acknowledged the presence of this special creature, who had come to be with me.

April, growing ever more frail, was asleep in the patch of sunlight that poured through the living-room window—oblivious to the distress in our household. Our activities are often beyond her caring these days.

Not so with Roscoe. He stayed with me until I got up again, and while I was heart-stabbingly aware of Joan's impending departure, I was also inescapably aware of Roscoe's continuing presence. It was in the pleasure—indeed, the wonder—of this special creature, during our hour together, that I felt a sense of tranquility come over me. All the grief about Joan's untimely death would be soothed by time, I realized, and the reminders of our precious friendship would be sweetened with gratitude. Life is sometimes difficult, and this was one of those days. But life is also beautiful, and this was surely one of those days, too.

Exhibiting another one of his perplexing ways, Roscoe has never again claimed me as his territory in this manner. Was he reading my mind, on that sad day, when I was too distracted even to know that anything was written there? I may never understand why my little boy-cat came to comfort me, but I can still hold close the lesson of his behavior: Cats know exquisitely well how to live in the moment—and, if we're very lucky, they can teach us how to claim for ourselves a spot in the sunshine.

Ellen Perry Berkeley

"Gotta go, Helen. My support group is here."

Time with Marky

Cats look beyond appearances—beyond species entirely, it seems—to peer into the heart.

Barbara L. Diamond

When I turned six, my dad bundled my family into the station wagon and drove us to a farm out in the country. By the time we finally rumbled up the dirt road that led to the barnyard, two hours of road ruts and winding turns had reduced my stomach to sheer nerves. Whenever the car jostled from side to side, my stomach lurched precariously as waves of nausea rolled over me.

The station wagon crested the last hill and rolled to a gentle stop. My sister and brother, Susan and Austin, a tangle of limbs fighting for the door, tumbled out and scrambled to the edge of a corral bordered by a weathered fence marked by fading chips of gray paint. Mr. White, the owner, was already leaning against the fence. A telltale din of yips and yaps punctuated by an occasional yelp rose up and captured our attention like an unexpected eruption of fireworks against a night sky. I followed slowly behind, still nursing my overwrought stomach.

The sight of several puppies frolicking in a patch of stamped grass lifted my spirits. Austin and Susan jumped up and down, pointing at each puppy in turn.

"That one!" shouted Austin. "The one with the white fur and black spots on his tail. I'll name him Spots!"

"*Noooooo,*" whined Susan. "I like the brown one over there in the corner. He's got golden highlights on his ears. We could name him Sunny!"

"I've changed my mind," continued Austin. "I like that gray one. He has ears longer than my hands. And look how furry they are!"

I stood as still as a statue, afraid that the energy generated by the dogs and my siblings would be the undoing of my queasy stomach.

Then, I saw Marky. He appeared as a streak out of the corner of my eye. In a split second, I realized that streak was a cat—*a cat!* He had wavy gray fur and faint black rings on his tail and around his eyes. He separated from the circle of puppies and darted to the edge of the corral, right where we stood. His eyes found mine. I looked back at him with a mixture of surprise and delight. But he wasn't the only one looking at me. Austin and Susan ceased their clamoring and studied us.

"This one here's Marky," said Mr. White. "He's not a dog, as you can see, but no one's bothered to tell him that. He's the life of the bunch, friendly as heck!"

I looked down at Marky again. His eyes, soulful and direct, held a question. I must have answered that question to his satisfaction because, a moment later, he swept his tail back and forth across the dusty ground. He was wagging his tail!

"He must like you," pronounced Mr. White with a chuckle. "He usually doesn't wag at strangers."

"Dad," I whispered, tugging at his sleeve, "I think he's the one for us. Just look at him." As if understanding my words, Marky turned his eyes toward my dad and gave him the same look he'd just given me.

We settled with Mr. White right then and there.

Marky had never been in a car. In the back of the wagon, he slid back and forth, expressing his excitement over the passing scenery. He got himself too excited, though, because after a short mew, Marky threw up. He whimpered, then fell silent. I scrambled to the back seat and gathered Marky into my arms. We drove all the way home that way, his head cradled in my lap.

In his new home, Marky soon became friends with just about anything that moved. His outgoing ways won over the entire neighborhood. Joey, my next-door neighbor's dog, whether duped by Marky's canine act or merely accepting of Marky's peculiarities, arrived by our sliding door every evening after dinner to call Marky out to play. Marky was only too happy to oblige.

But, when everyone was busy taking care of other business in their lives, Marky liked to plop down in one corner of our porch under a row of wooden benches. He sat there for hours, staring up into the pale-blue sky and out at the empty backyard. As soon as I stepped onto the porch and beckoned him, however, he'd scoot his hind legs out from underneath the bench and scramble eagerly over to me. We spent hours together roaming the woods behind the house. It really didn't matter what we did. Marky always had the time to play whenever I came looking for him.

Then, one day, Marky did not come home from one of his routine jaunts with Joey.

I went to school the next morning, hoping when I got home that I would find Marky biding his time in the corner of the porch. But he didn't appear, and a slow burning behind my eyes intensified. Crushed, I didn't tell anyone at school about Marky's disappearance. On the third day of his disappearance, a rumor began to circulate the school hallways that a dead cat lay by the creek bordering the school's soccer field. My thoughts weighed down with dread all day. As soon as school let out, too scared to go on my own, I ran home and told my parents the rumor. My dad, stern and quiet, flinched at the news and left the house. It was then that my heart emptied.

They found Marky by the creek. The vet told us that he was likely poisoned. The police told us there wasn't anything they could do to catch the culprit.

Several days after our discovery, I sat alone and forlorn in the corner of the porch where Marky once waited for me. I sat there remembering the happiness he had brought into my life. All the tears I had kept to myself coursed down my cheeks, and my body shook in small eruptions. After some time, I felt a presence by my side. I looked up, and, there, sitting next to me, looking up into the pale-blue sky, was Joey. I didn't move an inch. I didn't say one word. Joey looked over at me briefly, then turned his eyes back toward the sky. And there we sat, marking our times with Marky.

I would carry the memory of Marky for years to come. When my grandpa died, I spent time sitting with my dad in front of the television. When my best friend broke up with her first love, I spent time eating ice cream and watching movies in her dorm room. When my mom was diagnosed with cancer, I spent time at home with her while she lay in bed, suffering the effects of chemotherapy. No words were necessary. I'd learned from Marky that one of the best gifts you can give to the ones you love is simply your time.

Joanne Liu

6

FAREWELL, MY LOVE

But a family cat is not replaceable like a worn-out coat or a set of tires. Each new kitten becomes its own cat, and none is repeated. I am four cats old, measuring out my life in friends that have succeeded but not replaced one another.

Irving Townsend

A Postcard to Fremont

Fremont, the name of the highest peak in Wyoming, was also the name of my first cat.

In the late summer of 1980, I spent a month climbing in Wyoming's Wind River Range. In October of that same year, a kitten came to live with me.

"They're three-quarters Persian," the older woman who was selling the kittens pointed out, as if to impress and convince me that they were special and worth the thirty dollars that she was asking for each. But, even as she spoke, I knew that one of them was priceless. When I sat down next to the litter that gray October afternoon, Fremont almost immediately separated himself from his mewing brothers and sisters, and, on legs not yet sure, tottered over to me and crawled into my lap. His lineage was not important; I was already completely enchanted with him.

I was twenty-five, with summer skin tanned the color of sandstone, dark-eyed and dark-haired. Fremont was light in color—a soft, creamy-blond, longhaired fluff. Darker blond stripes on his forehead made him appear serious, as if he was always thinking about something important.

At home, he quickly learned to scale the highest objects

in the house. He could be found curled on top of the book-case, the refrigerator and the shelf in my closet where I kept my wool sweaters neatly folded. In those first few weeks, as we learned each other's habits, what struck me most about my new cat was his proclivity for the high and airy places. I decided to name him for the mountain I had climbed earlier that summer. We both shared a love of high places and the solitude they offer.

Despite our enjoyment of solitude, we discovered that we were good company for each other. I didn't mind when Fremont proved to be quite a conversationalist, comment-ing endlessly on the affairs of the neighborhood, the house and our relationship. While I made coffee in the morning or dinner in the evening, he would wind himself around and between my legs, crying, mewing and chatting in cat. He would complain loudly, appreciate softly and mutter to himself as he walked away. I listened with true interest and often talked back. In the mornings, I would ask him if he'd had a good sleep and if he'd dreamed. He always answered both questions. And, if he had dreamed, he would usually elaborate, recounting the details until he heard the clatter of breakfast in his bowl. Food was the one thing that quieted Fremont.

By the time he was twelve, Fremont had lived a pretty good cat's life. I moved a lot during those twelve years. Each time, Fremont adjusted easily. He made fast friends and was the only cat I ever knew who received his own mail. People sent Fremont postcards when they traveled. The first time it happened, a card arrived with a picture of the sun rising over the Grand Canyon. I tried reading the card aloud to Fremont. I sat him next to me on the couch, the way my father had with me when I was a child, and we read the Sunday funnies together. But Fremont would not sit still; instead, he jumped off the couch and went to play with the shoelaces on my running shoes. I decided he wasn't interested and left the card on the coffee table. Later, when I came back, Fremont was standing on the coffee table, straddling the card, looking down at it and talking. Since Fremont preferred to read aloud to himself, whenever a card came for him, I simply left it where he could find it.

In his thirteenth year, Fremont began to move differently. He stopped racing around the yard. Instead, he walked more carefully from place to place. He gave up hunting birds and focused instead on the occasional mouse or vole that wandered unsuspectingly into his grasp. One summer day, as I watched him coming toward the porch, I realized that he had become an old man. He climbed up to meet me, one step at a time. When he had settled in my lap, we had the first of what would be many talks about his eventual death. I told Fremont, who was by now familiar with my tears spilling onto the top of his head, that I did not want him to live in pain. I wanted him to die naturally, and, if he needed my help, he would have to let me know. It was a talk we would repeat every five or six months, whenever I thought he looked thinner or was moving with more difficulty. He always listened gravely, with none of the usual chatter. When I finished our talk, he would look at me and blink a long blink, as if he understood and was promising to ponder my comments. Then he would get up and walk slowly away.

Over the next five years, he lost weight and grew frailer. His gait slipped, his hind end lagging behind his front. Eventually, he moved like an articulated bus, which only endeared him more to his many friends. Once a hefty thirteen pounds, he shrunk to half that in his final year. People who were not fond of cats allowed this old man to sit beside them on the couch; those who loved him offered their laps willingly. Eventually, though, he preferred to sleep by himself. Although he still talked, his voice grew noticeably quieter. It seemed he had turned inward.

It was early in October, almost eighteen years to the day that he picked me as a life companion. I was packing to leave town for a two-week trip and ran upstairs to get something. Fremont was standing completely still beside the wall. "Fremont?" He didn't answer or even look. I knelt down and touched him gently. His legs buckled, and I scooped him up—already knowing what he was telling me. I called our vet. It was a Sunday evening at dinner-time, but the vet said she would meet me at the clinic.

As I drove out of our driveway with Fremont wrapped in a towel on my lap, I stroked his head. He didn't purr. He was already far away. I cried as I drove the seven miles into town, saying all kinds of things: how much I loved him, what a good cat he'd been, how I didn't want him to go, but didn't want him to stay—hurting—either. I prayed to God to help me do the right thing.

Later, as I stood watching, the vet examined him. At one point, Fremont gave a feeble yowl as the vet prodded his belly. *Maybe he's just sick,* I thought. Finally, she finished the exam, removed her glasses and said, "My job is to save animals." She paused and looked down, "But given his age . . ." her voice trailed off.

"I'm going to cry," I said, the tears already starting. She left the room, and I knelt down, resting my head on the stainless examining table. Fremont's eyes were open, but there was no spark in them. I rubbed his ears, trying to memorize for-ever the softness of them. "I will always love you," I said, for him. "It's okay; don't be afraid," I said, for me.

When the vet returned, I stood up. She carried a small glass vile filled with a pink liquid. . . . *To help you over,* I said silently to Fremont.

The vet was very gentle. "Why don't you hold him?" she suggested.

I lifted Fremont one last time. My big cat was suddenly

small and light. The vet placed a little rubber tourniquet around his leg, and, as I held him close to my heart, she gave him the shot. It only took a second; his body sagged, then he was gone.

In that moment, I understood that it is spirit that fills the body with life, and it is through the wonder of the body that we meet the spirit. We fall in love with both.

Fremont has been gone almost four years, buried beneath an apple tree behind our house. He is bone now, dust, some bits of hair, a body returned to the earth. We have a good apple crop this year; perhaps it is one of his many blessings.

Recently, I sat down at my desk to work, but, instead, watched dust particles floating through a shaft of autumn sunlight. For quite a while, I watched the gold-flecked light softly illuminate every object that it fell upon: my computer keyboard, a stack of files, and, finally, a photograph of Fremont, taped to the wall.

It was late afternoon when I got up from my desk, the sun low in the autumn sky. Out in the orchard, I placed a postcard in the yellow grass:

Weather is glorious. Wish you were here.
Me

                                      Catherine Johnson

Angel Cat

I knew her for less than twenty-four hours, but she will live in my heart forever. I can't recall her name, so I call her Angel Cat.

I met Angel Cat during a sad time in my life, exactly one month after my beloved sixteen-year-old tortoiseshell, Couscous, was put to sleep. I adopted Cousy when I was a creative-writing student in Boulder, Colorado. Walking home from class one spring day, I headed up Pearl Street, Boulder's main drag that had recently been converted into a pedestrian mall. Pearl Street was always lively, and that day was no exception. I passed a street musician strumming a Bob Dylan tune; a mime dressed all in gold, his face spray-painted to match; a clown handing out red balloons; and a snake-wielding belly dancer. But none of these acts were half as interesting as the drama unfolding on the corner.

A young boy stood outside an ice-cream parlor with a large cardboard box at his feet. Overhead, he held a hand-lettered sign: "Free Kittens." A woman who must have been his mother, and who reminded me of Cruella DeVil, hovered beside him yelling, "I don't care what you do with them. You are not bringing those kittens home."

Without a moment's hesitation, I pushed my way through the crowd that had gathered, knelt down and scooped up the smallest kitten in the box. "I'll take this one," I said, "and I'm staying here until we find homes for the rest." Relief washed over the boy's face; his mother continued to scowl.

That first night, after Couscous and I split a can of tuna for supper, I crawled into bed and settled her on the soft flannel blanket I'd placed at my feet. As soon as I turned out the light, Cousy crawled up to my pillow, walked in a circle on top of my waist-length hair until it was flattened down to her liking, and then curled on top of it with her head on my shoulder. Her baby purr serenaded me to sleep and more than made up for the stiff neck I woke up with the next morning.

Couscous was my constant companion from the time I was twenty-four until a few months before my fortieth birthday. She was there when my first book was published. She was there when I met my spouse. She was there when my grandmother died. At the end of her life, she was suffering from an enlarged thyroid, cancer and congestive heart failure. I knew putting her down was the kindest thing I could do. Still, it wasn't easy.

Two weeks after Cousy died, I was scheduled to go on a book tour. I kissed my spouse good-bye and, with a heavy heart, flew to California. The tour was a big success. Not only did it help me sell many books, it also distracted me from my sorrow—during the day, anyway. After my work was done, alone in a different hotel room every night, I closed my eyes, saw Cousy's face and cried myself to sleep.

At the end of the tour, my dear friend Lili picked me up in San Francisco and drove me to her home in the country for a short visit and some much-needed R&R. It was late afternoon when we walked into her house. Orca, Lili's black-and-white cat, ran up to greet us. Seeing Orca, a cat whom I knew well, comforted and saddened me at the same time.

"Doesn't your housemate have a cat?" I asked Lili as we prepared supper.

"Yes, a sweet, little sixteen-year-old calico," Lili answered. "But you won't see her. She won't come out when my housemate is out of town. She's a one-woman cat."

"Here, kitty, kitty." I looked under the couch, in the closets and behind dressers, eager to meet the cat who was born in the same year as Couscous. But the little calico was nowhere to be found.

That night, Lili and I put on cotton nightgowns and climbed into bed like two young girls having a slumber party. Orca lay down in the doorway, standing guard against potential intruders. As soon as Lili turned out the light, something landed on the bed with a heavy thud.

"Hi, Orca," Lili mumbled. "Settle down now."

I let out a deep sigh as a great sadness engulfed me. I didn't have to explain anything to Lili. Being a cat person, she understood, and, without a word, handed me a tissue to wipe away my tears.

A moment later, something else landed on the bed with a thud, though a softer thud this time. "Who's that?" Lili whispered.

"Must be your housemate's cat," I whispered back.

"Impossible. Orca would never let her in here. They don't get along." Lili sat up and turned on the light. There, at the foot of the bed, was the sweet old calico, staring at me.

Lili was amazed. "I don't believe it," she said. "I've lived here for over two years, and Orca has never once let her into my bedroom, let alone up on the bed. She must like you." Lili turned from me to Orca. "Be nice," she said sternly. Orca merely purred. "What a good cat you're being," Lili crooned to her pet. "I'm very proud of you."

"Hi, pretty girl," I said to the little calico, who blinked her big yellow eyes slowly in reply. I lay back down, and, as soon as Lili turned out the light, the little calico crawled up to my pillow, walked around in a circle on top of my waist-length hair until it was flattened down to her liking, and then curled on top of it with her head on my shoulder. Her ancient purr serenaded me to sleep and more than made up for the stiff neck I woke up with the next morning.

I cried myself to sleep that night as I had every night for the past month, but these tears were different. Joy mixed with my sorrow, for I understood that Couscous had sent down a message from Kitty Heaven through this angel of a cat. Couscous wanted to let me know that she was all right, and that I would be all right, too. And, even though she was no longer with me, she was never far away.

Angel Cat was still on my pillow when I woke up the next morning. She stayed close to me as I ate breakfast, packed my bags and got ready to leave. It was hard to say good-bye to her. She died a few months after my visit. After Lili gave me the news, I decided it was time to get another cat. My spouse and I adopted Princess Sheba Darling, a white Turkish Van with gray markings on her head and tail, and Precious Sammy Dearest, an orange-and-white tom. I like to think Couscous and Angel Cat are looking down at the four of us from high above, purring with approval.

Lesléa Newman

Full Circle

*Animals are such agreeable friends—they ask
no questions; they pass no criticisms.*

George Eliot

Posh was a magnificent, white longhair cat, tall at the
shoulders and long-limbed, with a grand, plumed tail and
a set of white whiskers like antlers framing his mouth. He
had been abandoned after the death of his guardian—left
alone to fend for himself. Even though he had been locked
out, he stayed close to the empty house where he had
once lived. A month or so later, the man who eventually
became *his* man bought the house, listened to Posh's
indignant tale of woe, and took him inside, cementing
their friendship on the spot.

I met Posh a few years later, in 1992. He was most likely
beginning middle age and was in good health, appearing
to have completely overcome the effects of his earlier
abandonment. Though I was of a similar human age, I was
not as lucky. At the time, I found myself in an emotionally
fragmented state: A colleague had committed suicide over
business reverses, a mistake in my own law practice had

cost me my confidence in giving good legal judgment, and a declining personal relationship had shredded the rest of my self-esteem. Over the course of six months, I had become severely depressed and then had been institutionalized after a nervous breakdown. Posh's man was my friend, and he offered me a place to recuperate. Posh helped me begin my recovery.

At first, all I did was cry, too leaden to leave the house. While my friend was at work, I sat at his kitchen table, sobbing as I wrote in my journal or lay curled on his couch. I don't remember when Posh started slipping into my lap. Balancing himself on my thighs, he sat upright to face me, so I could put my arms around him, kiss him and cry on his shoulder. He absorbed my tears and troubles when I felt like talking, and silently loved me when I, too, grew silent. Posh was not a great talker.

Posh affected my heart and mind when no human could. When I felt frozen in lethargy, he was alive and warm. Rushing to occupy my pillow on the couch bed, he made me laugh. He lay down with me when I went to bed at night and was curled up near me when I awoke. Later, I learned that he went back and forth between my bed and my friend's during the night, each of us believing that Posh had slept with only the one of us. Posh offered no advice, letting me work out my grief in my own way. His warm, silken body and soft purrs eased my battered mind. Time did not matter for him. He was willing to be with me for however long I needed him. I loved him for his healing skills.

After several years, Posh's man and I married, combining our household goods, as well as other rescued and adopted cats. Posh stayed aloof from the others; they were bothersome youngsters. In my new life, I hand-stitched quilts, wrote unpublished crime fiction, volunteered my time at local animal shelters, and kept house for my husband and our cats. When I walked through the house, I stopped frequently to caress Posh as he slept on our bed.

Posh was my well-behaved eldest child, and I enjoyed his pleasant weight in my lap when I relaxed. He often curled up to rest there, while I petted his thinning coat and body. He still stalked through the house on the way to the kitchen as if he were hunting in the long grass, parting a path through the other cats as if they were invisible. He slept more, ate only a little and moved with the gait of the old man he was. My husband and I figured he must be at least seventeen or eighteen. I vowed that, when Posh's time came, I would be with him at home, allowing him to die in his own place and time.

That time came soon enough. One late October morning, seven years after I first met Posh, I noticed several of the younger cats milling around our bedroom, anxious that I come and see what was wrong. Posh lay almost motionless near my dresser, half under it, his head crowded next to the laundry basket. Raising his head slightly off the carpet, he strained his yellow eyes toward my voice. My heart knew that it was likely his last day.

Posh shunned the baby food and water I offered. He didn't seem to be in pain, so I gathered him in my arms and sat in our recliner. Settling him in my lap, his head on my chest, I tucked a fresh towel around him so he would feel snug and secure. He weighed so little—six pounds at most. The other cats did not jump up on the chair to cuddle, too, as they usually would. They sensed that death had come to our house.

Although I had many other things to attend to, I put them all aside. For the remainder of the day, I stroked and petted Posh's fragile old body, fingering bones so clearly defined through his meager fur. I talked to him of how we'd met, what he meant to me and how much I loved him. Touching and kissing his silken whiskers and face—

once so animated, but expressive no longer—I watched over him as he slipped into a coma. Still I talked, having so much more to tell him, cradling his body and holding his soft face against mine. Posh lingered until his man came home from work to be with him one last time. My husband, already grieving, couldn't bear to stay as we waited for Posh to slip away. This time, I was the strong one.

The sun through the blinds faded into the shadows and the hours ceased to matter as I comforted Posh in much the same way as he had once consoled me. He died at the end of the day, the light dimming from his fur and eyes. He passed away as he had lived—quietly and gently— reminding me in my last hours with him, as in his first with me, that love freely given is always generously returned.

Andrea Rolfingsmeier

The Long Good-Bye

The suitcase was packed; the dog was washed; the car was gassed up. I was going to spend the weekend at my parents' house, five hours away, and I was late. I put cans of cat food out for Helen, the old lady across the street who cares for my cats, Bob and Steve, when I go out of town. I put a spoon there, too. And a note: "Thanks again, Helen!"

But something was wrong. Bob didn't look right. He wasn't eating. His fur was funny. When you have lived for eleven years with an animal, you know.

"Bob," I said, "what's the deal?"

Bob just looked at me. I had taken him to the vet the week before, shortly after an evil monster cat had come into the yard and beaten him up. Or maybe he had beaten up the monster cat; it's hard to say. But Bob had yet another bite wound. We know this routine: vet, antibiotics, rest. But this time it wasn't working.

I called the vet. He said I should bring Bob back in. I called my mother to tell her I would be even later.

"You worry so much about those animals," she said. "See, that's why I don't have pets anymore. I have enough people to worry about."

"I know, Mom." She and I have had this conversation a

million times. She is not a pet person.

My vet likes Bob. Most people do. This is because Bob is not stingy with his love. Bob loves everybody. Bob loves the vet. Bob loves dogs. Bob even loves my mother. At the top of this pyramid of love, Bob has put me. He drools with pleasure at the very sight of me. He aches with misery when I leave town for more than a day. He lets me know this upon my return. He moans. I am not talking "mew." Bob moans, low and guttural—for hours. I have tried everything to console him. And I have learned that nothing works.

Anyway, the vet looked worried. He told me about feline immunodeficiency—a newly recognized virus in the family of viruses that causes progressive pneumonia in sheep, infectious anemia in horses, arthritis-encephalitis in goats, and AIDS in humans. This virus is species-specific. Cats typically get it from cat fights. There is no vaccine and no cure.

My vet did a blood test. He said if the little white dot turned blue, it would mean Bob was infected. He put the cat back in my blue cat carrier. He had on a blue shirt. We stood with two technicians in blue lab coats. All I remember is blue everywhere. Until my eyes welled up, and I couldn't see much of anything.

I thought, *I am not going to cry. This is just a cat.*

"I'm afraid I have some very bad news," the vet said. Not only was the dot blue, but the test also showed a "weak positive" for feline leukemia, meaning that Bob's recent booster apparently had not boosted him enough. His immune system was shot. He was dying.

I thought, *I am not going to cry. This is just a cat.*

Then I thought, *This is . . . Bob!* And I began to wail. I wailed for the loss of him, the same way he wails for the loss of me. Only this time, our loss would be permanent.

They sent Bob and me home with a bottle of antibiotics,

a feeding syringe and some liquid food. They said that, if I could get Bob to begin eating on his own, he'd at least have a little time.

I didn't go to my parents' that weekend; I took care of Bob. We watched movies for two solid days. We got into arguments over the flavor of his antibiotic. I put plates of real tuna before him, stuff that used to make him dash inside for even a whiff. Now, Bob turned away. He just stayed curled up on a bookshelf next to a game of Yahtzee.

But then came Monday. Bob stood up and crawled between my ankles. He said "Yo," or something like that. I put a plate of cottage cheese down for him, and he tore into it. He lapped up the whole thing.

I called everyone I knew. "Bob ate cottage cheese!" And then I ran out and loaded a shopping cart with designer cat foods—Savory Duck in Meaty Juices, Paté-Style Poultry Liver—all kinds of pleasures Bob had never had before. Maybe I could entice him to stay alive by wowing his taste buds. It was worth a try.

Three days earlier, after bringing Bob home from the vet's, I had called my mother to tell her I wouldn't be coming. "See, this is why I don't have pets," she said again. And, in that moment, I understood her reasoning. I thought about my other pets and imagined saying good-bye to them, too. I imagined living my mother's way: no pets. I imagined how much safer it would be to do her one better: no friends, no family. No love.

Say what you will about pets just being pets. I say: Loss is loss, and grief is grief.

And so now here we sit, me and Bob. I have just presented him with a plate of Select Halibut & Cod in Aspic. He looks up at me with an "Are you serious?" expression on his face.

"Go for it, Bob," I say, hearing in myself a lesson about

nourishment and love, and the impermanence and necessity of both.

Jeanne Marie Laskas
Originally published in The Washington Post Magazine

Walking with Ace

Ace, a black-and-white shorthair cat, gave new meaning to the words *loyal, steadfast* and *true*. He came when called, sat in my husband's lap at the end of the day and slept pressed up against me at night. His dependable, even-tempered nature and gentle demeanor earned him the title My Good Ace.

Ace was stoic; he never complained when neighborhood children carried him around the house like a sack of potatoes. Those of us who could read his soulful expression and doleful eyes understood his patient tolerance. He greeted houseguests inquisitively and politely, and then retreated to his private corner, only crossing the bounds of good manners occasionally to beg for treats at the dinner table. (Turkey was his absolute favorite! Running a close second was the shrimp my adult son would indulge him in from time to time.)

Ace was an indoor cat who took every opportunity to try to sneak out whenever someone opened the door. Understanding his "call of the wild," I would sometimes sit with him on the front porch and stroke his sun-warmed fur. More often, cradled in my arms, his back against my chest, I carried him for walks around the neighborhood.

He never once risked the privilege of further ventures by trying to jump out of my arms and escape. (Did I mention Ace was also very intelligent?) Whenever I looked down into his face during our walks, he blinked and purred in pure contentment, and I am absolutely certain that there was a smile playing around the corners of his mouth. He would divide his time between looking up into the trees, craning his face toward the sun and sky, or turning his head to observe the passing scene. Neighbors would sometimes call out, "Hey, how's Ace?" and I would always lift his front paw, wave and answer, "He's just fine!"

I am a runner, and these short walks were not my major form of exercise. But the walks invariably produced, if not an aerobic high, a sense of calm and well-being. Ace and I continued this routine for sixteen years. I ran in the mornings, pounding out the miles, noting those runners whose leashed dogs trotted at their heels with seriousness of purpose. And, in the golden-shadowed afternoons and balmy summer evenings, it became a ritual for me to walk and smile with my cat. We were a team, enjoying each other on a special level during these daily perambulations. I was certain no runner and his dog could ever know the intimacy of silent communication that a slow-measured pace brought. Ace and I were both in the moment, savoring the delight of our outing. As we neared the end of each walk, I'd give him a comforting squeeze and say, "Ace, it doesn't get any better than this."

Sixteen years is a very long time in the life of a cat, and, one day, I began to notice the telltale indicators of old age. On one of our walks, Ace's body, once sleek and well-muscled, showed signs of some weight loss. And then his thirst increased as his appetite decreased. It wasn't very long before our vet diagnosed Ace with kidney failure, a common ailment in cats his age. While he still responded to the carving of a freshly cooked turkey, it took him somewhat longer to get to the kitchen; gradually, his interest in food became less and less. In an attempt to stimulate his appetite, my son made trips to the fish market to entice him with succulent fresh shrimp. When Ace made only a token attempt to pick at the treat, we feared the worst.

It was a beautiful, crisp October that year. The skies were a breathtaking blue, and the colored leaves of the trees played against them like a Technicolor movie. When I carried Ace on our walks, he seemed lighter than a feather, and I could feel every bone in his body. He needed cushioning and a little protection against the cool fall air, so I wrapped him in an old, soft baby blanket. We took our walks at noon, when the day was at its warmest. His once-strong purr had become labored. Never a complainer, Ace made little mewing sounds as he lifted his face in the breeze, trying to gather warmth from the sun.

We didn't give up our walks, not even on the day that I knew would be Ace's last. I could barely feel him cuddle in the blanket, his brave little face peering out. I knew how much he was suffering, and I told him as we began our walk that it was all right if he wanted to give up.

We continued around the block, and he tried to look up at the sky and me, but he wasn't smiling anymore. I knew it was time. As we approached home from our last walk, I stroked his head, whispered my love and said my good-byes.

I still begin my days with a run, and I have not given up walks around the neighborhood. On the pale, new green days of spring, in the lush, heavy sweetness of summer and on the crimson-hued days of autumn, as I approach home, I look at the sky and say, "Ace, it doesn't get any better than this."

Edie Scher

Patches

When Bob awakened in the middle of the night, knowing he was dying, somehow, Patches knew, too. As I lay
beside the man I'd lived with for more than twenty years,
I felt a warm, furry creature push herself between us, inch
by inch, until her nose jammed under his chin. She
refused to leave, clinging to his T-shirt as if she could prevent his leaving—refusing to acknowledge that he'd
already left.

That ancient, weepy-eyed calico, who seemed more
human than cat, spent three days mourning, curled up on
his dirty clothes in the bottom of the closet. Emerging
finally to lie in the garden for the summer, she stretched in
the sun, watching the birds hop by her nose.

The following winter, I packed Patches in her travel bag,
and we headed down to Mexico for a few months on my
sailboat in Puerta Vallarta. She checked out the pelicans
and slept in the sun. Life went on.

When I flew down to Zihuatanejo to crew up the coast
with a friend, to make things easier on Patches I left her
with the vet in the local mall. She knew him and liked to
sit in the front window, watching the baby octopus in his
aquarium or flirting with passing shoppers until they

came in to visit the *gata bonita*. For an old girl, she was a shameless hussy.

When I returned ten days later, the sad, little bundle of bones had scabs on her face from crying.

"Your husband left her. She was afraid you'd abandoned her, too. She refused to eat," the vet told me. "The shopping ladies came in every day to cuddle her. They tried to get her to eat, but I think she wanted to kill herself."

When I picked up the scabby mess with the smelly breath, she stuck her head in my armpit. I carried her back to the boat under my cotton shirt and lay her down on the cushion in the cockpit. As I turned to retrieve my backpack from the dock, she threw herself down the three steps of the companionway and sprawled on the floor, too exhausted to make it to our bed.

I slept that night, her nose jammed under my chin, guilt fluttering around me like a wounded bird. In the morning, I felt something pulling at my tangled hair.

It was Patches. "Feed me. Feed me," she meowed as she circled on the covers. "The sun's out. It's time to watch the pelicans." Relief poured over me in a warm wave.

We sat on the dock in the morning sun, watching the pelicans bang into the sea. It was time to move on. Patches curled on my lap, then looked up at me as if she knew.

I ran my fingers under her chin. "Don't worry. I won't leave you again."

And I never did.

Carolyn Harris

The Bell Tolls for Annabelle

They sent him back to me in a white box that held a gleaming chest with a tiny latch. Sliding the latch aside, I expected to see a little urn. Instead, a plastic bag of ashes filled the cavity—Annabelle's ashes, the remains of his body.

His spirit is still all around. I see him at every turn. He is on the clothes dryer, relishing the heat and waiting for an opportunity to switch sides of the door. He is curled in a quiet, tucked-away carrier or snoozing on a downy comforter on the closet floor. He is on the corner of my bed during the day and on my pillow at night. And he always will be.

He'd spent the first four years of his life in abysmal conditions. I'd brought him home to help him pass peacefully. Instead, he revived. A name change to Alex Bell never stuck.

In his new home, he followed sun patches around the house, sat on my shoulder, slept on my head, gently demanded attention from company, looked deeply into people's eyes, chased butterflies across the lawn and startled himself by climbing a tree. No matter how much pain he was in, he sought delight and gave it.

With constant doctoring, slowly, the tenor of his days shifted from mostly bad to mostly good, but he always required care. One day he crashed—all systems down. The new medicine that had been so promising was losing.

I took him to the vet's for a last check and blood test. They gave us new meds and told us to wait for the results. The second afternoon, he just gave out. I wouldn't wait for the tests to tell me what I could see: Annabelle was leaving. His own doctor unavailable, I bundled him into a thick towel against the frigid temperature, holding him close while a friend drove us to a vet who promised to help him go painlessly. In the car, he seemed fascinated by the lights, the passing vehicles and the holiday decorations.

Sensing my reluctance, the vet said he could keep him comfortable for a day until we knew for sure what the tests said, even though he was so sick. So, Annabelle's skinny body was hydrated and steroidized. Bundled up, he returned home with me to spend a peaceful night.

Doc called the next morning at eleven. Renal failure. Extreme. Aggressive measures could be taken, but why not let him go peacefully on a good day? There wouldn't be many more, if any. I took the last appointment of the day.

All afternoon, I held him, thinking peaceful thoughts. When other thoughts intruded, I said *peace and love, peace and love,* over and over again in my mind. No histrionics were going to upset his last moments. At one point, he jumped to the counter where I'd potioned and pilled his ever more reluctant mouth and cleaned this end and that. Lately, even his food had been forced. All unwanted attentions. His eyes asked where the dropper was. I held him close again.

We got into the car to make our slow way to Doc's. Since Annabelle had loved the scenery the night before, I didn't put him in his carrier. He relished this calmly until we entered the parkway. Then, he scurried from window to window to take in the excitement. I pulled over and put him in the carrier, promising to let him watch the traffic when we parked near Doc's.

I didn't take the turn to Doc's; instead, I drove to the ocean, and Annabelle and I sat in the car and watched the day end, with the waves gently foaming along the shore. Off in the distance, a freighter edged toward the horizon. Light from a nearby condo's foyer gleamed on faces hurrying across the ice. Annabelle looked deep into my eyes as I told him the ocean's Maker would be waiting for him.

The clock kept moving. We drove to Doc's. Annabelle crawled into my lap, rested his paws on the window and watched life outside the car. I parked in the clinic parking lot and sat, allowing Annabelle to watch the traffic and the travelers. Slowly, his eyes moved to Doc's window where everyone was busy at work. Still, the clock kept moving. It was time. *Peace and love, peace and love.*

Inside, we were immediately taken to a room where Doc examined Annabelle. He said that, although Annabelle was comfortable right now, he was still terribly ill. He explained that aggressive treatment would mean leaving him in the hospital for several days on an IV. Given his many conditions, he might not survive. If he did, he would be consigned to even more medicines, even more treatment. We were left together to decide. I asked him. He walked into his carrier—his signal for fatigue. He didn't want to try anymore. I didn't want to force anymore.

A vet-in-training held Annabelle tenderly while Doc gently cradled his paw in his hand. I caressed his other paw. He wouldn't look at me. Instead, his eyes were fixed on Doc, who softly told him that he had fought the good fight; now, it was time for him to rest . . . time for him to be at peace. And, just that quickly, he was gone. His body stretched out on the table—his face reflecting the pain

that my sunseeker had hidden with a smile, a chipper attitude and insatiable curiosity.

He was beyond pain now. I placed him into the bag for
cremation.

Now, the little chest of ashes sits on my desk, reminding me of his life and the promises we made to each other.
I promised to help those penned in filth and fear and illness, and he promised to teach me how. Promises we will
both keep—in peace and in love.

Madelyn Filipski

The Funeral

The old stone church is a fixture at what has become a busy intersection in my growing town. The church's crumbling foundation houses the catacombs, accessible to both rodents and the colony of feral cats that took up residence years ago. The cats keep the rodent population under control, but no one monitors the cats' numbers closely. Parishioners occasionally feed the strays, and one kind woman has tried to trap, tame and adopt out some of the many kittens that the colony produces.

I pass the church daily on my way to and from work, always marveling at the array of cats adorning the steps and stone walls, or sitting atop gravestones. With six cats of my own, I can't adopt any more, no matter how much I want to.

The cat colony has its own social hierarchy, based on the principle that only the fittest survive. At one point, one red male tabby appeared to be the patriarch. With ripped ears and scars across his wide face, he swaggered around the neighborhood, secure in his position as top cat. Challenges to his authority—from subordinate colony members or the neighborhood's indoor/outdoor house cats—were met fiercely. Screaming vocalizations, slashing claws and sharp bites kept the red tabby in power. He might not have been popular among the local male cats or their owners, but his prowess was legendary among the female cats. Many red kittens appeared during his reign.

Returning home extremely late one evening, I heard the squeal of brakes and then the revving of an engine as a car peeled out somewhere ahead of me. Rounding the corner where the church stood, my headlights illuminated a still, red form in the middle of the road. With emergency flashers on, I stopped in the middle of the now, deserted street. Before I could get out of my car to check the cat, a black-and-white cat came dashing out of the catacombs and rushed to the tabby. With a tentative paw, it gently touched the prone cat, sniffing him from head to tail. The tabby never moved; neither did I.

The black-and-white cat sat down next to the tabby's body, threw back its head and howled. Within seconds, cats came pouring out of the church foundation, dozens of them, of every size and color. In a well-ordered procession, each one circled the body and its black-and-white guardian, then headed back under the church. As the last of the cortege disappeared into the catacombs, the black-and-white cat continued its vigil for a few more minutes, gazing at the tabby. Once again, it reached out and touched the tabby with a paw, then followed the others.

Stunned at what I'd just witnessed, what I can only describe as a feline funeral, I sat silently crying, awed by the display and saddened by the red cat's death. Not wanting to leave him for the road department's inglorious disposal, I took the tabby home and buried him alongside my own departed pets. I wish I'd been able to bury him in the church graveyard, but I'm sure he's happy two blocks over, where his spirit can still wander his familiar territory forever.

Linda Mihatov

Merlyn's Magic

As Eric and I pulled into our farmhouse driveway, the headlights swept across the dark expanse of the yard. There, in a large clump of catnip growing by the front walk, I spotted a huge black-and-white cat. Perhaps tipsy from the catnip or just unusually brazen, the cat did not budge as we approached. Eric took the groceries into the house while I reached out for the cat. Because of the darkness, I wasn't prepared for the brittle, dry, matted fur and grossly bloated belly that met my hand. The cat responded swiftly by purring loudly and diving repeatedly into my hand for more. I scooped up the cat and plopped down in the porch swing.

I so enjoyed the cat nestling in my lap that I did not immediately notice the tears on my face. Crying was my worst fear—I knew in my heart that if I started again, I might never stop. I took quick inventory and realized I was sobbing not only for this poor, mangy cat in my lap, but also for the cats I'd lost (and still missed) as a result of my divorce the previous year. I sobbed for the three family members I had lost in eight short months. I cried because I had jumped into a rebound relationship with a man I barely knew. Although Eric treated me like I was a queen, I knew there must be heartache coming. It always did.

The more I cried, the harder the cat purred and twisted in my lap. I was mystified why this pitiful excuse for a cat had triggered such an emotional reaction in me. My roving hands began to register another disaster in the making. The huge belly could mean only one thing: I had a very pregnant female who would deliver an impossibly cute, writhing litter of kittens on my doorstep. Kittens I would get attached to. Kittens I would have to find homes for. I cried even harder now. Emotionally spent, I put food and water out for our expectant mother and went to bed, worried sick and bawling.

The next day, the bright morning sun revealed a hideously dirty, but clearly intact male cat! Although the darkness might have masked the full extent of his shabby exterior—not to mention his true gender—it had not dulled his friendly, ebullient personality, which was still in overdrive in the bright light of day. He purred, rubbed and wove figure-eights around us as if it were his job. Eric and I quickly fell in love with him, naming him Merlyn; however, we agreed that he had to stay in the garage until we could get his bloated belly wormed and his coat detangled.

On the third morning after Merlyn's arrival, Eric called to me from the garage. "Lori, you better come here." His tone was flat and serious.

"It's the cat, isn't it?" I asked.

"Yes, but I think you better see this," Eric replied.

Fearing the worst, I slowly stepped into the garage. I didn't see anything.

"Call, 'kitty, kitty, kitty,'" Eric begged.

Confused, I went along with his game. Tentatively, I called, "Here, kitty, kitty, kitty." Again, nothing. I called a little louder. "Here, kitty, kitty, kitty."

From underneath the lawn tractor came a tiny black

kitten. Swaggering behind it came Merlyn.

"See," said Eric beaming, "it wasn't something bad."

Merlyn sat on his haunches and watched as I scooped up the kitten. "It's a girl," I announced as if I had delivered her to new, expectant parents. Then reality set in. I looked at Merlyn dubiously.

"You know what this means, don't you?" I asked Eric. Not waiting for his reply, I continued, "This means she probably came from a litter of males. You know what tomcats do to male offspring?"

Eric gave me a puzzled look as his answer. "Intact males sometimes kill the male kittens because they are future breeding competition," I said dully.

We both peered down at Merlyn, who, I swear, looked smug. He blinked, never taking his gaze from us. Was he a ruthless kitten killer who brought us his only daughter to raise? Was she just some homeless kitten who hitched onto his mangy black-and-white tuxedo tails? Who had ever heard of anything like a male cat bringing home a barely weaned female kitten?

Because we were so besotted with Merlyn, we readily chose to believe that he brought us his precious daughter to raise, since he had checked us out and found us to be affectionate surrogate parents. We named the tiny girl Elke, a nickname I once had, but her prima donna ways soon earned her the expanded title of Miss Elke.

Elke and Merlyn happily took over our home, our bed and our greyhound, Hector. Neutered, well-fed, loved and vaccinated, Merlyn flourished into a magnificent cat. His black-and-white tuxedo markings shone in the sun as he groomed himself on the farmhouse porch.

Elke soon forgot her humble beginnings and blossomed, in her mind, into Bastet, the worshipped cat of ancient Egypt. The only time she would abandon my lap or her regal ways was when she would entice Merlyn into wrestling matches. Her small, lithe body was hardly a match for Merlyn's bulk, but she held her own quite fiercely. Merlyn educated her, like her mother would have, teaching her to hunt like a warrior. The two of them soon had every mouse and vole cleared from the property. At night she slept wrapped around my head like a hat. Merlyn curled up at the foot of the bed, riding out the constantly shifting legs that buffeted him all night long.

The years passed quickly, as they often do with busy schedules and a house full of animals. The two cats rolled effortlessly with every punch we threw them. Other cats came and went—I guess the word was out on our hospitality. Neither Merlyn nor Elke cared. We were married in their mouse-free yard. They willingly joined the reception. We brought them home a real, live, crying baby. They loved him just as much as we did. We started a business in the back room. They sat on my desk. Elke liked to be carried in my arms like an infant, and Merlyn never tired of being touched; in fact, he solicited stroking at every possible turn. It did not matter if he was eating, napping or sitting next to us. His affection was endless—or so we thought.

One spring morning, I heard Eric pull into the gravel driveway and stop suddenly, the tires sliding in the chunky rocks. I heard him yell, "No!" in a strained voice. As I ran to the front door, I saw Eric standing in the middle of the drive, Merlyn lifeless at his feet.

As I ran to them, the story was easy to piece together. Before Merlyn lay a flattened mouse. Merlyn didn't have a mark on him. He apparently broke his neck as he charged into the passing car during his hunt.

With a broken heart and an old shovel, Eric began to dig a hole under the rose of Sharon tree in the front flower garden. I sat in the grass with Merlyn one last time, his black-and-white tuxedo coat still gleaming brilliantly in the April sun. I touched him, weeping uncontrollably, coming to the realization that as we had met, so would we part—my life with Merlyn had started and ended with tears.

But there was one crucial difference. The memories I had that dark night I first held Merlyn in my lap were full of heartache and self-doubt from years of sad events, tempered with a tiny shred of hope. The memories I had today, as I stroked Merlyn one last time, were full of the happy events he had seen me relish, this time tempered by the breaking of my heart at losing him. A heart that would be forever enriched by Merlyn's loving presence in my life.

Lori Hess

Ring of Fire

My friend Kathy and I are both therapists. For the last ten years, we have met twice a month to offer each other support and guidance in our work and in our lives. Recently, we discussed grief.

A client of Kathy's felt that he should be "further along" in the grieving process. It was two years after the death of his much-loved father, and he said he was still afraid he could get lost in the pain if he really let himself feel it. Instantly, the image formed in my mind of grief as a ring of fire, frightening to approach and painful to step through. And so, for most of us, like Kathy's client, the temptation is to ease on down the denial road, pretending that the loss really wasn't so great.

Working with my own clients, I make no distinction between the loss of a human or animal companion. Love is just love, no matter what body it wears. In fact, my own primary guides in learning about grief have been animals. I have grieved for humans as well, but those relationships are much more complex, and their endings can contain a mixture of many other feelings along with the grief. My feelings for my animal loved ones are far less conflicted, and so their passing has been experienced much more simply and clearly as a piercing sadness.

Five members of my animal family are now buried underneath the towering white pine in my front yard: four cats and my rickety, eighteen-year-old miniature poodle. A thirteen-year-old orange cat with a scarred white nose and serrated ears named George is the most recent. He was my dear companion and guide in life, and has continued in these roles since his death.

To deal with my grief at George's death, I've used the same process that I recommend to my clients. First, I had a picture of George in his prime enlarged and framed. The picture sits on an end table next to the chair I usually use. Several times a day, I relate to the picture in some way and, thereby, to his memory. I brush the back of my hand across the photo in the same way that I used to brush his cheek. I pick up the picture and hold it. Or I just speak to it, saying, "I love you" or "I miss you." I visit with George and enjoy the thought of him.

Then, maybe once or twice a month, I step through the ring of fire and let the grief burn me. I feel completely my love of this special friend—and my loss. And, in these feelings, we meet again as intimately as we did in life. I feel my throat tighten and the tears come, and it is as though the water coming from my eyes acts as a conductor for the energy that connected us. In my sadness, George is alive to me once more.

As soon as I step inside the ring of fire, I can remember George very clearly: his chin on my pillow and his paw cupped in my hand as we slept. I can feel it! I can see the scars on his nose and the little bites in his ears, remnants of his time on the road before he accepted me as his life assignment. I can hear the chirp of his singing purr during one of our many conversations. I can see the little spot of black fur in the corner of one eye, so unusual on an orange-and-white creamsicle cat. These details bring him to life again, details I cannot remember—even so soon after his death—unless I allow myself to step into the grief.

But there is even more treasure inside the burning ring. I find that, when I let the grief in, I am not only in contact again with my beloved, but he becomes my guide in his new world. He shows me a place where life never ends and limits never bind. He allows me to know that there is no death. In life, we live as single drops of rain. George and the other loved ones who have passed show me the ocean we become.

Unfortunately, this holy state doesn't last, and I find myself back outside the ring, feeling cold and alone. Grief is composed mostly of slogging through lonely patches. Much of the time, I just want my animals' warm and squishy fur-bodies back!

I remember when my twenty-one-year-old cat Ivan died. Three days after his death, I found myself walking around the house saying, "Okay. This hasn't been too bad. I've been good. I've been brave. Three days is just about enough. I want my cat back. Now!"

Once, after the death of Simon, another of my elderly and ailing foundling cats, he and I were having a "conversation" late at night. Suddenly, I dropped into the grief and said, "I just miss you. I want you here."

And he answered, "I *am* here. Every time you hold another cat, I'm right there."

And, you know, I've noticed since then that he really is! I can feel him or Ivan or George—any of them that I want to hold—in the warm, yielding body of the living cat in my arms!

Still, I don't know anyone who isn't afraid of grief. It burns—so we tend to push it away. But by not attending to it, we allow it to become an undertow in our lives, the weight pulling us downward.

The road of life isn't straight. There are sharp turns.

We're going to have losses. And, if we're going to experience them, and they're going to hurt, we might as well go
for the diamonds in the coal. Our loved ones can show us
the way through the ring of fire—if we let them.

Sara Wye

A Cat's Gift of Faith

He was a marmalade tabby kitten with sapphire eyes that I adopted from the Massachusetts SPCA. Fitting perfectly in my palm, he promptly chewed his way into my thumb—and my heart. "You're a feisty little peppercorn, aren't you?" I yelped, and so he got his name.

Described by many as "an extraordinary cat," Peppercorn grew from diminutive to nearly three feet long—measured from orange-whiskered nose to pumpkin-tipped tail—punctuated by burnt-orange eyes that could stare you down. I learned that he was an excellent judge of character. A quick once-over, and he would sum you up with a flick of his tail, then either deign to advance for a pat or glower at you from the sofa armrest.

My apartment was his oyster—as was the warm spot on my neck or next to my tummy at night. He had an uncanny ability to sense my moods: He lashed his tail when I was angry and cuddled up to me when I was down. When he wanted to know what I was thinking, he meowed and gave my hand a gentle paw pat. We would mutter at each other throughout the day, often to the profound consternation of my non-cat friends.

To me, Pep was a four-footed person. I loved him as a

furry son and believed he loved me with the same fierce loyalty.

And so, at age twelve, when he began to pass blood in his urine, and the doctor diagnosed bladder cancer, I was confronted with the unbearable possibility that my "little love" of a cat was not going to live forever—or even the seventeen-plus years for which I had hoped. And I found myself praying for his life, even though my belief in God could be best described as "casual"—as in, he might exist, he might not, but why take a chance?

A week after his surgery, Peppercorn seemed to be gradually recovering. As I bustled around getting ready for work, it was the first day in weeks I had felt positive about his future. I knelt down to give him a head scratch as he slowly followed me around. He pushed his head hard against my hand, rumbling away with his unique triple-noted purr, which I have never heard any other cat make, before or since. "I love you, my little love," I said with a final stroke. "I'll see you tonight." As I walked out the door, I glanced back and saw him silhouetted against the sunlight, aglow in orange and gold.

He lay stretched on the floor when I got home. The vet surmised that a blood clot had broken loose, and that Pep had died instantly. My heart died with him, and no amount of crying would help. I railed against everything for taking away my beloved cat. As I placed flowers on his headstone, inscribed with his nickname "my little love," I asked why this had been done to me. I believed it showed that there was no God and challenged anyone to prove me wrong.

The weeks oozed by as I came back to the empty hollow of my home, staring at the litter tray, food bowls and scratching post that I could not bring myself to put away.

One night, after I had sobbed so long that my eyes were dry, I dreamed of Peppercorn—if it was a dream. It was not like any other dream I had ever had; they are always fragmented snippets of images, with no rhyme or reason, and no continuity.

In my dream I stood in my living room, and Pep marched up to me, the picture of feline health, eyes alight with happiness. I scooped him up, felt his weight in my arms that had so longed to hold him again, stroked his soft fur and felt the three-noted purr rumbling against my chest. "Pep, oh Pep! I dreamed you were dead," I told him as I wept and laughed into his neck. His purr deepened, and he patted my cheek with his paw, as he always had.

After a bit, he wriggled, asking to be put down. Reluctantly, I did so, and he turned and strode to the front door, glancing over his shoulder for me to follow. At the door, he asked to be let out. "You're not allowed outside," I reminded him, puzzled and afraid. He gazed at me, and I knew I had to open the door, as much as I did not want to.

Outside, a beautiful summer's day garlanded everything with sunlight, overarched by a brilliant blue sky. Peppercorn gazed up at me for a long moment, curling himself about my legs one more time. Then he walked away over the grass. I began to sob, reaching for him, begging him to come back.

He paused, turning to look back at me once more. Then, before my eyes, he gently changed from his familiar shape to a glowing ball of golden light. I stared as he rose from the grass and up into the heavens, then disappeared into the sunlight.

I jerked upright in bed in the early morning light, struggling to hold on to the dream, resisting chill reality. I still could feel the sensation of him in my arms, hear his beloved purr. And slowly, as I sat there, I realized that the raw wound that was my heart didn't hurt the same way it had for months, soothed by Peppercorn's final visit to me.

He had been permitted to return and tell me he was

okay, allowed to let me glimpse what he had become. We had been granted the final good-bye that had been denied before.

And, in that gesture of compassionate love, I felt the hand and the grace of God—Pep's final and greatest gift to me.

Claudia Newcorn

7

RESCUE ME!

If a homeless cat could talk, it would probably say, "Give me shelter, food, companionship and love, and I will be yours for life!"

Susan Easterly

A Miracle Called Faith

The morning was no different from any other—except for the persistent cry from a determined little cat. The school principal and I both froze when we saw her, a small, bedraggled, black-striped, gray kitten with a very mangled front leg. Howling plaintively, she didn't scamper away; she just leaned forward, her front leg deformed, muddied and matted with dried blood.

We found a small box, and the principal took the broken kitten to his office. As a second-year teacher, I couldn't leave my class to take her to the vet, so I did what pretty much all kids do when they're in trouble: I called my dad. Even with a very hectic schedule, he made time for things that really mattered, including a stray kitten with injuries. He said he'd pick her up within an hour. During that time, the kitten continued howling: first for milk (which she heartily lapped up), then for attention and, finally, as if she wanted to tell her story. Her yellow eyes were wide, and she wanted to see everything. We decided that she must have been hit by a car to receive such an awful injury, but she didn't seem to be in pain.

Later in the morning, I called my dad again to get an update on the kitten. "She's okay for now, but the prognosis isn't good," he explained. "The vet said that the injury is at least a day or two old, infected, and the nerves in that leg are dead. He said that she should either be put to sleep or have her front leg amputated."

It was shaping up to be one bad day. My students had been particularly horrible to me and to each other. The school is in a low socioeconomic area, and it has produced rough students who seem only to know how to be tough so they don't get hurt. One student in particular, Darren,* was a quiet but very angry boy. He refused to complete any of the activities, work with the other students or answer me. Instead, he'd sit at his desk and stare straight ahead. The rest of the class knew better than to provoke Darren. Although he didn't go out and pick fights, he had no qualms about giving a hard wallop to any kid who crossed him. Earlier in the year, he slammed a boy taller than himself into a wall for going through his book bag. Darren was feared by all.

At the end of the school day, I rushed over to the vet's office. He repeated to me the same options that he had outlined to my dad. Questions flooded my mind: *How could I even afford such a procedure? A three-legged cat? What kind of life is that for an animal?* I'd have to put it on my credit card—along with many other, older charges that amounted to quite a large figure.

"Could I at least say good-bye to her?" I asked.

They brought me to the back, where she was sleeping in her litter pan on the floor of a cold, metal cage.

"Hello," I called to her, carefully opening the wire-mesh door. "Hello, little lady."

She sleepily lifted her head, her yellow eyes mere slits. Her ears drooped lazily, but she let out a little squeak, then yawned. I reached in and gently picked her up,

---

*Names have been changed to protect privacy.

avoiding the hurt leg that was now bandaged all the way to her shoulder. I could feel her little purr-box working away, and I held her close. "Meow, meow, meow," she responded, as if she were informing me of her trip to the vet and how her stay had been up to that point. I started to cry. In my arms rested a little life that was about to end, and all she could do was purr and talk.

"You know, if you think you might want to save this cat, Sergeant has only three legs, too," the vet said, pointing to a white fur ball who was very busily stalking something. "And he's still a very happy cat."

"Really?" I asked, looking closely at the three-legged feline.

"Sure!" he replied, retrieving a very plump and very three-legged Sergeant. "He hurt his leg a few years ago, and his owners brought him here. I amputated the leg, and he's been the office cat ever since. Why, he isn't slowed down a bit by that missing leg." Sergeant sprang off the examining table onto the floor, swatted at a loose rolling ball of fur, then scurried down the hallway.

No sooner had I decided to have her leg taken off than ideas began to fill my mind—ideas of how to include this little kitten in my classes. The more advanced students could organize bake sales to help pay for the medical expenses. I would assign all my students a research project to learn more about any animal they chose. And the vet agreed to come and talk with them once the kitten had recovered enough to visit the school.

Three days later, I called the vet to check on the kitten's surgery. "The vet's still in with her," his receptionist said. "But don't worry. He's done this before. It just takes a while."

My students were also disappointed that I couldn't update them on her status. Finally, we learned that the kitten had pulled through just fine. It was safe for the students to finally choose a name for her. Every child either suggested a name or voted, except for Darren. He thought the entire event was absolutely stupid and beneath his efforts. The students finally settled on the name Faith.

One month, 120 research projects (ranging from a picture of a duck to elaborately designed displays) and five bake sales later, the day arrived for Faith and the vet to visit the class. The students were wired and restless, but they knew the rules: stay in your seats and speak only when it's your turn, or the visitors go home.

Darren was particularly ugly that morning, slamming his books, mumbling about stupid cats and boring visitors. Such an angry kid! Faith introduced herself with a squeaky howl from inside her carrier. I couldn't believe how well the students behaved. Faith sat bravely in the vet's arms as they gathered around and gently ran their fingers over her soft fur. Darren watched from his seat.

"Does she still hurt?"

"Has she fallen?"

"Can she wash her face?"

"Can she really walk?"

The vet placed her on the ground, and the students jumped back as though she might explode. Even Darren craned his neck so he could see through the students standing in front of him.

"Wow!"

"She hops!"

"She can walk!"

Faith scampered about the classroom, meowing, squeaking and exploring. She loved when someone scratched her back at the base of her tail. Standing a little wobbly on her three legs, she arched her back and stood on her hind toes.

Later, my principal told me that a reporter from the

local paper wanted to visit the students who had adopted Faith, the three-legged cat. We were going to be in the paper!

Everyone wanted something to do or to show for the reporter's visit. One group arranged Faith's progress pictures on a poster board; another presented bake-sale signs; I prepared two students as greeters and hosts. Only Darren, the good-ole-grouch, was left out. All he could do was give me a whaddaya-gonna-do-about-it? glare.

I was going to be the one to watch over Faith. Then I had an idea. I announced, "Darren, you will watch over Faith."

His reaction was, "Huh?"

"She needs someone to hold her cage and make sure nothing goes wrong when the reporter tries to pet her."

The reaction from the class was:

"I want to do that!"

"No! Let me!"

"No, me! Darren can show the projects."

"This job is for Darren and Darren alone," I said firmly. "If he doesn't want to do it, then I will. So there will be no fighting about it."

"I'll do it," Darren said, looking back over his shoulder and grinning slyly at his classmates. "I'll watch Faith."

The reporter's visit was a smashing success—Darren carefully opened the carrier door so the reporter could take Faith out, pet her and see her scar, which was nearly covered over by her grown-back fur. Darren watched over Faith and was her strongest protector. When the reporter left, the students cleaned up and put the room back in order.

"You did a good job," I told Darren, and I meant it.

He nodded, then looked into her carrier. "Can I pick her up?"

Startled by the question, I hesitated at first, which he

didn't notice. "Yes," I replied. "You know to be careful."

"Yes, ma'am, I know."

I watched, holding my breath, as he slowly opened the door, extending both arms into the cage, talking in a voice so soft, I could barely hear him. He cradled Faith to his chest, and she purred and purred. Quietly, I backed away. Something was going on here, and I was not going to interrupt it. He sat down and gently placed her on the desk in front of him. She stood on her three legs, meowed, squeaked and purred, but didn't try to leave. The street-hardened Darren softly scratched under her chin, petted her between her ears, on her neck, down her back. He was gentle and focused.

Something changed in Darren that day. Something that had long been dormant came alive and grew each time he saw Faith. Every Friday, when Faith came to visit, Darren was her special guardian. He made sure the classroom door was shut tight and no one was rough with her. But, most of all, he watched her. Something deep within him connected to that once-broken little kitten.

Darren's transformation continued beyond his Fridays with Faith. The tough exterior and the anger were gone, leaving an eager student who raised his hand to answer questions, completed his work and participated in class. He even smiled just a little more.

I believe that finding Faith in the school hall was no accident. Forces greater than we can ever understand worked through that mangled little kitten—forces that gave me hope as a teacher, brought smiles to a classroom of kids and a little peace to an angry and hardened young heart. Faith, a little gray kitten with three good legs, wandered into a school of tough kids and created a miracle.

Heather L. Sanborn

Black Jellybeans

I've never read an official study on the matter, but I've noticed that in animal shelters, black cats are the most overlooked. Black seems to be the least preferred of cat colors, ranking below all combinations of white, orange, gray, spotted and striped. Black cats are still stereotyped as Halloween cats, creatures of bad luck, more appropriate on a witch's broomstick than curled up on your pillow. To make matters worse, in cages, black cats become close to invisible, fading into the dark shadows in the back of a stainless-steel cage.

For eleven years, starting when I was ten years old, I volunteered at an urban animal shelter. It always struck me as particularly unfair that, time after time, I'd get to know affectionate, adorable black cats, only to watch them be passed over by adopters merely because of their color. I assumed there was nothing that could be done.

One day, many years into my work at the shelter, I spent a few minutes petting a sweet, black half-grown kitten, who had been found as a stray and brought to the shelter. The slender thing purred warmly at my attention, gently playful as she patted my hand with one paw. I thought about what a shame it was that the kitten was already too big to be adopted on baby-kitten appeal alone, and so solidly black that most people wouldn't even pause in front of her cage. I noticed there was no name written on the informational card on her cage. Since volunteers were welcome to name the strays that came to the shelter, I thought for a moment about what I could name this black kitten. I wanted to think of a name that could give the kitten the kind of appealing "color" that might encourage an adopter to take a second look. The name Jellybean popped into my head, and I wrote it on the card, just as I'd named thousands of cats in the past.

I was taken entirely by surprise when, later that afternoon, I overheard a woman walking through the cat room say, "Jellybean! What a wonderful name!" She stopped to look more closely at the kitten, now batting at a piece of loose newspaper in the cage. She asked me if she could hold Jellybean, and, as I opened the cage, I sheepishly admitted that the kitten didn't know her name, as I'd named her just hours before. I lifted her into the woman's arms, and the kitten leaned into the woman, looking up into her eyes with a purr of kitten bliss. After a few minutes, the woman told me that she'd like to adopt this black kitten, and, when the paperwork was approved a few days later, she took Jellybean home.

I was pleased, of course—adoptions were always what nourished my soul—but I chalked it up to a lucky break for one black kitten, and moved on.

I was surprised again a few weeks later when the woman came back to the shelter. She found me refilling water bowls in a cat room and said, "You were the one who helped me adopt that black kitten a few weeks ago, remember? Jellybean? I know you were the one who named her, and I've been wanting to stop back to thank you. She's the sweetest thing—I just love her to pieces. But I don't know if I would have noticed her if she hadn't had that great name. It just suits her perfectly. She's so bouncy and colorful—I know that sounds crazy. Anyway, I wanted to say thank you."

I told her I was touched that she had stopped by and thrilled to hear that Jellybean was doing well in her new home. Then I explained how I thought black cats were often unfairly overlooked and admitted the name had been my conscious attempt to get someone to notice a cat who would probably not have been adopted otherwise. She said, "Well, it worked! You should name all the black cats Jellybean."

I smiled politely at the suggestion, thinking to myself that this woman knew nothing of the harsh realities of animal shelters. Just because I named one kitten Jellybean and it had gotten adopted didn't mean anything—it had just been a stroke of luck. Black cats were still black cats, after all, and most people didn't want them.

As the day went on, I kept thinking about the woman's advice: "You should name all the black cats Jellybean." As crazy as it seemed, I decided I had nothing to lose. Pen in hand, I walked along the cages, looking for a black cat without a name. There was only one, a small black kitten alone in a cage, sleeping. I wrote "Jellybean" on its cage card. Later that afternoon, someone came along and said they'd like to adopt that little Jellybean. *Well,* I thought to myself, *that wasn't really a fair test—it was so cute and tiny.*

A few days later, a nameless black cat came along, fully grown. I named it Jellybean. It was adopted. Days later, another. Adopted. The process repeated itself enough times that, after a while, I had to admit that maybe there was some magic in the name, after all. It began to seem morally wrong *not* to name black cats Jellybean, especially ones who had a bounce in their step and a spark of joy in their eyes. Although I'd usually refrained from using the same name for more than one cat, after a while, my fellow volunteers ceased to be surprised when they came across another of my Jellybeans.

Of course, we'll need more far-reaching solutions to ensure that every cat has a home. But for my black Jellybeans, sitting in sunny windows, sniffing at ladybugs walking across the kitchen floor, snuggling in beds with their adopted people, a name made all the difference. "Jellybean" allowed some humans to see beyond a dark midnight coat into the rainbow of riches in a cat's heart.

Dorian Solot

Persian Love

Lindsey's white Persian head—a snowball with huge golden eyes and a flat, upturned nose—gave her a look of perpetual sourness. Her fully feathered tail and paws were worthy of a pedigreed show cat. But everything in between—her skinny little torso and legs—had been shorn to the skin, ridding her of years of heavily matted fur. Still, with a wiggle of her rear and her head held high, she approached everyone as if she were a fashion model sauntering up the runway and displaying the latest in designer feline styles.

She didn't care that the sight of her caused people to giggle. She felt no shame or humiliation, nor did it cause her to think less of any human—all humans were her friends and deserved her affection. I, too, was a guilty party: She made me laugh, that spunky little sprite.

Lindsey, a rescued cat I was fostering, didn't realize my halfway house for homeless animals was not her real home. It was the best she had ever known. She had spent eight years in a shopping cart topped with fencing. Her former people, elderly themselves, meant well and often took in homeless cats. They prevented reproduction by housing each cat individually in carriers. The cats never left their cages. The couple had rescued Lindsey as a kitten when she was tossed from a moving car. The white Persian had been lucky to be given deluxe accommodations—the shopping cart—but now she had been rescued from her rescuers. I promised her daily that the best was yet to come.

At first, Lindsey could barely walk. A lifetime of confinement left her shaky and unsteady on her feet. Her muscles protested. She wobbled and stumbled. But she refused to give up, and, with practice, she soon began jogging and exploring. Lindsey found such glory in being able to run.

She adored the other foster cats and loved to snuggle with them. At long last, she could touch other cats instead of just watching them through bars. She had never seen a dog before, but that didn't matter—they were living creatures. She approached them without fear, confident of a loving reception.

One day, I found Lindsey upstairs in resident cat territory, with cats she had not yet met. Odessa and Abigail sat together, peering down their long alley-cat noses, wondering what the heck *this creature* was. They had never seen a Persian before, much less a bald Persian—and such a bold one, who would dare to come in and act like she was everyone's lifelong friend. I let them be.

A while later, I returned to investigate. At the sound of my entry, two heads emerged from a cat bed in the window, cheeks fused as one. The white, fluffy Persian head seemed dwarfed by the huge, coal-black head of my antisocial cat, Claude, who, years before, had lost a paw at the hand of a cruel human. The four-eyed, "Do-you-mind?" glare hastened my respectful retreat. Claude had found a new friend.

Then, suddenly, Lindsey became ill. Refusal to eat and drink sent her to the hospital—and a convalescent cage. It was touch-and-go for a while, but, finally, Lindsey regained her appetite. She joyfully returned to her foster home, free once again of the hated confinement. Tests showed some irregularities, possibly the result of past nutritional deficiencies. I was sure her retests would be fine, since Lindsey's appetite was back. In fact, Lindsey acted like her old self. As the adoption applications started rolling in, I felt certain that the best was now within reach.

Her story touched people, and interest in adopting her grew, despite Lindsey's advanced age. My duty as a good foster mom meant careful scrutiny of prospective homes. Not just any home would do, only the right home—a home suited perfectly for Lindsey's needs.

That mounting feeling of excitement, that intuitive knowing *this is the one*, ran through me as I studied one couple's application. Laura and Mike, who already had Fredo the Himalayan and Penny the Persian, wanted Lindsey to share their quiet, peaceful and loving home, where cats were cherished family members. A call to their veterinarian confirmed them as the best of pet guardians. Lindsey would meet them and go home the very next day!

No sooner had the arrangements been made than my vet called with the long-forgotten test results. I knew he would not be calling in person if everything were normal. The news hit me hard. Lindsey had kidney disease, and the prognosis was grim. "Make what time she has left quality time," the doctor advised.

With a heavy heart, I relayed the sad news to Laura. "We would still like to meet her," she told me. The ache in my throat eased at her kind words. Nothing could have lifted my spirits or restored my faith in humans more. Not only were Laura and Mike the committed pet guardians I hoped to find, but their selflessness put Lindsey's needs above their own, even knowing their attachment to her could only last a short time.

Although Laura, Mike and I were strangers, we hugged, linked by our common goal to make Lindsey's remaining time special. They signed the adoption papers, but more important to me was the verbal commitment they made— a promise to call it a day when Lindsey's health started to fail. Suffering was not to be part of the deal.

Lindsey settled nicely into her new home. Fredo fell in love with her, grooming Lindsey at every opportunity. Penny had to adjust, but soon found Lindsey more than willing to share Fredo's attentions. The three became friends. Lindsey spent her days exploring her new home and basking in a bed of sunshine streaming through the windows. She spent her nights sleeping comfortably wrapped around either Laura or Mike's head. This *was* the best—exactly what I had hoped for when I'd made that promise to Lindsey.

It lasted two months. Lindsey became weaker, and when she no longer rallied with treatments and medication, Laura and Mike lovingly allowed her to leave life, peacefully and with dignity. Tears flowed freely in grief, but also in appreciation for having known her.

Lindsey had emerged from her long years of isolation and confinement miraculously unscathed in spirit. The love and sweetness she radiated enriched the lives of everyone she touched. I was comforted, knowing that she had experienced a life worthy of her, even though only for a short time. Against all odds, she had achieved the best.

Daniela Wagstaff

My Life as a Midwife

I used to lead two separate lives. In one, I took advantage of my six-foot frame and three-hundred-plus pounds of brawn to earn an adequate living as a bouncer. I broke up fights, and, occasionally, had to throw a punch or two. In the ten years that I pursued this profession, I had my nose broken no less than six times. My knuckles will never be a normal size again. I had a minor reputation as a very tough guy.

Then there was my other life—my secret life, in which I served as a midwife for pregnant cats. Imagine, if you will, an outsized, middle-aged man coaching tired and cranky female cats through the pain of childbirth. I have always suspected that I do this because I was unable to be present at the births of my stepchildren and my grandchildren, but that's for my therapist and me to find out.

My split life started when my first cat, Bacall, got herself pregnant before I could afford to have her spayed. She was expecting kittens around the time of my birthday. I arranged for my friend (and future wife) Janet to watch Bacall while I spent that weekend at a conference. Like many conferences I have attended, there was much talk late into the night, and, as a result, I had not gotten a lot of sleep. During the eight-hour drive back from the conference, I was getting more and more tired. All I wanted to do was to get home and go to bed. So, of course, about an hour before I got home, Bacall went into labor.

I pause here for character identification. I was an exhausted, surly and totally unpleasant representative of humanity at this point. My first impulse was to go to bed and let Bacall handle the birth by herself. After all, it was a most natural thing, and her motherly instincts would kick in, wouldn't they? Of course they would. But, somehow, I found myself sitting on my bed, my favorite blanket under Bacall, while I rubbed her ears and back during labor. She gave birth to four healthy kittens, two of whom still share my home today. I was so pleased with her that I sat up half the night trying to get her to eat and drink something.

And so my life as an animal rescuer began.

Unfortunately, the kittens kept coming because pregnant strays kept finding their way to our doorstep. There have been seven mothers-to-be in our house since that night, and I have participated in the births of all twenty-six kittens. I am a sucker for the process, even though, these days, I spend most of my time trying to avoid the whole situation—by convincing people to show some responsibility and have their pets fixed before they can produce offspring!

After Bacall's midnight delivery, the next litter born in our house was Baby's. Baby was a stray who came to stay with us on Christmas day in 1996. Her four kittens, born in January 1997, actually arrived while I slept, but I participated in the birth by giving up my thirty-five-dollar white dress shirt as the birthing bed. Baby must have known that I had only worn the shirt once, and that it was in the laundry basket so I could wash it and wear it to work again.

Shan Li was a calico who came to us when a friend of

our son's found her wandering the streets. She was dirty, undernourished and traumatized, as well as de-clawed and pregnant! Five weeks after her arrival, she gave birth to five kittens we ended up calling The Pile—four females and one male. We named the single male Watson, and ended up keeping him because he developed an eye infection and needed "special attention." (This is the excuse we almost always use when my wife and I have fallen in love with a kitten and decide that it can't leave.)

Pregnant cats kept showing up in our lives. Once we had two cats—Tiffany and Lenore—deliver litters within twelve hours of each other! When Tiffany ultimately rejected her litter, Lenore came to the rescue. Lenore was a tiny cat with a constant harassed look upon her face. After giving birth to her own four kittens, she then took in Tiffany's abandoned three and nursed all seven to health with some assistance (and feedings) from us. By the time the kittens were weaned, she was exhausted. Lenore was the only cat I ever thought was *glad* to be spayed. We were able to find homes for all seven kittens, and for the mothers as well.

We were especially pleased with the home we found for our beleaguered ex-super-mom. Today, Lenore, aka Lenny, is living a quiet, reflective life in a local retirement home for Franciscan nuns. The good sisters offer prayers every day for our efforts; sometimes, I think it is the only reason we are able to keep doing what we do.

I don't work as a bouncer anymore, but I'm still delivering kittens. We took in another cat just a few weeks ago, and—no surprise—she's pregnant. Any day now, probably in the middle of the night (of course), I'll be playing midwife again. I enjoy the experience, but I wish with all my being that I didn't have to do it. It gets tiring looking for homes for healthy cats with nowhere to go. My wife and I always take the kittens to the vet, getting them altered and inoculated with their first shots before we start looking for homes for them—we want to make sure that we don't perpetuate the problem! This process costs us a few hundred dollars each time, and our vet always lectures about being such soft touches. Still, I'm sure that we'll continue to do it in the future. As long as there are pregnant cats who need help, I am willing to play midwife.

Brian Baker

The Kitten Who Saved His Mom

You become responsible forever for what you have tamed.

Antoine de Saint-Exupéry

The mother cat would have done anything to save her kittens. This is the story of how one of her kittens managed to save her instead.

One night, Jim was driving home late from the office. His "office" wasn't a cubicle in a city high-rise, but a room in one of the stucco buildings on the grounds of Best Friends Animal Sanctuary, nestled in the red rock canyons of southern Utah. Best Friends offers a cage-free, no-kill environment to more than eighteen hundred homeless pets, and Jim worked on its publications.

To Jim, a well-furnished office meant plenty of dog and cat hair, and an office with a view meant he could see the canyons and sky. His daily commute was a little different, too. Driving home that night at nine o'clock, his was the only car on the road. As he wound along a dark stretch of narrow highway, something unusual caught his eye.

It was a cardboard box. *Why would anyone stop on a*

winding highway in the middle of red-rock canyons, unload a cardboard box, then drive away again? Jim had a bad feeling and pulled over. When he got closer, he saw six adorable baby kittens cuddled inside the box. Each was no bigger than the palm of his hand, and they seemed to have made a nest of their cardboard container. He was just about to pick one up, when something made him look around. He had the feeling he was being watched.

There, just around the corner of the box and watching him like a mother lion, was an adult cat—the kittens' mom. When he met her eyes, she meowed warnings at him. He assured her that he meant the babies no harm. Averting his eyes, he noticed something about the cardboard box he hadn't seen before: It was completely sealed—taped shut—except for the hole through which he could see the kittens. That opening must have been made by the mother cat clawing her way out. He realized with shock that the seven of them—mother cat and six kittens—had been sealed up in the box, then cruelly left at the side of the road. But the mother cat had been determined to escape—and then had stayed around to look after her babies.

Jim decided that they should all be brought to the animal sanctuary. It wasn't safe out there. At night, temperatures drop dramatically in the desert, and, if they didn't get to the warmth of the sanctuary where Mom could nurse her babies without predators lurking about, they might not make it through the night. Knowing she would be a greater challenge than the kittens, he grabbed Mom first. But she wasn't about to leave her babies! She struggled fiercely, keeping her eyes on the cardboard box. It took a lot of effort to get her into the back seat of the car; she was so determined not to lose sight of her little treasures. Finally, he got her inside and relieved her by putting the babies in after her. He wished he had a cat carrier, but he didn't; he would have to trust Mom in the back seat.

It wasn't far to the sanctuary, but by the time he reached the clinic, it was closed for the night. He made his way to the bird area, where people were still tending homeless pet parrots. He asked whether they had a cat carrier for the mother cat. They gave him something that seemed like it would do. When he and the bird folks opened up the back car door to get Mom—*vroom!*—she ran for it. There was just no stopping her. She wasn't going to spend another moment in this stranger's car. She would rather face the wild. Jim ran after her into the trees, but couldn't get her to come. He looked at the kittens and felt heartsick. Their mom. He had lost their mom. Who knew what would happen to her out there in the wilderness?

Frantic, Jim called the clinic manager, Judah, at home. Judah was in the shower, but when he heard the story, he said he'd be right over. He raced over, still wet, and, after hearing another hectic retelling of the tale, he told Jim he'd take care of it from there. There was nothing else that Jim could do; it had been a long-enough night already. Jim should go home, knowing that the kittens were safe, and Judah would do everything in his power to find Mama Cat. Judah was right. Reluctantly, Jim drove home, worry lines creasing his forehead. All he could think about was the cat he had found . . . and then lost.

In the meantime, Judah had a plan. He had long ago learned how to "speak cat." If he meowed at just the right pitch, a cat would always meow back. So he ventured out into the trees and practiced his meow, grateful there weren't too many people around to hear. At last, he hit just the right note, and, from somewhere in the distance, a cat meowed back. Now, he knew where the mother cat was. He called again, and she called back. But she would not come. A long-distance conversation was just fine with her! If he tried to get too close, she might take off, but

Judah wasn't out of ideas yet. She wouldn't run to him, but he was pretty sure he knew someone for whom she would come. In fact, he knew *six* little someones for whom she'd probably face a lion or a bear—and, certainly, the likes of him. He went and fetched one of them, a little brown tabby with white markings, stroking the furry little kitten as he held him in his palm. Right on cue, the kitten called out to his mom. Maybe he was saying, "Mom, come back!" or maybe, "Hey, who's this guy?" Whatever it was, it worked.

The mother cat bounded at Judah, trying to rip the baby from his hands. He caught her gently and carried her over to the rest of her kittens. "Don't worry," he said. "I won't separate you." And he drove them off to the cats-only section of the sanctuary where they could all get warm and cozy for the night.

Jim, on the other hand, slept restlessly. He kept imagining coyotes circling round the mother cat—and her babies never seeing her again. He thought about the way she'd fended him off out by that cardboard box, and wished he could start all over again and get her safely to the sanctuary this time. He drove to work in the morning with dark circles under his eyes. First stop: check on the kittens. He could do that much for their mom, keep an eye on them for her. He knew it's what she would have wanted.

When he arrived at the cat section of the sanctuary, he was met with a wonderful surprise. There they were: six healthy kittens lazing in a patch of sunshine in a big room painted white—with Mom snuggling them and purring them to sleep.

Someone told a delighted Jim the story of last night's happenings. As far as Jim was concerned, it was a miracle. He had seen firsthand how scared the mother cat had been, kittens or no kittens. He'd thought she was lost forever.

Now, he tried to catch the mother cat's eye, but couldn't. She wasn't interested in him; she was enjoying the bright, warm morning—content to be surrounded by her favorite little bundles as they rested after a good meal. He gave up trying to get her attention, and, instead, caught the eye of one of the little dinner roll-like kittens curled at her belly. The round, striped fur ball had a grateful, contented little spark in his eye. Jim couldn't help wondering whether the little guy knew that his was the meow that had saved his mom.

Elizabeth Doyle

Bogie's Search for His Forever Home

One must love a cat on its own terms.

Paul Gray

I first met Bogie during a volunteer-training class at Pittsburgh's Animal Friends, Inc., my community's no-kill shelter. As the facilitating volunteer spoke to the recruits gathered in the resident feline room, I couldn't help but notice the gray-and-white shorthair cat sleeping in his cage. The nametag on the cage informed me that Bogie, a four-and-a-half-year-old male, was the current occupant of cage 12. *Poor thing,* I thought as I knelt down before his cage to get a better look.

"Hey, little guy," I whispered, anticipating a meow or purr in response to my hello. But this cat was not happy that I woke him. Instead of purrs, Bogie hissed and spat, growling and staring at me with eyes that looked possessed. I was positive that, given the opportunity, he would have bitten my face off. I quickly apologized to Bogie, assuring him that I meant no harm. The rest of the group, distracted by this rather loud how-do-you-do, looked over at us.

The facilitator explained, "That's Bogie, the shelter's longest-term resident, and, as you can see and hear, he also happens to be our problem child."

Bogie seemed fully aware that he was being talked about, and his body language confirmed his irritation as his tail swished violently back and forth. The group chuckled at the facilitator's words, then began milling around the room, oohing and aahing at the friendlier cats that occupied the other cages. Bogie just sat there, growling.

After the training class, I began volunteering at the shelter every Sunday. Although I love all animals, I am particularly fond of cats, so I spent my time there socializing the cats—hours of playing, brushing, kissing, massaging and loving my furry little feline friends. Every cat received equal amounts of my love and attention—that is, every cat but Bogie. Bogie was strictly off-limits to volunteers because of his history of biting. This type of behavior isn't all that unusual for de-clawed cats, and poor Bogie had been a victim of that unfortunate and inhumane surgery prior to coming to the shelter. For Bogie, who felt defenseless and vulnerable without his claws, biting was the only way to protect himself against any perceived harm. As a result, Bogie was left to sit in his cage and observe all that went on around him.

Although Bogie was labeled a "Staff Only" cat, I didn't ignore him. From the moment I met Bogie, I was determined to break through his tough exterior to uncover his beautiful but hidden, loving spirit. The trick was how to go about it. My first thought was to make him feel important, so, every Sunday when I walked through the door, I would sing out his name before addressing any of the other cats. "Hi, Bogie! How are you? Boy, did I miss you Bogie!" Then I gave him his favorite fishy treats while telling him that his new family would be coming any day to take him home. I felt that it was important for him not to give up hope. I know it sounds crazy, but I believe that Bogie understood—if not my words, then at least my soft, reassuring tone. There were a few times that I actually snuck my finger though the cage bars and scratched behind Bogie's ears, until he discovered this intrusion and swiftly let me know that he did not approve. I brought Bogie a new bed and sprayed it with lavender oil, hoping that the aroma would calm him—it didn't. I brought him toys, hoping that he would play and find even the tiniest bit of pleasure in something—he was not interested. Day in and day out, he lay in that cage with his back facing the world. It was a pathetic sight; despite my efforts, Bogie had given up hope.

Because I already shared my home with five felines and two dogs, adopting Bogie was out of the question. But I had to do something—his situation tore at my heart. I began a campaign to find him a suitable home. Hoping that someone would be interested in giving him a second chance at a happy life, I told Bogie's sad story to anyone who would listen. Bogie was found wandering a beach in South Carolina. How he got there is anyone's guess. Perhaps he lost his way or maybe he was purposely abandoned. Only Bogie knows what really happened. He was rescued from the beach by a vacationing shelter employee and was brought back to Pittsburgh, where he weighed in at a frail six pounds and was diagnosed with hemolytic anemia. Medical treatment was successful, and, soon, Bogie was on the road to recovery. With Bogie's illness under control, he was eligible for adoption. The day finally came when a family adopted Bogie—only to return him days later because of litter-box aversion. Rejected, Bogie, in turn, seemed to reject the world. I told everyone that he was just waiting for his perfect person. Bogie needed someone who would be committed to working with him to help overcome the many traumas of his life, someone who actually embraced his cranky disposition and wouldn't give up on him, even if he did have an accident in the house—in short, someone who would make him feel safe and loved. I was sure that someone was out there . . . somewhere.

Finally, to my great joy, after a very long two years and four months of living at the shelter, Bogie was adopted in May 2002. Bogie's adjustment to life outside the shelter wasn't always easy, but his adoptive family constantly reassured him that he was finally in his forever home. The progress he made was slow, but definitely steady. Within two days, he allowed his new mom to briefly scratch him under his chin. Within a week, he was playing like a kitten, and, so far, he's only had one accident! The daily doses of hugs and kisses that he receives are healing his little heart, enabling him to trust once again.

When I think of Bogie and all the positive changes he's experienced since he found his forever home, I have to smile—especially when I see him sitting on his window perch, watching the birds while his tail swishes playfully.

That's right: *I* am Bogie's new mom, and there isn't a day that goes by that my formerly cranky cat doesn't thank me for giving him the chance to prove that, underneath all that attitude, he's just a big bundle of love.

Lorra E. Allen

Alley's Gift

On the small Florida farm where I grew up, the veterinarian did not treat our family pets because they weren't our livelihood. As a result, I knew almost nothing about the proper care and medical requirements of companion animals. After marrying and moving away from home, I got Nicky, a gorgeous Turkish Van-mix. As a new "mother," I wanted nothing but the best for my "baby." Nicky received excellent veterinary care, and I followed all the doctor's recommendations without question. My sweet boy thrived. He was my best friend and made being away from my family a lot less painful.

The first time I saw Alley, she was slinking around the wooded edge of the yard during a cookout. She was scrawny, looked like she hadn't eaten in days, and her coat was a scruffy brown. I remember thinking how pitiful she looked compared to my handsome Nicky. I threw scraps to her and watched as she swallowed them whole. The food was good, but not good enough to bring her within twenty feet of me. Eventually, she stopped being so afraid, and I began to feed her regularly. She wouldn't allow me to hold her, but I was able to trap her and get her spayed and given a rabies shot. We tried to keep her indoors, but she paced and howled until she was allowed back outside. At the time, I thought I had done everything necessary for her.

Alley blossomed, and her once-scruffy coat soon showed perfect brown tabby stripes. She loved living on our heavily wooded ten-acre lot. Nicky spent his days outside, sleeping on the porch, and his nights inside, sleeping on our bed. Alley adored Nicky and was his constant companion when he was out. I believe she stayed around only because he was there.

One night, Alley disappeared. Although she had disappeared before, she always came back in a day or two. When she didn't return after three days, I searched the woods. I kept Nicky with me, hoping Alley would seek him as she had in the past, but she was gone.

Around this time, I had begun studying technical drawing and was relieved when I landed my first job. I wasn't thrilled with my chosen profession, but it was a job. Almost a week after Alley disappeared, on the morning I was to start my new job, Alley came home. She could barely get up the steps to our porch. I could tell that something was terribly wrong. She was so weak that she even let me pick her up and hold her in my arms for the very first time. I had to go to work—I couldn't miss my first day—but I couldn't leave her. So I compromised: I would just have to be late. While I was supposed to be checking in with my new boss, instead, I was checking in at the veterinary hospital. I explained the situation to the receptionist, and gave her a blank check and my work phone number.

Thankfully, the supervisor at my new job was an animal lover, and, when I told her the reason for my late arrival, she sympathized. An hour later, the vet called with bad news. Alley had many cancerous tumors in her abdomen, as well as feline leukemia. The vet asked permission over the phone to humanely euthanize Alley because she didn't want the cat to suffer any further. Sadly, I agreed.

After work, I returned to the hospital. The doctor had stayed after hours to speak with me. She explained how leukemia affects cats and the importance of testing and immunization. My heart was broken. Alley had not been tested for leukemia and had only been to the vet when I trapped her for spaying and then for annual rabies vaccinations. When she mentioned how contagious feline leukemia is, I worried about Nicky. The vet checked Nicky's medical record, which showed that he had been vaccinated annually against the virus and had tested negative for it as a kitten. I was grateful that I had trusted Nicky's first veterinarian and followed his advice, even without completely understanding it.

Alley's death hit me hard. I was already going through a difficult time in my life—my marriage was in trouble, I didn't like technical drawing, I was plagued by my ever-present homesickness—and now I missed Alley, too. I hadn't realized how attached to her I was until she was gone. I also kept thinking about how tragic it would have been to lose both my cats and never have known that feline leukemia is preventable. I felt lost and alone.

The week after Alley died, I received a card from the state university's school of veterinary medicine. A monetary donation had been made in Alley's name. It lifted my spirits to think that she would be remembered somehow. My veterinarian had sent the donation, so I made a card for her on my home computer, thanking her for her compassion and for taking the time to talk with me. After I finished the card, I continued to sit at my desk. I couldn't stop thinking about my lack of education about feline leukemia. I spent another two hours on the computer, designing a poster to help others avoid the mistake I'd made with Alley.

I printed it. The bold type at the top read: "Do You Love

Your Cat?" In the middle was a picture of a cat. At the bottom was another line of bold type: "Love Can't Cure Feline Diseases. Have Your Cat Tested and Vaccinated for Feline Leukemia." Below that, in tiny print at the bottom of the sheet, it read: "This poster is dedicated to Alley, a shy, little cat whom I loved and lost." I mailed the card and the poster to my veterinarian.

A few months later, the company I worked for went bankrupt, and I was let go. I started sending out resumes again. I wasn't as upset by the loss of my job as I should have been.

Alley's vet remembered me when she read in the newspaper that the drafting company was going under. She called and offered to train me as a veterinary technician. She believed my desire to educate pet owners would benefit her practice.

On my first day of work at the veterinary hospital, my heart soared when I saw my Alley poster hanging on the wall. I immediately loved my new job and felt I had finally found a purpose in life. But my husband, who cared very little for my personal happiness, was not happy about my new—low—salary. He filed for divorce, and I moved back to be with my family. Back home, I was hired at a local veterinary hospital. The hours were long, but I thrived.

Then, almost two years after my divorce, a handsome new client walked into the office with his wounded cat, Shadowmar. My coworkers and I counted the days until "the cat guy" would be back for a recheck appointment. At the follow-up visit, we noticed that the wound on Shadowmar's head was not healing well. Testing revealed feline leukemia as the reason for Shadowmar's suppressed immune system. My own painful experience with the deadly virus was obvious as I discussed Shadowmar's diagnosis with his teary-eyed owner. When "the cat guy" left the office, I handed him my business card (just in case he had questions). I returned home that evening to find his message on my answering machine. We began dating, and I was there to comfort him on the awful day we had to end Shadowmar's life. Two years later, I married him.

Today, we are still happily married, and our family includes many wonderful furry "babies." I cannot imagine how things would have turned out if I had not met Alley and been so affected by her disease—the entire course of my life was changed by that one small cat.

Lori Pitts

Romeo and Juliet

Working for an animal-rescue organization, one sees a lot of loneliness: abandoned animals, unwanted animals, animals who've never had a companion in their lives. Perhaps the loneliest existence is that of the feral cat. Born to stray mothers, these kittens have never known the soft touch of a loving hand. They fear humans as their most adept and deadly enemy. Nor do they find solace from their own kind. Feral cats lead a fairly solitary existence in the wild, and, once weaned, often have to fend for themselves completely, fearing other cats as well.

Our rescue group included a team of self-proclaimed "crazy cat ladies," who helped manage the feral colonies typically found in alleys, barns and, especially, behind fast-food establishments. Using a box with a trapdoor, they would catch as many of these cats as they could and have them vaccinated and spayed or neutered. Sadly, many remained too wild to place into homes. So, once vaccinated and "fixed" to prevent more unwanted kittens from being born, they released the cats where they had been trapped.

The cat ladies had altered every cat living behind one particular fast-food restaurant—except for a wily male and female too cagey to fall for the trap. Trying to catch them without a trap simply wasn't an option. These two, extremely wary of humans, acted as if death had come to scoop them up every time a human came near.

The problem is, two ferals make six ferals, who, in turn, make dozens. And most business owners tolerate only so many cats before they decide to have them put down.

The cat ladies stepped up their plan. Trapping attempts went on night after cold night. Our rescuers were getting tired. Frustration starts to wear on even the best of us after a while.

Then it happened.

The scrappy black female was in the trap! She was furious, howling and pawing frantically at the door, but they had her! The big male tabby had presumably disappeared into the woods because of all the noise. Although the black female was angry now, vaccinations and spaying would help prolong her life. Everyone celebrated when she and the box were placed into the back seat of the car.

Calling it a night, the volunteers walked away from the car to collect the other trap. They knew the gray tabby male remained on the prowl, wildcat eyes probably glaring from the brush somewhere nearby. Still, everyone agreed they'd enjoyed a successful evening.

The first person to return to the car gasped, frozen.

There in the back seat was the big gray tabby, struggling to help the female break free of the box. He was so intent on saving her, he didn't even hear the car door slam behind him. It only took a tap to have him in a box next to her.

He had faced his greatest fear, braving his most dangerous enemies—humans and cars—to try to save her.

Once they were spayed and neutered, an interesting thing happened. These two, the wildest of the bunch and the least trusting of people, were so content during their vet visit, so happy to be together, that they were willing to accept a human into their lives. Dubbed Romeo and Juliet, the devoted couple, now safe in a home, will never be separated by infectious disease, predators or violent death.

What's more, they found the only thing still missing from their lives: a human pet.

E. V. Noechel

Happy Endings

It was a Saturday afternoon. As the shelter's cat-program director, I had just completed an adoption. Now, I stood in the adult-cat room, looking around. The doors of the cat cages—we call them cat condos—were open, yet some cats still lounged on the brightly colored, flannel-covered pads inside them. There were a few cats lying on the wide, sunny window ledge, watching the world out-side or just snoozing contentedly. I looked up and saw Otis walking along the catwalk, a network of boards sus-pended from the ceiling that cats access by climbing a tall, rope-covered column in the corner that doubles as a scratching post. Moo stuck his head through the cat door from the screened-in porch, just to make sure he wasn't missing anything important. Satisfied I wasn't bearing food, he withdrew his furry black-and-white head, and, through the window, I saw him leap gracefully onto one of the chairs on the porch to resume his nap in the dappled sunlight. The scene was one of pleasant, clean, feline serenity.

What a difference a year makes, I thought. A year ago, Noah's Ark Animal Foundation's cats were all in foster care, as well as some cramped temporary housing in my own home. It hadn't been easy, but we'd made it through. It had been just one more stage in our journey—rising from the ashes of the tragedy that had nearly destroyed us seven years before.

In March 1997, local teenage boys broke into our shelter, killing seventeen cats and seriously injuring a dozen more. The story generated headlines across the country—it was even voted *People* magazine's 1997 "Story of the Year," based on the level of reader response. When the young men were found guilty of only misdemeanors, many animal lovers were outraged, feeling the boys had been let off with too light a punishment. Yet even this dark cloud had a silver lining: Using the incident as a banner, we at Noah's Ark, along with other animal-welfare organizations, were able to persuade state legislators to stiffen the animal-cruelty laws in Iowa, and in several other states as well.

But, as an organization, we experienced some tough times. The tragedy had been traumatic for all involved, and it took a while to recover emotionally. Then, five years later, we were forced to move from the facility we had been using for more than ten years. We scrambled and found a temporary home for our shelter dogs on the farm of a generous couple who supported the foundation's work. The cats were scattered in homes throughout the area.

We kept our doors open—rescuing and finding homes for as many dogs and cats as we could, as well as promoting spay/neuter education and activities. In the meantime, we were slowly raising money to buy land to build a new shelter. We were doing the best we could under the circumstances. The strain was enormous, and, privately, I wondered how much longer we could go on that way.

Then a miracle happened—the kind that makes you pinch yourself to be sure you aren't dreaming. A fairy godmother appeared, waved her magic wand, and—

poof!—we had our very own brand-new shelter. Well, not exactly, but close! The administrator of a charitable foundation heard about our work. Our benefactress, who was appropriately named Miss Kitty, made a sizable donation, which—in addition to the money we had already raised— enabled us to build a shelter: the beautiful, modern, designed-for-animals building in which I now stood.

Of course, it took a lot more than a *"poof!"* to build the shelter. A great deal of work went into the research, design and building of our facility, because not only is our shelter clean and comfortable for animals, staff, volunteers and visitors, it is also kind to the Earth. Our building is "green," which means it is energy-efficient and has healthy interior-air quality because it was built with nontoxic construction materials and designed to take advantage of the sun for lighting and thermal power. The cats and dogs at Noah's Ark really seem to like the building. This is important because, even though we hope their stays will be brief, some animals spend a long time with us. Once we take an animal in, it remains with us until we find it a home—no matter how long that takes.

Doing rescue work isn't always fun. There is a high level of frustration because we can't save them all, and also because we worry when an animal doesn't seem to be adjusting well to shelter life or is returned after an unsuccessful adoption. Nevertheless, there are a lot of happy endings—and they are what keep us going.

I smiled, thinking of the adoption I had just completed. Kenny left this afternoon in the arms of a woman who couldn't see him, but loved him all the same. Kimberly, who is blind, immediately fell in love with Kenny, a longtime Noah's Ark resident, who had been passed over repeatedly by other potential adopters, probably because he was considered too ordinary: a black shorthair cat, no longer a kitten.

Of course, Kenny had done his part. Kimberly wanted a cat who would be drawn to her. Just a few moments after she took a seat in the adoption-room rocking chair, Kenny was on her lap, extolling his own virtues in his own way. Sometimes, I can only marvel at how these cat adoptions transpire; so often, it seems that it is the cat or kitten who adopts a human family, not the other way around. In any case, Kenny and Kimberly connected in a way that was beyond mere visual attraction. It was a particularly satisfying happy ending for me because I knew how much Kenny had to give.

Leaving the cat room, I looked around and said, "Don't worry, guys. Soon, it'll be your turn to go home with someone nice." Then I closed the door and walked through the happiest ending of all—Noah's Ark's new building, which houses our reborn spirit and provides shelter for the steady stream of animals who need and receive our care.

Janet Mullen

8

ONE OF THE FAMILY

This house is owned and operated solely for the comfort and convenience of the CATS!

Unknown

Elvis Has Left the Building

He had been my best friend and companion for more than twelve years, a first-year anniversary present from my husband when I told him I wanted something soft and warm to take care of. He had been with me through several jobs, earthquakes, fires, the L.A. riots, and five or six moves to different apartments. He was my surrogate child, my baby, my pal and protector when my husband was working late. He took care of me, followed me everywhere and loved me unconditionally.

So, when the veterinary surgeon told me that my beloved cat Elvis would die within a few weeks, I was devastated. I had just become pregnant with my first child, and so badly wanted my baby to know Elvis and come to love him as much as my husband and I did.

It had happened so quickly: One week, my husband and I noticed that our usually healthy and robust black-and-white cat was rapidly losing weight. After a few more days passed, we noticed a distinct loss of energy, and we took Elvis to be examined.

Finding an abnormality in the blood, the vet referred us to a wonderful internal-medicine group for animals. There, Elvis suffered through a battery of tests, which eventually determined his fate. He had a rare form of mast-cell cancer that was untreatable. But that didn't stop him from befriending the receptionists and lab technicians, who quickly grew to love him. Whenever we would come to pick him up, we could hear them in the back yelling, "Elvis has left the building!"

As the weeks went on, the doctor taking care of Elvis left it to us to decide how to proceed. We decided to try anything we could to keep Elvis alive and give him a chance to fight. That meant spending more than five thousand dollars, and coming in two to three times a week to give Elvis blood transfusions and chemotherapy—none of which guaranteed his recovery. But we had to try.

At night, Elvis slept cuddled up in bed near us. He was so gaunt and weak that he needed our body heat to stay warm, and he would press his head against my arm as if to say, "Stay close." During the days he was home, he would lie on the couch and sleep, occasionally raising his head and giving me his trademark meow, a strange, nasal *"maaaaa!"*

As the baby inside me grew bigger, Elvis grew weaker, and my husband and I realized he was losing his battle with cancer. It was January, and my baby was due in March. If only Elvis could hold on a little longer—but, as the month wore on, it was obvious the chemo was not working. Elvis had lost more than half his body weight, and he could barely move. His blood levels were dangerously anemic. The doctor didn't even think he could handle another transfusion.

So, on a cold day at the end of January, my husband and I carried Elvis back to the doctor's office one final time. In what seemed like a surreal dream, we were led through the surgery area to a room in the back called "the grieving room." It was a peaceful, friendly room with a couch and curtains, designed to make a painful process a little more comfortable. We were given a half hour to say our final good-byes. Then the doctor came in, said a prayer for Elvis, and injected a syringe into a vein.

As I felt my friend, my beloved Elvis, go limp in my arms, I held him close to my huge belly, hoping that maybe part of his spirit would go into my unborn child. It was a silly fantasy, but it kept me going long enough to leave the office without crying—until I heard one of the lab techs say sadly, "Elvis has left the building." The receptionist was crying, and, as she hugged me, I broke down in tears.

It took a few weeks before I could get through the day without weeping. Reminders of Elvis were everywhere. But, as March approached, my focus turned to my upcoming C-section. Our little boy, Max, was about to make his appearance into the world. My husband and I had picked out his name, Maxwell Gordon Jones, and, on March 19, as scheduled, he was born—big and bouncy and healthy.

During Max's first night in the hospital, he made all kinds of strange baby noises, including a very distinct nasal *"maaaaa!"* My husband and I gasped, staring at each other. Could it be? *"Maaaaa!"* We laughed as we pondered the idea that our child had somehow absorbed Elvis's spirit. And, when Max napped next to me in the bed, I melted when he pressed his head against my arm, as if to say, "Stay close."

When we filled out the birth certificate, we decided to add a little something special to Max's name: Maxwell Gordon Elvis Jones. Now, six months later, Max acts more and more like the feline brother he will never meet—loving, affectionate and cuddly—and this comforts me.

I took Max grocery shopping recently. As I stood in line, holding him in my arms, I noticed a tabloid headline and had to laugh. It read: "Elvis Lives!"

No kidding, I thought, as I squeezed my son and kissed him on the cheek.

Marie D. Jones

A Tale of Two Kitties

They say that cats have nine lives. Well, I don't know about that, but I do know one cat who had two lives. His name was Smokey; at least, that is what I called him. He was a gray-striped tom with a pink nose, four white paws and a silky-furred right ear that folded over at the tip. I found him shivering in our garage as a kitten when I was nine years old and kept him hidden in my bedroom for a week until I was sure that my mom would let me keep him. A stranger might not have thought him much to look at, but, to me, he was the cutest kitten in the world. My mother used to joke about how I was the only girl in Indian Hills, Colorado, who'd fall in love with a "dog-eared" cat.

By the time I was eleven, Smokey had pretty much established his own daily routine of returning home in time for dinner, after which he'd curl up on my bed. When I'd slip beneath the covers for the night, he'd move close to my face, nudge his head right under my chin, and, snuggled safe and warm, purr like a small-appliance motor. I never had a bad dream when Smokey slept beside me. He liked my three brothers, but it was obvious that he was a one-kid cat. And I was his girl. Or so I thought.

One night in July, Smokey didn't come home. I was upset, but my mother assured me that it wasn't unusual for a cat to wander off for an adventure now and then. I spent the next few days searching for him, calling his name and expecting to see him any minute, but there was no sign of him. By the end of the week, we were all upset.

My mother agreed that I should go to the general store and put up a missing-cat notice with Smokey's picture. I picked out a photo of him lying sphinx-like across my pillow, his bent ear and white paws clearly visible. As I completed the sign, describing his coloring and distinguishing marks, it was hard to keep from crying. My brother Dave went with me to the store to post the sign. Once it was up, we stood back to see if it was in a good spot. Sure enough, it was—right next to a notice for another missing cat named Ranger. In fact, the only difference between the two cats was their names; their descriptions were identical.

I wrote down the phone number on the other sign and called the moment we got home. The girl who answered said that her missing cat, Ranger, always stayed out at night and came home in the morning, but hadn't shown up in a week. I told her that my cat, Smokey—same coloring, same bent right ear—went out in the morning and came home in the evening, and that he hadn't shown up in a week. It was just too much of a coincidence to *be* a coincidence. With an unspoken pang of betrayal, we both conceded that her Ranger and my Smokey were one and the same cat—and that he had been living a double life! So much for a one-kid cat. But two-timing tom or not, both of us loved him, and he was still missing.

The girl's name was Evelyn, and we arranged to meet the following day. She was a year older than I, which was probably why we hadn't known each other, even though she lived just a quarter-mile away. She brought over her pictures of Ranger, and I brought out my pictures of

Smokey. We spent the afternoon sharing stories about our "dog-eared, one-kid cat," alternately sniffling and laughing at the similarity of his two-household antics. By dinnertime, we'd gone through more than half a box of Kleenex and had become best friends.

Together, Evelyn and I handmade flyers for our missing cat ("answers to the names of Smokey and Ranger"), passed them out all around town, and kept each other from giving up hope by recounting amazing stories of lost animals who'd miraculously found their way home after years. But, by the end of August, even these took on a hollow ring.

Then, a week before school started, we got a phone call that seemed too good to be true. It was from a woman in Golden, about ten miles away, saying she'd seen our flyer in a gas station and believed she had our cat. Her son had found him about a month ago on the side of the road, bloody and near death from an animal attack, and she'd been nursing him back to health. She said that she'd named him Marker because of his bent ear.

My mother drove Evelyn and me to Golden that same afternoon, cautioning us not to get too excited in case the cat wasn't ours. *How many dog-eared cats could there be?* we wondered, but really didn't want to know. Squeezing each other's hand tightly, we followed the woman into the house where she said Marker was resting. But, the moment we saw him, we had no doubt that Marker wasn't Marker: He was Smokey; he was Ranger. He was ours—and he was alive! His nonstop purring all the way home told us that he was as happy to be found as we were to find him.

Smokey/Ranger continued to live his two lives—dividing his days and nights and love between Evelyn's house and ours—until advancing age and illness got the better of him. When his health worsened, we knew the kindest thing to do was to set him free from his suffering. Evelyn and I were both with him when he died. He seemed to know that we were both there—stroking his white paws, caressing his bent ear—and he drifted from us peacefully, purring to the end.

No, Smokey wasn't the one-kid cat I once thought he was. He was just the best cat that ever was.

P.S. Evelyn, who's remained my best friend for all these years, says the same thing about Ranger.

June Torrence
As told to Hester J. Mundis

Etcetera, Etcetera, Etcetera

"LUCILLE! Get over here right now!"

Silence.

The cross voice boomed again, "LUCILLE! What are you doing?"

Lucille, my small, quiet mother, looked puzzled. "Hanging up the diapers," she answered.

I opened the back door and laughed. "Mom, that guy across the alley is yelling for Lucille, his *dog*. Not you." I adjusted my newborn baby on my shoulder and walked to the back gate. "Make sure this gate stays locked because that dog is ornery."

I lay the baby down in her buggy and watched my six-year-old daughter put our Siamese in her doll buggy. The cat's clear blue eyes looked worried, but he remained on his back wearing a doll's nightgown and bonnet like a good baby should. When I was little, I remember my elderly neighbor's warning: "It's not good to have Siamese cats around small children. They have a mean streak, you know." She dropped her voice, "*And cats will suck the breath out of a baby.* Anyone with small children should think about getting rid of a cat."

No way would I dream of getting rid of our cat! Etcetera

was an important member of our family. Even naming him had been a family decision. We all enjoyed listening to my record of Rodgers and Hammerstein's musical *The King and I*. The kids particularly liked the part when the King of Siam says, "Etcetera, etcetera, etcetera." And that was how our pretty, fine-boned Siamese kitten became Etcetera.

Etcetera grew up with our children. He demonstrated his good nature by never complaining and sometimes even taking the blame for their antics. The boys ended up with very sticky hair after devouring a whole package of gum. When I asked how this happened, they assured me that our cat had chewed the gum and deposited it in their hair. Another time, the owner of a pair of wet underpants told me, "Etcetera did it!"

Etcetera showed his patience by being the load carried in a big dump truck in the sandbox. He morphed into a ferocious lion and sat still for the construction of a building-block fence around him. He purred contentedly while a chubby little arm anchored him down during naptime. Was this the same breed of cat that had a mean streak?

When the new baby was two weeks old, Grandma Lucille went home, and I settled into raising our four children. One morning, during the baby's bath time, I heard frightened cries from the kids playing outside. I wrapped the baby in a towel and opened the back door. I noticed that the back gate stood open. Without warning, Etcetera whipped past me out of the house—eyes wild and tail straight out.

He made a beeline to the sandbox, where I now saw the children had been cornered by Lucille. Etcetera pounced. Lucille's threatening growl stopped. Lucille, the loser in round one, streaked out the gate yelping. Etcetera, the victor, climbed into the dump truck for a ride. After meeting our attack cat, Lucille wouldn't be over again anytime soon. I shut and locked the back gate, dried tears, watched the road building begin in the sandbox and listened as praises for our cat filled the air.

"Wasn't Etcetera brave?"

"He saved our lives."

"He flew faster than Superman."

"Our little cat's tougher than that big dog."

Etcetera, etcetera, etcetera.

Sharon Landeen

Machiavelli

Arthur, a cat of discriminating taste, largely ignored them, these oversized, fluffless males who came and went. In Arthur's opinion, they practiced less-than-meticulous personal hygiene. They bathed no more than once a day, he guessed, and rarely smoothed their hair. Not like Arthur. He twisted and ran his tongue down his dazzling white back. Arthur's personal assistant liked clean cats. Her name was Beth, or maybe Brenda. He couldn't remember. Arthur didn't concern himself with details.

They were easy to get rid of, the fluffless males. Arthur figured this out back when his personal assistant was married to Bill, or was it Bruce? Whatever his name, the husband liked to sit in Arthur's chair and sleep on Arthur's side of the bed. The worst offense, however, was the day that the husband came home smelling of some other male cat. *Unacceptable.* Arthur had no choice but to soil a pair of wingtips. The husband yelled. Arthur targeted some running shoes.

"Either that cat goes or I do," the husband said.

Hardly a difficult choice, Arthur thought, but his personal assistant cried and hesitated. However, she only hesitated until she found out that the other cat belonged to another woman. Arthur stayed, and the husband went.

Then came other fluffless males. Arthur let each one stay for a while—until the man did something unforgivably crass, such as calling Arthur "kitty." Then Arthur would soil a pair of shoes or a jacket or a gym bag. Arthur's personal assistant would cry and accuse. The male would defend himself. She would counter that her cat had an uncanny sense about these things. Arthur would hit the shoes one more time. Another fluffless male would disappear. Life was good.

Then came George, or was his name Jeff? The New One heard about Arthur and the shoes. When he came to dinner, he brought roses for the personal assistant and some expensive, catnip-scented bauble for Arthur. Arthur accepted the bribe, but, when he was sure the New One was watching, he would cast a long look at the shoes: leather topsiders. The New One understood that look. He smiled at Arthur, scratched his ear gently and called him "Machiavelli." Arthur didn't know what Machiavelli meant, but it sounded cool.

One weekend, the New One came over with tools in tow. From his comfortable perch, Arthur could hear pounding in the backyard. He disliked the noise and went looking for a pair of shoes, but the New One never left them lying around. Finally, the pounding stopped, and the New One opened the back door and called Arthur. Outdoors? He wasn't allowed outdoors. But the New One had screened in the back porch and built a special platform for Arthur. They sat on that porch all day: the two humans curled together, and Arthur stretched out, eyes closed, face lifted to the sun. He felt the warm, scented air ruffle his dazzling fur. *I suppose,* Arthur thought, *this one can stay.*

Susan Hasler

Training Camp for Wheezy

My wife Sue returned on a Monday afternoon from the veterinarian, crying. Wheezy, one of our three cats, was still in his carrier, and I feared the worst.

"The vet gave me this," she sniffled and handed me a blue pamphlet. Trembling, I unfolded it and read: "A Fat Cat Is Not a Happy Cat."

"The doctor says he's got to lose weight and get in shape," my wife added, as she unhinged the carrier's gate. Wheezy, who almost qualifies for his own ZIP code, bounded out of his kitty cab and sprinted toward the basement door and his favorite spot: the twenty-four-hour buffet we call his dinner dish.

"Funny, he didn't appear to need a Prozac on his way to lunch just then, sweetheart," I said.

Oops. Every married man knows the feeling of letting a wisecrack accelerate through the intersection of good judgment without hitting the brake in time. This was one of those moments.

Sue's eyes welled at my insensitivity, and I did what every self-respecting doofus of a husband does when he knows he's in trouble—I promised to fix things.

"Honey, don't worry. I'll get ol' Wheeze on a workout

plan. I'll whip him into shape in no time, no problem. By Sunday, you'll see success. Our cat will be a happy cat, just you wait and see."

Tuesday

As a near world-class athlete myself (I hold my high-school basketball record for fouling out of a game the fastest), I knew I was the man for the job. The first day of training camp meant stoking the fires of motivation. I rented all my favorite macho videos and sat Wheezy down on the sofa for a gut check. Actually, Wheezy struggles in the sitting position because gravity tends to force him to roll over—but that's not important.

We sat through all the *Rocky* movies, all the *Terminators* and then a bunch of military flicks. Right after the scene in *An Officer and a Gentleman* when Louis Gossett, Jr. berates all the new recruits, I got inspired. I quickly searched the house for military garb—the best I could find was Sue's Girl Scout camp sweatshirt. It was greenish and would have to do.

I puffed out my chest and tried to make all the veins in my neck stick out. I approached the sprawled-out Private Wheezy on the couch and shouted: "Hey, you mangy fur ball, ATTENTION! On your feet . . . uhhh, paws . . . whatever."

Wheezy stirred awake from his nap, shook his head a bit and gave me a confused gaze. I continued on my roll: "Don't look me in the eye, private. I am your superior!" I began to wobble with the dizziness brought on by trying to make my neck veins stand out, and I felt like I was going to keel over.

Wheezy flopped off the couch and walked right past me on his way to the basement.

Wednesday

All right, so the boot camp approach failed—I wasn't discouraged. The more I thought about it, the more I realized that this had to be fun and exciting for Wheezy. It had to be something different, something everyone liked. That meant just one thing: Tae-bo.

I popped in the tape and got in a nice uniform line with Wheezy. It started out with some deep breathing. I glanced at my exercise buddy; he looked like he was getting it, so far. Next, it was time to throw something called reverse punches.

As I neared a state of hyperventilation, Wheezy just tilted his head. I wasn't sure whether he was trying to figure out just how a cat is supposed to throw a reverse punch, or was staring at the grinning instructor on the tape and wondering if those were really his teeth or not.

To be a good role model, I decided to keep on with my workout. I went to throw some sort of crazy triple-side, ax-murderer kick, and I thought I heard the street's power lines snap.

An instant later, the burning in my leg told me that this wasn't a problem for the power company—it was a leg muscle shredding like the piano wire in a 300-year-old Steinway.

As I writhed on the floor, gasping, Wheezy stepped on my chest on his way to the basement stairs. I'm not positive, but I think I heard my furry little buddy laugh as he went down the steps.

Thursday

After a night's rest and the application of some Ben-Gay, it was time to go to the fitness store. I figured it made sense to keep it simple. And what could be simpler than running? Wheezy and I were going to do some roadwork. This created a slight problem because Wheezy never leaves the house, and it was going to be difficult for my little would-be marathoner to actually do "road" work. The answer was a treadmill. After much deliberation and handing over the equivalent of the gross national product of some lesser-developed countries, it was delivered.

Any fitness enthusiast knows you have to stretch before you run. So I sat facing my chubby buddy with one leg stretched out and the other tucked in as I bent toward my knee.

Wheezy arched his back.

I switched legs and bent toward that knee.

Wheezy stretched his front paws.

I couldn't believe what I was seeing—he was getting it! I stretched my back.

Wheezy did that funky cat stretch that always makes him look like a TV with bad horizontal hold.

I took strides in place.

Wheezy kneaded the carpet in front of him.

I was loose; I was ready.

Wheezy took one last *lo-o-o-o-ong* stretch and . . . fell asleep.

Deciding not to let this get me down, I carried my training partner to the treadmill and put him between my legs. I turned on the treadmill and started to jog. Wheezy abruptly awoke, took a few steps, then slid down the belt like an old Samsonite on an airport's luggage conveyor belt.

It wasn't good.

Friday

I couldn't sleep. Wheezy could. I guess we all handle stress differently.

I was up all night flipping through the channels with my training partner on my lap. Then I found our answer: personal power.

Self-improvement guru of gurus, Tony Robbins, was promising us a new life. Some of the world's greatest achievers have called on the hyper-intense, bright-eyed, big-toothed leader.

I perked right up and nudged Wheezy awake.

Tony said we needed to feel the fire. Wheezy cocked an ear.

Tony told us to dream and visualize big things. Wheezy started to breathe harder.

Tony yelled at us to become who we really wanted to be! Wheezy started to shake.

Tony implored us to reach deep down within ourselves and stir our insides!

Wheezy did—and then coughed a large hairball into my lap.

Saturday

So much for personal power. It was only a day before the weigh-in, and I still needed a map to make it all the way around Wheezy. I had to make one last-ditch effort. It was time for the Tummy-O-Matic.

The Tummy-O-Matic is this mass of twisted plastic pipe that has a pillow in the middle for the user's head and guarantees the user six-pack abs after using it for just eight minutes a day. I figured we didn't have much time, so Wheezy and I would do twice as much in half the time.

As I finished setting up the apparatus, I caught my training partner heading for the basement stairs. I snatched him up (using proper body mechanics) and placed his head on the headrest. Wheezy's paws didn't reach the handles, so I was going to have to do the rolling while he crunched his six-pack.

By the time I got positioned and reached for the handles, Wheezy was drooling and sound asleep, apparently impervious to the potential of the Tummy-O-Matic. It dawned on me that it didn't say anywhere that you had to be awake to develop a six-pack of steel, so I began to roll away while Wheezy took his catnap.

It was going so well.

With each ab crunch, more drool dripped out of Wheezy's mouth, and, in my eagerness for success, I guess I sacrificed good body mechanics. On Wheezy's fourth unconscious rep, I slipped in the pool of drool, snapped the stabilizing bar on the Tummy-O-Matic, crashed onto the hardwood floor and re-injured my leg.

Once again, I was rolling around on my living-room floor, overcome with pain.

Wheezy started to snore.

Sunday

Our day of reckoning upon us, I scooped up my dedicated fitness enthusiast and marched to the bathroom scale to get it over with. Gently lowering Wheezy to the scale, I braced myself for failure. As the digits stopped spinning, I glanced down and couldn't believe my eyes:

"HOLY OCEAN-FISH FORMULA!!!! WHEEZY LOST A POUND!!!!" I heard myself shout.

Immediately, I ran through the house pumping my fist, doing that foolish "raise-the-roof" gesture, along with my best end-zone dance. Rhetorically, I shouted, "Who DA Man? Who DA Man? I DA Man, that's who DA man is!" I hadn't felt this good since I broke that foul-out record.

Wheezy was sound asleep on the scale.

While I was high-stepping through the house, Sue came in through the side door. I could not contain myself: "Wheezy lost a pound! I did it! I DA man! I DA cat-trainin' man! Like I always say, honey, 'If you can do it, it ain't braggin'—*I DA man!*"

Sue was clearly pleased. She rubbed her chin, deep in thought , then said, "Gee, I wonder if that new food I've been giving Wheezy, 'Cat Food for the Almost Never Active Cat,' helped? Either way, he looks happier."

Wheezy and I know the real deal, but I'll let Sue think what she wants.

And as for Wheezy, well, of course, he's happier—he's in shape.

Tom Schreck

The Call of the Lobster

Basil Rathcoon and his half-sister Agatha Coonstie were the first Maine Coon cats that I had ever had, and I quickly became accustomed to their trilling, musical sounds, which my husband and I refer to as "talking." Basil, a twenty-pound male, is, by far, the more vocal of the two; as a kitten, he developed a particular language for talking to his favorite plaything, a stuffed toy lobster.

The "call of the lobster" always occurred when Basil, carefully clutching the red toy in his jaws, moved his little friend. Every day, the lobster was taken to breakfast, to naptime in Basil's bed, to watch television on the sofa, to dinner and, finally, to bed. Of course, the lobster, "Mr. Johnny-on-the-Spot," helped with various household chores, such as doing the dishes or the laundry. Basil made sure that he and his friend participated in every activity that involved the family, so, each time Basil moved his lobster, he would pick him up and explain to him—using his entire lung capacity—the next task on their agenda. No matter where I was in the house, I could always hear them coming.

As so often happens in childhood friendships, I feared that the two would grow apart as Basil matured. But the two remained fast friends, even though the poor lobster suffered many tragedies, such as being dropped into the water bowl by Basil's jealous brother Rochester, a longhair red tabby. The lobster had to be washed, dried and refitted with catnip—via a minor surgical procedure—before he was fit to travel again. All seemed well. Until one day, when the toy disappeared, and the call of the lobster ceased.

My husband and I were saddened by the loss of the musical cries, but what we found even more distressing was the change in Basil's behavior. Although he had always been a fantastic jumper, energetic and a little too intelligent for his own good, he had never destroyed the furniture or broken anything fragile. So when he started stretching his arms through the upstairs banister in order to swipe at the artificial long-stem flowers in an antique vase that had belonged to my deceased mother-in-law, I became upset. I feared that the sometimes-naughty Rochester had taught Basil the art of attacking fake flowers.

For several months, I moved the vase of flowers around the house to different locations. Each time, Basil would try amazing stunts to reach it. One day, disgusted by yet another of Basil's attempts to massacre the flowers, I picked up the vase to move it. My husband, who was standing nearby, said, "Why is there a pair of eyes looking at me?"

Startled, I set the vase down on the dining-room table and backed away. My fearless husband reached into the flowers and pulled out—Basil's lobster.

We sat down on the floor, called Basil to us and reunited him with his wayward friend. Basil sniffed the lobster, then picked up his pal and marched him upstairs to the bedroom and placed him in a circular cat bed. For two days, the lobster remained grounded in the bedroom, but at the end of the lobster's detention, he was allowed to resume his normal traveling duties.

Basil is now five years old. Sadly, the irreplaceable lobster was dunked one too many times in the water-bowl by Rochester, so Basil adopted a red catnip-stuffed mouse, and a new loving friendship has developed.

Even our female tortie, Pyewacket, caterwauls to her favorite friend, a green sparkling glitter ball—though she is not able to make the same musical sounds that Basil can. I am the only person I know whose pets have pets of their own, which makes for a happy, if somewhat loud, family.

Susan Isaac

Jingle, Jingle

When I play with my cat, who knows if I am not a pastime to her more than she to me?

Montaigne

As a responsible pet guardian, I make sure to keep up on the latest recommendations and innovations in pet care by reading the ripped and wadded-up back issues of cat magazines at my vet's office, every six months when I herd the cats there for their semi-annual shots.

The most recent article I read discussed the importance of playtime with your feline companions. Pets, the article emphasized, *love* and *rely* on playtime with their humans. It is a time of bonding, and, if done regularly, will be something a pet looks forward to with excited anticipation every day.

See, here all along I had assumed our cats were happy stuffing their faces, then lying belly up in the sun for eight-hour stretches. Little did I suspect that behind those full bellies and warm fur, kitty hearts were breaking because they did not have a regularly scheduled playtime with me. I set about to remedy the situation.

Walking in the door with purchases from the pet store, I felt confident that one of the bags I held contained the secret to unlocking shared fun for me and my cats. I started out simple, with their favorite toy from kittenhood, the cotton mouse.

"Here, kitty," I said, dangling a bright-yellow cotton mouse by its tail. "Come play."

The cat scratched her nose in her sleep and rolled over.

I tried the kitten. "See the mouse? Want to get the mouse?"

The kitten sat up and yawned. I was encouraged. At least one of them was awake.

I dug in the bag and pulled out rubber cheese.

"*Oooooh!*" I exclaimed. "Look at the pretty cheese. Who wants to try to eat the pretty cheese?"

The kitten looked at the cat, who gave an I-have-no-idea-but-just-ignore-her-and-maybe-she'll-leave shrug.

I clapped my hands. "Hey! You are supposed to want to play with me. I bought all these toys, so get with the program," I announced.

I yanked two identical candy-cane-striped jingle balls out of the bag. *Jingle, jingle. Jingle, jingle.* They made a happy noise.

The cats turned their backs to me.

"Aw, c'mon!" I begged. "One round of 'chase the jingle ball.' Here, I'll show you how."

And so it was that I found myself rolling a jingle ball down the hallway, then running after it to retrieve and roll it—again and again. I was panting when I returned to the cats after five rounds.

"See?" I huffed. "It's not so . . ."

But they were gone. I searched the house until I found the cat munching nibbles out of the kitten's dish, and the kitten wedging herself under the dining-room credenza in the hopes of hiding from me.

"Fine, you win," I said, abandoning the toys in the middle of the floor. "We won't play."

Cut to two in the morning: My husband and I are warm under the blankets and deep in our dreams.

Jingle, jingle. Jingle, jingle.

My husband rolled over. "Wass that?" he mumbled.

Jingle, jingle.

"I bought the cats some toys," I said. "They hated them. Just wait a minute, and they'll quit."

Jingle, jingle. Jingle, jingle. Jingle, jingle. Annoying, but bearable. Bearable, that is, until the cats discovered how much better the balls sounded on hardwood floors.

JNGLE JINGLE. JINGLE JINGLE. JINGLE JINGLE JINGLE JINGLE JINGLE JINGLE JINGLE JINGLE JINGLE. Pause. *JINGLE JINGLE JINGLE JINGLE JINGLE JINGLE JINGLE JINGLE.*

Two hours later, and there was no end in sight. Not only were the cats enthralled with their new playtime of "chase the jingle ball," but they also discovered a love of the game "keep-away." Every time we got out of bed to take the balls from them, they hid them somewhere unfindable, sitting and staring at us until we returned to bed. Then they retrieved the balls and reinstated soccer practice on the hardwoods outside our bedroom.

It's been a week, and I still can't find those jingle balls. The cats obviously have some secret hiding place they won't divulge. But I know they're out there. Because late at night, deep in the recesses of the house, drawing closer, we hear them coming.

Jingle, jingle.

Sometimes, we hold each other and cry.

Stupid pet magazines.

Dena Harris

Confessions of a Cat Hater— Who Got Lucky

I remember most clearly watching our daughter carry a young kitten down the path leading to my office. Why, I wondered, would Jenny be bringing a cat to me? She knew quite well that I was not fond of cats. Only recently, we'd had an argument over her decision to bring a cat into the family. I opposed her—and lost. My grandfather disliked cats, my father disliked cats, and, ever the obedient son, I learned at an early age that cats were sinister, evil and altogether disreputable animals. They had no legitimate place in the homes of civilized people, I thought.

My question was quickly answered. Jenny had rescued the cat from a group of stick-wielding young ruffians at a nearby trailer park. At first glance, one might think she'd been too late. The cat looked awful. He was emaciated and had numerous sores on his body, as well as an injured jaw. Obviously, he needed medical attention.

As Jenny held the cat, she reassured him that everything would be all right. And then she said, "Daddy will take you to see Dr. Waggoner."

"Jenny," I said, "you know I don't like cats. Get someone else to take him to the vet."

"I don't have time, Daddy. I'm already late for class. (She was a music student at a local university.) Oh, Daddy," she continued, almost tearfully, "you don't want him to suffer, do you?"

"Well, no," I replied. (I might not have liked cats, but I wasn't a monster!) "All right," I said reluctantly, "I'll take him to see Dr. Waggoner. But when I bring him back, *you* will be his caregiver. And when he has recovered, I want *you* to find a home for him." It was a done deal. Or so I thought.

Dr. Waggoner was acquainted with my feelings about cats—or, more accurately, my lack thereof. After express-ing amazement that *I* had been chosen to bring this unfor-tunate feline in for his ministrations, he examined the animal, cleaning his wounds and making a few minor adjustments to his injured jaw. Then he gave me some medication for the cat, with instructions to administer it orally two times a day. He said the cat was lucky to be alive, very lucky. "Lucky," I repeated, and the name stuck.

I had never administered medication to a cat before and was surprised by the strength of Lucky's jaws, despite his injury. On my first attempt, he clamped them shut tight, in effect saying, "I ain't taking no medicine for nobody." Fortunately, anticipating this, Dr. Waggoner had shown me how to apply pressure to both sides of the jaw simul-taneously, thus forcing the cat's mouth open. As the win-dow of opportunity appeared, I stuck the dropper in the little beast's mouth, squeezed the bulb, and the job was done until the next time.

Day followed day, and I saw very little change in Lucky's attitude. Finally, after ten days, I brought him back to Dr. Waggoner for a follow-up exam. I was dismayed to learn that we needed to continue the treatment for another ten days. This was not what I wanted to hear, but I had gotten the procedure down, and I thought that, just maybe, Lucky's resistance was becoming a little less savage.

Sometime during the second ten-day period, I noticed a few changes. Lucky would occasionally jump up on my computer desk and lie down on the papers that I happened to be working on. Then I noticed that, at feeding time, he would walk around my ankles and purr very softly. One day, he jumped up on the back of my chair, where he curled up and actually went to sleep for a short while.

As the second ten-day period reached its end, I asked Jenny (who seemed to be suspiciously overwhelmed with her work schedule during this time) if she had found a nice home for Lucky. "Not yet," she said. "I'm still looking." Then, casting an eye on Lucky snoozing comfortably on my desk, she said, "It looks to me as though Lucky thinks he has found just the right home."

"Not with me," I said. "You made a promise when I agreed to take him to Dr. Waggoner; now, keep that promise and go find this cat a nice home." But Jenny realized what Lucky had already decided—and I had yet to find out: Those four paws of his were right where they wanted to be.

So, true to the wily personality of the cat, Lucky had worked his way into my life and made himself a very important part of my routine. Evidence of this came as I recognized that I actually had started looking for him at the window and listening for his greeting—a very loud purr as he approached the small office building where I worked and he was determined to live. I even built a small window perch for him (carpeted, no less) and placed a heavy wire screen outside to protect him from the neighborhood dogs. This also made an escape more difficult, if he ever entertained such an idea. These were not steps taken by someone who hated cats. I didn't realize it at the moment, but, soon, it began to sink in.

It sank in for sure (and forever) when I brought him to the vet for the last checkup with my University of Florida colors—orange and blue ribbons—proudly tied to the door of his pet carrier. That's when Dr. Waggoner confessed that Lucky had not strictly needed the second sequence of medication. "Lucky was doing well enough," he explained. "You just needed a little extra time for the bonding process to take hold."

Marshall Powers
As told Hester Mundis

[EDITORS' NOTE: *The bonding process took a deep hold on Marshall Powers, who enjoyed the love and company of Lucky for nearly ten years. A year after his death, Lucky the Cat was named cofounder, with Marshall Powers, of the Gato Press. Dedicated to publishing cat-oriented stories designed to educate and enrich young readers, Gato Press now has a series of books about Lucky's adventures in cat heaven. The stories are told from Lucky's point of view—but all are written by Marshall, a man who discovered the incomparable joy of opening his heart to a cat.*]

"They always seem to know when
someone doesn't like cats."

The Gift of Acceptance

When we brought Doogie, a four-month-old gray-and-white kitten, home to live with us, Calvin, our two-year-old tabby, was not happy. He greeted us at the door with suspicion, hissing loudly at the box that contained the kitten. That first meeting was a flop. Doogie wanted to be friends right away, and Calvin would have none of it.

The first few days were rocky. Doogie continued to try to make friends with Calvin, and Calvin continued to hiss and swat. I felt stressed, thinking that maybe we'd made a mistake adopting a second cat. I knew that Calvin needed a feline playmate, but, apparently, he wasn't pleased with my choice.

To make matters worse, Doogie had a problem digesting the expensive, specially formulated cat food that we fed him and was producing some mighty bad odors. My husband Steven, who hadn't been too enthusiastic about getting a second cat to begin with, turned to me after another one of Doogie's "fragrant" moments and said, "Out of all the cats at the rescue, why did you have to get a smelly one?"

It didn't look promising.

However, after Doogie had been with us for a full week, he made another attempt to make friends with Calvin, and

Calvin, in a moment of benevolence, allowed it. Doogie bumped his little head up against Calvin's face, then rubbed the entire length of his body against him. I was marveling at how well the boys were finally getting along, when an incensed meow roared out of Calvin, and he smacked his little brother. Before I could scold the older cat, I smelled it. Doogie had chosen the moment his little rump reached Calvin's face to have a digestive problem erupt. I had to laugh.

In spite of Doogie's impolite greeting, relations between the two cats improved significantly from that point on. They began wrestling with one another and playing games of chase all over the house. Although they were getting along, Calvin still thought that he should make it very clear to Doogie that he, Calvin, was the dominant cat who deigned to allow Doogie to share his home. If Doogie had something that Calvin wanted, usually a coveted warm spot to sleep in, he didn't hesitate to boot Doogie out of the way and take what he wanted. Thankfully, Doogie agreed to this arrangement.

Meanwhile, Doogie's digestive problems worsened. He ceased to be smelly, but also stopped keeping his food down. Concerned, I took him to the vet. I learned Doogie had a sensitive tummy and needed to eat a special diet. We came home with a bag of neutral cat food, specially prescribed.

This posed a problem. The boys were used to having their food sitting out for them to snack on whenever the mood hit. We couldn't continue to keep the rich food out all the time. We exchanged the rich food for the neutral, thinking that the problem was solved. We were wrong.

The first time Calvin approached the bowl for a snack, he took one sniff and loudly voiced his indignation. That one meow plainly said, "What is this garbage in my bowl?!"

To appease Calvin, Steven and I began keeping his rich

food in the pantry. When he wanted a snack, he would stand at the pantry door and meow loudly until one of us opened the door to let him in. We would stand there until he was done, then shut the door behind him once he exited the pantry. This effectively kept Doogie away from the food that made him sick.

There's something magical about things we can't have. We begin to want more than anything the very thing that we aren't allowed. This applies to cats, as well as humans. Doogie soon realized that there was something special in the pantry that he was being denied. Whenever the door would be opened for Calvin to have a snack, Doogie was on his brother's heels, trying his hardest to get at the mystery that was Calvin's food. We denied him access every time.

If cats can have pity, Calvin had it for Doogie. He knew that he was getting the good stuff, while Doogie ate what Calvin considered to be inferior food.

One day, after this arrangement had been going for weeks, Calvin went into the pantry, as usual, to eat. As he backed out, I quickly closed the door so Doogie, who was hot on his heels, wouldn't get in. This day, though, Calvin refused to go on his merry way. He stopped in front of Doogie and opened his mouth. A cascade of cat food poured out into a pile at Doogie's feet. Doogie gobbled gratefully.

I marveled at what had just taken place. My cat had not only shown great ingenuity, but had also given Doogie the greatest gift of all—final and total acceptance.

Anne Marie Davis

"Oh come on now. . . it's not that bad."

Learning the Rules

Most cats do not approach humans recklessly . . . Much ceremony must be observed, and a number of diplomatic feelers put out, before establishing a state of truce.

Lloyd Alexander

Hazel and Stormy had no clue it was coming. One day, my husband stayed home from work, then we both were gone for two days; when we returned, we had a human kitten.

Frightened, neither cat wanted to see the baby at first. Stormy had been rescued at four weeks of age and believed in her little feline heart that she was a larval form of human. She had lived her first two years convinced that, one day, she would shed her fur and grow to be six feet tall. She viewed my husband as her mother and tried her best to walk on her two hind legs. Seeing an actual human baby shattered her faith, and I'm afraid she's never regained her equilibrium.

Hazel—with a deep, self-preserving instinct developed after months on the street—had a more worldly view. She understood that I was now a "Mother Animal," and, as such, I was dangerous. She avoided me. Defending my young, I might become unpredictable. Although she had always slept on my pillow, now Hazel refused to jump on the bed when I was on it. My reassurances meant nothing. Hazel clearly wanted the baby to grow up and leave. She would patiently wait for that time to arrive.

The baby was born in the middle of July. By the middle of August, Hazel grew concerned, as the baby was not yet walking or talking—or showing any signs of moving to its own apartment. Clearly, this called for a compromise: She needed to open diplomatic relations with the baby.

It was a Friday afternoon, and the baby had finally stopped squawking and settled to sleep. I laid him down in the middle of my queen-size bed and sat reading. A moment later, Hazel leaped up to the foot of the bed, then retreated to the farthest inch of the mattress. She watched me. Her question was clear from her posture: *May I be on the bed while the baby is on the bed?*

I made clicking noises to her, and she relaxed. Still watching me, she took two steps forward, then stopped. Again her question was obvious: *May I get near the baby?*

I sat relaxed, watching her, so that my body language said yes.

Hazel made her way around the perimeter of the bed, then put her head under my hands. *May I get petted while you're with the baby?* Yes, Hazel, you may get petted.

Next, she straightened her tail and walked right toward my son, a clear, *May I step on the baby?* This I answered by lifting her and placing her on the other side of me. No, Hazel. You may walk on us, but you may not walk on the baby.

Still watching me, Hazel put her head near the baby's hands. *May I try to get the baby to pet me?* Yes, Hazel, but it's no use.

May I cuddle up next to the baby? Yes, particularly if you purr like you're doing now, but watch those back paws.

The cuddling issue took some time to resolve. I had to keep pivoting Hazel so her back was to the baby. She disliked that position because she couldn't see me. She had done her best to maintain eye contact the entire time.

Hazel stood, and still with her gaze locked onto mine, she went to the next step in negotiations: carefully laying one paw with claws retracted on my son's forehead. I sat up sharply, and she pulled back her paw and didn't try that again.

Negotiations completed, Hazel settled again beside the baby, this time not hesitating to turn her back toward me. She had forged some clearly defined boundaries for how to treat our human kitten, and, seven years and three babies later, our little diplomat still adheres to those rules.

Jane Lebak

George Washington Cat and Family

We were moving into our new house. I had just opened the door to get more things from the car when "something" rushed by me. "What . . . ?" I started. The neighbor across the way gave me a big grin, saying, "I think you have a new friend. He's a stray cat who's been hanging around here."

A cat? We already had a dog, a sweet little sable Shetland sheepdog named Greta. What would she do with a cat? In the past, Greta had shown a great affinity for all types of friends. She loved all dogs. At our old house, a parade of them had shown up on a regular basis, all of them wearing the expression, "Can Greta come out to play?" Our favorite of her friends was a little toad that used to sit on our front porch in the evenings. Greta would touch noses with him, and then sit beside him under the porch light. We even took photos of this strange friendship. But a cat?

The only cat she had known was a black-striped tabby down the street from us. We walked Greta by her house every evening. The cat would come out, arch her back and hiss. Greta would bark once or twice, the tabby would turn and leave, and Greta would continue her walk. The man who owned the cat was highly amused. "I think they like each other, but can't admit it," he told me. When Greta was hospitalized for a throat infection, the cat's owner came to our house to inquire after her. "My cat misses her," he explained.

The new house was filled with many large boxes of our things. Looking around in the rooms, all I could see were boxes and boxes—and no cat. Maybe when we finished unpacking, I'd be able to find him. In the meantime, I decided to put out cat food and leave the patio door open in case he decided to leave. The food disappeared on a regular basis. The door stayed open, but it did not seem as if anyone was leaving.

When I finally got down to the last packing box, we found him. He was the dirtiest white cat I have ever seen. His ears were a strange green hue, and his nose was black. His white coat was streaked with various shades of brown, gray and orange. Not knowing if he was feral, I reached for him gingerly. But he came to my arms as if he belonged there.

One trip to the vet's produced a bill six inches long. He had a mold infection in his ears, as well as ear mites and fleas. Plus, he had to have a bath, shots and a license. Through all this, the cat remained as patient and uncon-cerned as could be.

In the weeks before we found him, Greta sensed that he had been in the boxes, but didn't seem to care. When the newly cleaned and vetted cat showed up, she offered him a nose, and he nosed her back: Their relationship was cemented. We named him George Washington Cat because of the upright way he sat in our club chair with one foreleg on the arm of the chair as he regally surveyed his new home.

A few years later, we bred Greta to a wonderful working Sheltie, and she had four puppies. I was a little worried how George Washington Cat would take to the new strangers. Georgie walked over to the whelping box and sat in his Egyptian way with his tail curled around him. I watched him as he eyed the box for a while; suddenly, he started to purr. The purrs got louder and louder. Finally, he stepped carefully into the box, wrapped himself around the sleeping group and went to sleep, too. Greta came back and took a peek. From the expression on her face, I could almost hear her thinking, *Baby-sitter! I have a baby-sitter!* And she went to her favorite place to nap, without the puppies to nag at her.

As the puppies grew, Georgie participated with even more energy. Every morning, Greta would leave for her breakfast, and Georgie would jump into the box and start the morning wash-up. He cleaned ears (eight of them), noses (four), fronts (four), and eyes (another eight), and, when he was through, his little pink tongue hung out of his mouth. I didn't dare laugh; he took all this very seriously. When a very nice family adopted one of the puppies, Georgie hunted for him for days. Heartbroken, he meowed over the whelping box. We decided we didn't want to put him through this anguish again and never bred Greta after that.

A second puppy was given to a very dear friend, and, because Georgie could not bear to be parted from "his" brood, we kept the last two puppies. For the rest of his life, it was Uncle Georgie's morning ritual to clean them up. The now-grown dogs would dutifully come to him each morning, and he would clean their ears, eyes, face and fronts. Commenting on how wonderfully white the fronts of the Shelties were, people would ask me what I used to wash the dogs. I never told them about the boys' Uncle Georgie.

After Greta died, he looked for her constantly, and his cleaning ritual seemed a little less thorough. Georgie lingered only one short year before following his beloved canine friend. The boys missed him after he died, and, for months, went to the same spot under the table every morning for their "cleaning."

These wonderful members of our family are all gone now, but I like to think that Uncle Georgie has "his" family back, and is busy once more, cleaning all of them up with his little pink tongue.

Peggy Seo Oba

More Chicken Soup?

Many of the stories and poems you have read in this book were submitted by readers like you who had read earlier *Chicken Soup for the Soul* books. We publish at least five or six *Chicken Soup for the Soul* books every year. We invite you to contribute a story to one of these future volumes.

Stories may be up to twelve hundred words and must uplift or inspire. You may submit an original piece, something you have read or your favorite quotation on your refrigerator door.

To obtain a copy of our submission guidelines and a listing of upcoming *Chicken Soup* books, please write, fax or check our Web site.

Please send your submissions to:

Chicken Soup for the Soul
Web site: *www.chickensoup.com*
P.O. Box 30880
Santa Barbara, CA 93130
fax: 805-563-2945

We will be sure that both you and the author are credited for your submission.

For information about speaking engagements, other books, audiotapes, workshops and training programs, please contact any of our authors directly.

Supporting Others

Join us in Supporting
Pets to Stay in Their Homes "For Life"

The stories in this book celebrate the loving relationship between people and their animal companions. Yet in
spite of all this love, an estimated four to six million animals are brought to shelters throughout the United States
every year! Contrary to popular belief, most animals in
shelters weren't abused, nor did they do anything "wrong"
that caused them to lose their homes. Most animals are
abandoned for "people reasons" like allergies, divorce and
moving or because of behaviors that pet owners don't
understand and don't know how to address. If these reasons, which break the bond between pets and their
families, could be eliminated, just imagine how many animals could remain in their homes.

That's the premise behind the Pets for Life program of
the Humane Society of the United States (HSUS). Through
Pets for Life, the HSUS provides information on the most
common behavior problems and how to solve them, deal-
ing with allergies, finding pet-friendly rental housing, and
other issues affecting pets and their people. The HSUS
also provides information on choosing the right pet,
whether from a shelter or a reputable breeder. For information, go to *www.PetsForLife.org* or write to the address on
the next page.

Of course, pet overpopulation is still a factor that contributes to the large number of animals that end up in
shelters. The HSUS continues to work to reduce pet overpopulation through education and programs like the
Rural Area Veterinary Services (RAVS).

The Humane Society of the United States is the nation's
largest animal-protection organization with more than

8.5 million members and constituents. This nonprofit organization is a mainstream voice for animals, with active programs in companion animal and equine protection, disaster preparedness and response, wildlife and habitat protection, research and farm-animal advocacy, and the development of sustainable agriculture. The HSUS protects all animals through legislation, litigation, investigation, education, advocacy and fieldwork. The group is based in Washington, D.C., and has numerous field representatives across the country.

The HSUS depends on donations for its lifesaving work. To donate, go to *www.hsus.org*, or send your contribution to: The HSUS, 2100 L Street NW, Washington, DC 20037. The HSUS can be reached at 202-452-1100.

Who Is Jack Canfield?

Jack Canfield is one of America's leading experts in the development of human potential and personal effectiveness. He is both a dynamic, entertaining speaker and a highly sought-after trainer. Jack has a wonderful ability to inform and inspire audiences toward increased levels of self-esteem and peak performance. Jack most recently released a book for success entitled *The Success Principles: How to Get from Where You Are to Where You Want to Be.*

He is the author and narrator of several bestselling audio- and videocassette programs, including *Self-Esteem and Peak Performance, How to Build High Self-Esteem, Self-Esteem in the Classroom* and *Chicken Soup for the Soul—Live.* He is regularly seen on television shows such as *Good Morning America, 20/20* and *NBC Nightly News.* Jack has co-authored numerous books, including the *Chicken Soup for the Soul* series, *Dare to Win* and *The Aladdin Factor* (all with Mark Victor Hansen), *100 Ways to Build Self-Concept in the Classroom* (with Harold C. Wells), *Heart at Work* (with Jacqueline Miller) and *The Power of Focus* (with Les Hewitt and Mark Victor Hansen).

Jack is a regularly featured speaker for professional associations, school districts, government agencies, churches, hospitals, sales organizations and corporations. His clients have included the American Dental Association, the American Management Association, AT&T, Campbell's Soup, Clairol, Domino's Pizza, GE, Hartford Insurance, ITT, Johnson & Johnson, the Million Dollar Roundtable, NCR, New England Telephone, Re/Max, Scott Paper, TRW and Virgin Records. Jack has taught on the faculty of Income Builders International, a school for entrepreneurs.

Jack conducts an annual seven-day training called Breakthrough to Success. It attracts entrepreneurs, educators, counselors, parenting trainers, corporate trainers, professional speakers, ministers and others interested in improving their lives and the lives of others.

For free gifts from Jack and information on all his material and availability, contact:

Self-Esteem Seminars
P.O. Box 30880
Santa Barbara, CA 93130
phone: 805-563-2935 • fax: 805-563-2945
www.jackcanfield.com

Who Is Mark Victor Hansen?

In the area of human potential, no one is more respected than Mark Victor Hansen. For more than thirty years, Mark has focused solely on helping people from all walks of life reshape their personal vision of what's possible. His powerful messages of possibility, opportunity and action have created powerful change in thousands of organizations and millions of individuals worldwide.

He is a sought-after keynote speaker, bestselling author and marketing maven. Mark's credentials include a lifetime of entrepreneurial success and an extensive academic background. He is a prolific writer with many bestselling books, such as *The One Minute Millionaire, The Power of Focus, The Aladdin Factor* and *Dare to Win,* in addition to the *Chicken Soup for the Soul* series. Mark has had a profound influence through his library of audios, videos and articles in the areas of big thinking, sales achievement, wealth building, publishing success, and personal and professional development.

Mark is the founder of the MEGA Seminar Series. MEGA Book Marketing University and Building Your MEGA Speaking Empire are annual conferences where Mark coaches and teaches new and aspiring authors, speakers and experts on building lucrative publishing and speaking careers. Other MEGA events include MEGA Marketing Magic and My MEGA Life.

He has appeared on television (*Oprah,* CNN and *The Today Show*), in print (*Time, U.S. News & World Report, USA Today, New York Times* and *Entrepreneur*) and on countless radio interviews, assuring our planet's people that, "You can easily create the life you deserve."

As a philanthropist and humanitarian, Mark works tirelessly for organizations such as Habitat for Humanity, American Red Cross, March of Dimes, Childhelp USA and many others. He is the recipient of numerous awards that honor his entrepreneurial spirit, philanthropic heart and business acumen. He is a lifetime member of the Horatio Alger Association of Distinguished Americans, an organization that honored Mark with the prestigious Horatio Alger Award for his extraordinary life achievements.

Mark Victor Hansen is an enthusiastic crusader of what's possible and is driven to make the world a better place.

Mark Victor Hansen & Associates, Inc.
P.O. Box 7665
Newport Beach, CA 92658
phone: 949-764-2640 • fax: 949-722-6912
www.markvictorhansen.com

Who Is Marty Becker, D.V.M.?

What Jacques Cousteau did for the oceans, what Carl Sagan did for space, Dr. Marty Becker is doing for pets.

As a veterinarian, author, university educator, media personality and pet lover, Dr. Becker is one of the most widely recognized animal-health authorities in the world. He is also passionate about his work, fostering the affection-connection between pets and people that we call "The Bond."

Marty coauthored *Chicken Soup for the Pet Lover's Soul, Chicken Soup for the Cat & Dog Lover's Soul, Chicken Soup for the Horse Lover's Soul* and *The Healing Power of Pets*, which was awarded a prestigious silver award in the National Health Information Awards.

Dr. Becker has powerful media platforms, including seven years as the popular veterinary contributor to ABC-TV's *Good Morning America*. Dr. Becker authors two highly regarded newspaper columns that are internationally distributed by Knight Ridder Tribune (KRT) Services. And in association with the American Animal Hospital Association (AAHA), Dr. Becker hosts a nationally syndicated radio program, *Top Vet Talk Pets*, on the Health Radio Network.

Dr. Becker has been featured on ABC, NBC, CBS, CNN, PBS, *Unsolved Mysteries* and in *USA Today, The New York Times, Washington Post, Reader's Digest, Forbes, Better Homes & Gardens, Christian Science Monitor, Woman's Day, National Geographic Traveler, Cosmopolitan, Glamour, Parents* and major Web sites such as *ABCNews.com, Amazon.com, Prevention.com, Forbes.com* and *iVillage.com*.

The recipient of many awards, Dr. Becker holds one especially dear. In 2002, the Delta Society and the American Veterinary Medical Association (AVMA) presented Dr. Becker with the prestigious Bustad Award as the Companion Animal Veterinarian of the Year for the United States.

Marty and his family enjoy life in northern Idaho and share Almost Heaven Ranch with two dogs, five cats and five quarter horses.

Contact Marty Becker at:

P.O. Box 2775
Twin Falls, ID 83303
phone: 208-734-8174
Web site: *www.drmartybecker.com*

Who Is Carol Kline?

Carol Kline is passionate about cats! In addition to being a doting "pet parent," she is active in animal-rescue work. Although she has recently relocated to California, she is still a member of the board of directors of the Noah's Ark Animal Foundation, *www.noahsark.org*, located in Fairfield, Iowa—a limited-access, "cageless" no-kill shelter that rescues lost, stray and abandoned dogs and cats. For the last eight years, Carol has spent many hours a week monitoring the fate of dogs and cats at Noah's Ark and working to find them good permanent homes. She also administered the Caring Community Spay/Neuter Assistance Program (CCSNAP), a fund especially designated for financially assisting pet owners to spay and neuter their pets. Carol says, "The reward of helping these animals is more fulfilling than any paycheck I could ever receive. Volunteering time with the animals fills my heart and brings great joy to my life."

A freelance writer/editor for nineteen years, Carol, who has a B.A. in literature, has written for newspapers, newsletters and other publications. In addition to her own *Chicken Soup* books, she has also contributed stories and her editing talents to many other books in the *Chicken Soup for the Soul* series.

In addition to her writing and animal work, Carol is a motivational speaker and gives presentations to animal-welfare groups around the country on a variety of topics. She has also taught stress-management techniques to the general public since 1975.

Carol has the good fortune to be married to Larry and is a proud stepmother to Lorin, twenty-three, and McKenna, twenty. She has three dogs—all rescues—Beau, Beethoven and Jimmy.

To contact Carol:

P.O. Box 521
Ojai, CA 93024
e-mail: *ckline@lisco.com*

Who Is Amy D. Shojai?

Amy D. Shojai is an animal-behavior consultant, award-winning author, lecturer, and a nationally known authority on pet care and behavior. She is a passionate proponent of owner education in her books, articles, columns and media appearances, and has been recognized by her peers as "one of the most authoritative and thorough pet reporters."

The former veterinary technician has been a full-time pet journalist for more than two decades. She is a member of the International Association of Animal Behavior Consultants and consults with a wide range of animal-care professionals, researchers and other experts. She specializes in translating "medicalese" into easily understood jargon-free language to make it accessible to all pet lovers. Amy answers pet questions in her weekly "Emotional Health" column at *www.catchow.com*, hosts "Your Pet's Well-Being with Amy Shojai" at *iVillage.com* and is section leader for the Holistic and Behavior/Care portions of the PetsForum. She is also the author of twenty-one nonfiction pet books, including *PETiquette: Solving Behavior Problems in Your Multipet Household* and *Complete Care for Your Aging Dog,* and a coauthor of *Chicken Soup for the Cat Lover's Soul.*

In addition to writing and pet-care consulting, Amy's performance background (B.A. in music and theater) aids in her media work as a corporate spokesperson and pet-product consultant. She has appeared on *Petsburgh USA/Disney Channel Animal Planet* series, *Good Day New York, Fox News: Pet News, NBC Today Show* and hundreds of radio appearances, including *Animal Planet Radio.* Amy has been featured in *USA Weekend, The New York Times, Washington Post, Reader's Digest, Woman's Day, Family Circle* and *Woman's World,* as well as the "pet press." As a founder and president emeritus of the Cat Writers' Association, a member of the Dog Writers Association of America and the Association of Pet Dog Trainers, her work has been honored with over two dozen writing awards from these and many other organizations.

Amy and her husband, Mahmoud, live among 700-plus antique roses and assorted critters at Rosemont, their thirteen-acre "spread" in north Texas.

To contact Amy:

P.O. Box 1904
Sherman, TX 75091
e-mail: *amy@shojai.com*
Web site: *www.shojai.com*

Contributors

Barbara (Bobby) Adrian has loved animals all of her life and is particularly partial to cats. She is a published artist and muralist, and for fifteen years has taken the love of God into the nursing home through her ministry. Please e-mail her at *churchlady777@comcast.net.*

Marlene Alexander is a freelance writer whose work has been seen in *Reader's Digest, The Toronto Star* and other publications. Her interests include travel and home decor. She is currently working on a project for the budget-conscious decorator called "Dollar Store Style." Contact her at *marlene.alexander@ sympatico.ca.*

Lorra E. Allen shares her home in Pittsburgh, Pennsylvania, with an adorable assortment of rescued felines and canines. She is an avid animal-rights activist and PETA member and enjoys spending time with friends, family and volunteering at Animal Friends Inc., a local no-kill shelter. Lorra can be reached at *Tabby0108@aol.com.*

Brian Baker is a husband, father, grandfather and cat lover. He works with Safe Haven (*www.SafeHavenForPets.org*)in Elizabeth, Illinois, and with feral and stray cats in his hometown of Dubuque, Idaho. He is a moderator at the Web site *www.ForumPets.com* and an active writer. He plans to continue writing, and can be reached at *bbaker563@aol.com.*

Maryjean Ballner has videotapes and books that teach cat massage and dog massage. She teaches cat and dog massage workshops both in the USA and internationally. She still volunteers at her local animal shelter. Contact Maryjean at *www.dogandcatmassage.com.*

Silvia Baroni is a writer living in northern California.

Syndee A. Barwick works in Manhattan for one of the world's best-known comics publishers. An ordained interfaith minister trained in many alternative spiritual and mental disciplines, she is also an animal/nature-inspired jewelry designer. Inspirational and otherworldly books are in progress. Please e-mail her at *syndeebar@hotmail.com.*

Karen S. Bentley lives in the north Georgia mountains where she teaches college business courses, consults, gardens and enjoys the company of two feline companions, Skipper and Xander. Her nonfiction writing has appeared in newspapers, magazines, trade journals and books.

Ellen Perry Berkeley's *Maverick Cats: Encounters with Feral Cats* (1982; expanded/updated, 2001) remains the most comprehensive volume about domestic cats gone wild. Her *TNR Past, Present, and Future: A History of the Trap-Neuter-Return Movement* (2004) was published by Alley Cat Allies, the national resource for feral cats.

Staff Sergeant **Rick Bousfield** retired from the U.S. Army last April after almost twenty-one years.

Art Bouthillier resides on Whidbey Island with his wife, Jennifer, daughter, Sierra, and their two dogs, Kaos and Karma. Art currently freelances his work to several magazines and is editorial cartoonist for his local paper. To reach Art, you may e-mail him at *artb@whidbey.com.*

Linda Bruno is a speaker and writer. She is writing a devotional book based on how our interactions with pets mirror our relationship with God. She and husband Guy have one grown daughter, four grandchildren and four fur-kids. Linda can be reached at 877-216-5781.

Dr. Mary Bryant graduated from the University of Pennsylvania in 1995. After practicing for nine years, she currently works in the veterinary pharmaceutical industry. She is also an adjunct assistant professor at the University of Pennsylvania's Veterinary School. An enthusiastic birder, she lives in West Chester, Pennsylvania, with her husband and furry four-legged children.

Renie Burghardt, who was born in Hungary, is a freelance writer with many credits. She has also been published in two previous *Chicken Soup* books: *Chicken Soup for the Christian Family Soul* and *Chicken Soup for the Horse Lover's Soul.* She lives in the country and loves nature and animals. E-mail her at *Renie_burghardt@yahoo.com.*

Vanni Cappelli is a freelance journalist who has covered wars in the Horn of Africa, the Balkans and Central Asia for more than a dozen years. He has done his best to be kind to cats in all of these places, besides caring for his American felines back home.

M.L. Charendoff lives in Elkins Park, Pennsylvania, with her husband, four kids, one dog, and her two ancient cats Morris and Chloe. An at-home mom and freelance writer, Meg is currently working on a novel and a collection of essays. Please e-mail her at *MLCharendoff@comcast.net.*

Anne Marie Davis is a graduate of Baylor University with a degree in English. She is a former secondary English teacher. She enjoys reading, writing, singing, working with her church's youth group, and spending time with family and friends. Anne Marie can be reached at *annebellomydavis@hotmail.com*

Edi dePencier is a Certified General Accountant working for a charity in White Rock, B.C. She loves reading and kayaking. Edi is just finishing a screenplay and is at the research stage in her historical novel. Her passions are her family, her cat and history. E-mail her at *edidep@telus.net.*

Elizabeth Doyle is a multi-published romance novelist and a staff writer at Best Friends Animal Society.

Lisa Duffy-Korpics is a freelance writer and social studies teacher at Valley Central High School in Montgomery, New York. Lisa's work has appeared in several *Chicken Soup for the Soul* books. She lives in New York's Hudson Valley with her husband Jason, son Charles and daughter Emmaleigh.

Toni Eames lives with Golden Retriever guide dog Keebler and four cats. She is a founder and board member of the International Association of Assistance Dog Partners. Toni and husband Ed are authors, lecturers and advocates. She can be reached by e-mail at *eeames@csufresno.edu.*

Rebecca A. Eckland received her Bachelor of Liberal Arts with high distinction from the University of Nevada, Reno, in 2004. She is currently working as a research intern for the Tahoe Maritime Museum on the west shore of Lake Tahoe. She enjoys writing, painting and the outdoors. To contact her, e-mail *rebeccae@unr.nevada.edu.*

Gwen Ellis retired after many years in publishing to start her own company, Seaside Creative Services. She writes books and screenplays, edits, conceptualizes products, and consults. Having beaten ovarian cancer, Gwen seizes life with both hands. She doesn't want to miss life because of fear or unwillingness to act upon a dream.

Joseph Farris is a staff cartoonist and cover artist with *The New Yorker* and works for many national and international publications. He also paints and his work is in many collections. He has published many books, his latest being *Money Inc.* He may be reached at *jfarris1@sbcglobal.net.*

Madelyn Filipski received a Bachelor of Arts from Newark State College in New Jersey. A retired English teacher, she relishes reading, traveling, kayaking, spoiling her cats and lobbying on behalf of animals. She is currently compiling a book of stories about her animal friends. Please e-mail her at *capemews@hotmail.com.*

Valerie Gawthrop is a freelance writer from Tulsa, Oklahoma. She shares her home with her husband and "several" assorted rescued cats. E-mail her at *gawthrop@worldnet.att.net.*

Kerri Glynn graduated from Vassar College in 1971. For thirty-two years she taught high-school English and ran the theater program. An animal lover, Kerri's menagerie includes five cats, a llama, a miniature horse and two parrots. She writes the newsletter for the Save-A-Pet animal shelter and does rehabilitation work with sea turtles and seals at the Riverhead Foundation for Marine Research and Preservation.

Speaker-artist **Bonnie Compton Hanson** is author of several books for adults and children, including the popular Ponytail Girls series, plus hundreds of published articles and poems. Her family includes husband Don, sons, grandchildren, cats, birds and possums! Contact her at 3330 S. Lowell St., Santa Ana, CA 92707; 714-751-7824; b*onnieh1@worldnet.att.net.*

Shirley Harmison is the United Nations representative for the Art of Living (AOL) Foundation. This story was inspired by her spiritual teacher Sri Sri Ravi Shankar and the cat that stays outside of his *kutir* in Bangalore, India. She travels the world working for humanitarian causes with the AOL Foundation. For more information about AOL, please visit *www.artofliving.org* or e-mail Shirley at *ahimsa108@aol.com.*

Carolyn Harris lives in the Cascade Mountains with her husband, Dave, and three cats. Her book *RV in NZ: How to Spend Your Winters in New Zealand* can be seen at *www.rvinnz.com*. Wednesday's Child, a novel set in a 1949 northern California logging camp will be available in 2006.

Dena Harris is a freelance writer, humorist and public speaker whose work appears in magazines and newspapers around the country. Her humor book, *Lessons in Stalking*, recounts Dena and her husband's faithful service to their two cuddly, if somewhat demonic, cats and is available through her Web site at *www.denaharris.com*.

Susan Hasler received degrees in Russian Language and Literature from the University of Virginia and the University of California, Berkeley. After two decades of working as an intelligence analyst for the federal government, she now lives in the Shenandoah Valley of Virginia where she writes about and rescues cats.

Jonny Hawkins has been cartooning professionally since 1986. Over 300 publications and over sixty-five books have showcased his work. His books, *Wild and Wacky Animal Cartoons for Kids, Laughter from the Pearly Gates, The Awesome Book of Heavenly Humor* and *A Tackle Box of Fishing Funnies*, along with his three cartoon-a-day calendars, *365 Laughtershocks, Medical Cartoon-A-Day* and *Fishing Cartoon-a-Day*, are available in stores and on-line. He can be reached at *Jonnyhawkins2nz@yahoo.com*.

Lori Hess graduated from Purdue with a degree in English and a desire to teach, but an abrupt change led her to self-employment in telecommunications. She volunteers for English teachers in her son's school, aspires to travel and yearns to find a published outlet for her sardonic musings. E-mail her *lhess@indy.rr.com*.

Susan Isaac received her Master of Arts in English from East Tennessee State University. She teaches Composition, American Literature, and Creative Writing at Georgia Military College. Susan enjoys reading, listening to music and writing. She completed her first mystery novel and hopes to publish it. Please e-mail her at *sisaac@gmc.cc.ga.us*.

Joan Shaddox Isom is the author of *The First Starry Night*, a book about Van Gogh, and coeditor of *The Leap Years* (Beacon Press). The animals that have shared Persimmon Hill with her and her husband offer ample inspiration. You may e-mail her at *jsisom@intellex.com*.

Dr. Vivian Jamieson received her D.V.M. from the Ontario Veterinary College in 1979 and completed her residency in Veterinary Ophthalmology in 1990. She currently practices at Veterinary Eye Care in Charleston, South Carolina. Vivian enjoys world travel, photography, tennis and writing. She has coauthored a book and several magazine articles.

Catherine Johnson is a writer and educator. Her essays have appeared in *Face to Face, Scent of Cedars* and *Teaching with Fire*. When not writing, Catherine serves as a faculty member at The Leadership Institute of Seattle (LIOS), developing therapists and consultants who practice with integrity.

Cori Jones teaches at Raritan Valley Community College in North Branch, New Jersey. She enjoys traveling, hiking, running and reading. A fiction writer, she has published stories in such journals as *The Iowa Review, The North American Review* and *Playgirl,* and has won several grants and awards for her work. She is at work on a novel, and likes to have Henry and Billu close by when she writes. Please e-mail her at *cjones@raritanval.edu.*

Marie D. Jones is an ordained New Thought minister and author of *Looking for God in All the Wrong Places,* as well as over three dozen inspirational books, essays and magazine articles. She lives in San Marcos, California, with her husband, toddler son and two crazy cats.

Kathleen Kennedy has lived in Atlanta all her life. Throughout that time period, much to her parents' chagrin, Kathleen has rescued everything from vultures to alligator snapping turtles. Since suburban sprawl has pushed horse-country out of her reach, Kathleen now volunteers her time at Good Mews, an animal shelter in Marietta, Georgia. She still fancies the notion of creating a haven in Georgia for unwanted animals large and small. All it will take is a winning lottery ticket! E-mail her at *cdkblk@earthlink.net.*

Author **Roger Dean Kiser's** stories take you into the heart of a child abused by the system. Through his stories he relives the sadness of growing up in a Jacksonville, Florida, orphanage. He publishes most of his work at "American Orphan," *www.rogerdeankiser.com.* E-mai him at *trampolineone@webtv.net.*

Mary Knight is a professional writer, speaker and workshop facilitator. Her story is excerpted from *My Mystical Life with Muggins the Cat,* a memoir about her search for intimacy and the cat that showed her the way. Muggins is now fourteen years old and still purring. E-mail Mary at *singleye@whidbey.com.*

Nancy Kucik is a copywriter for a home health and hospice agency in Birmingham, Alabama, and also does freelance writing. She enjoys reading, traveling, aerobics and volunteering with her therapy cat. Nancy and her husband currently share their home with two cats and two dogs. E-mail her at *nancykucik@yahoo.com.*

Sharon Landeen, a retired elementary-school teacher, enjoys working with youth. She's a 4-H leader (for twenty-plus years), a volunteer teacher in reading and art, and "grandmother superior." She still finds time to be an enthusiastic University of Arizona sports fan and a good pal to her dog, Dusty. She can be reached at: *sllandeen@theriver.com.*

Jeanne Marie Laskas is a weekly columnist for the *Washington Post Magazine* and a writer for *GQ.* She teaches writing at the University of Pittsburgh, and is author of four books, including *Fifty Acres and a Poodle* and *The Exact Same Moon.* She and her husband and daughters live on a farm in Scenery Hill, Pennsylvania.

Jane Lebak lives in sunny New England with her husband, three kids and three kitties. She published her first novel at age twenty-one and has had several publications since, including a fantasy story in *Catfantastic IV*. Check out her bio, upcoming books and articles for writers at *www.janelebak.com*.

Joanne Liu is a writer and attorney who lives with her husband and cat in Austin, Texas. She is currently working on a young adult novel about cats. Please e-mail her at *jliutex@yahoo.com*.

Roberta Lockwood received her Master's Degree in Counseling from Washington State University in 1978. She is a life coach, specializing in personal environmental design and creative expression. She enjoys writing, painting, traveling, knitting, quilting, handmade books, animals, nature and gardening. E-mail her at *robertalockwood@hotmail.com*.

Wolfie and **Michael McGaulley** have collaborated on a self-help book for cats: *Eat Well and Get Plenty of Rest: Wolfie's Guide to the Good Life (catSelfHelp.com)*. Michael, a lawyer/management consultant, has written *The Grail Conspiracies*, a spiritual thriller (*GrailConspiracies.com*) and several training programs on business, personal effectiveness and sales.

Sharon Melnicer is a writer, artist and teacher in Winnipeg, Manitoba, Canada. She also frequently broadcasts the "slice-of-life" pieces that she pens on CBC local and national radio. A high-school English teacher on leave, she teaches "Lifestory Writing" to seniors for "Creative Retirement Manitoba." As well, she is a busy, working artist who shows and sells throughout Canada.

Linda Mihatov is a wildlife rehabilitator, caring for orphaned and injured wildlife until they can be returned to nature. Her stories have appeared in many books and magazines.

Janet Mullen is Director of the Cat and Kitten Adoption Program at Noah's Ark Animal Foundation (*www.noahsark.org*). She enjoys traveling, reading and grandparenting. Please e-mail her at *cats@noahsark.org*.

Hester J. Mundis is a permanent, pressed-to-the-heart animal lover, comedy writer and author of numerous books, including the autobiographical, *No, He's Not a Monkey, He's an Ape and He's My Son*. She and husband Ron VanWarmer currently share their upstate New York lives with a Wheaten Terrier and a suave cockatiel.

Bev Nielsen is a native of California and teaches high school English in Los Angeles. In all her travels, the Kona Coast of Hawaii is her favorite spot, where she plans to retire. Her interests include gardening, vegetarian cooking, and getting together with friends and family.

Claudia Newcorn graduated from Wellesley College, earned an MBA from Northeastern University, then spent the next twenty years as a marketing executive. Underneath it all was a writer waiting to emerge. In 1993, she launched her own marketing communications firm, Acorn Enterprises, and is writing her first novel. E-mail her at *Claudia@acornmarketing.com*.

Lesléa Newman is the author of *The Best Cat in the World,* a picture book about grieving the loss of an old cat while adjusting to life with a new kitten, and *CATS, CATS, CATS!,* a picture book about a woman's sixty cats. To learn about her books, visit *www.lesleakisa.com*.

E. V. Noechel oversees Raleigh Rodent Rescue in North Carolina. Her writing is widely published. She was the recipient of the Kelty Award for Outstanding Local Animal Activism, and grants from the North Carolina Arts Council, the United Arts Council, and The Culture and Animals Foundation. Contact her at *veronica@evnoechel.com*.

Born in Brooklyn, **Don Orehek** attended the High School of Industrial Arts and the School of Visual Arts. His cartoons have appeared in *The Saturday Evening Post, Good Housekeeping, Cosmopolitan* and *Playboy*—to name a few! Don has illustrated over thirty joke books, does caricatures and teaches cartooning to kids. He has won the National Cartoonists Society's Best Gag cartoonist award four times. He can be reached by e-mail at *suztwo@aol.com*.

Lisa-Maria Padilla writes regular humor columns for the *Cat Fancier's Association Almanac,* and South Africa's *Cat's Life* magazine. Her articles on cat fancy have also appeared in magazines in Europe and the UK. Her online webzine, *www.MEOWclick.com,* features more of her real-life, feline-inspired writing and photo-illustration work.

Mark Parisi's "off the mark" comic panel has been syndicated since 1987 and is distributed by United Media. Mark's humor also graces greeting cards, T-shirts, calendars, magazines, newsletters and books. Please visit his Web site at *www.offthemark.com*. Lynn, his wife/business partner and their daughter, Jenny, contribute with inspiration (as do three cats).

Lori Pitts is a Licensed Veterinary Technician currently residing in Coweta County, Georgia. She has worked in small-animal veterinary practices for over twelve years. She and her husband share their home with many feline friends. Lori enjoys spending time with her family and friends, scrapbooking and reading.

Russian-born and award-winning international circus star **Gregory Popovich** developed his performing talents at the famed Moscow Circus School. Popovich excelled at juggling and became one of the most proficient masters of the art of juggling before creating his wonderful Comedy Pet Theater. For more information, visit *www.gregorypopovich.com*.

Kate Reynolds, a freelance writer and novelist, lives in Arizona with her husband and cats. She writes articles for local and national magazines, and also enjoys writing historical fiction. Her current project is a coming-of-age novel set in Phoenix during World War II. She can be reached at *kate@waldenpond.com*.

Andrea Rolfingsmeier, a Texas native, is a retired attorney living in Kansas City, Kansas. She received her B.A. in Art History from the University of Kansas, and her law degree from the University of Missouri at Kansas City. She has five cats, and enjoys reading, writing, quilting, refinishing furniture and rescuing animals. She can be contacted at *arti@vaughns.com*.

Michael Ruemmler is managed by four Abyssinian cats and a Cornish Rex. He edits a cat-rescue newsletter for the Cat Network and keeps the house in cat food and litter working as a Child Abuse and Neglect Social Worker. He can be reached at *netmews@yahoo.com*.

Heather L. Sanborn lives in Florida with her husband, Robert Ramirez, and five cats and two dogs. An educator for nine years, Heather hopes to one day have her own horse farm and work with troubled adolescents. Feel free to e-mail her at *heatherandzoo@hotmail.com*.

Harriet May Savitz has had twenty-two books published and an ABC Afterschool Special produced by Henry Winkler. Her recent book of essays, *More Than Ever—A View from My 70s*, is available through *Authorhouse.com*. Visit her at *www.harrietmaysavitz.com* or reach her by e-mail at *hmaysavitz@aol.com*.

Edie Scher and her cat, Bix (named after the jazz musician), live in Scotch Plains, New Jersey, where she teaches Shakespeare at a Magnet High School. She is a published writer whose credits include *The New York Times, Hearst Publications, Runners' World,* and the anthology *A Cup of Comfort*.

Tom Schreck lives with his wife Sue, their two cats and three hounds in Albany, New York. He regularly contributes to pet, boxing and fitness magazines. His novel, *Duffy's Nuts*, a murder mystery involving social work, professional boxing and Al the basset hound, will be released soon. He can be reached at *tschreck@wildwood.edu*.

Patti Schroeder is Professor of English at Ursinus College in Pennsylvania, where she teaches American literature. She can often be found hanging around blues clubs, sailing on blues cruises or attending Phillies games. She adores Italy. When at home, she is usually reading with cats on her lap.

Peggy Seo Oba is a dental hygienist with graduate degrees in public and business administration. She currently works for the Fetal Alcohol Spectrum Disorders Center for Excellence (SAMHSA). She is "grandma" to three Shelties and "Mom" to a college freshman.

Carol Shenold is a freelance writer who lives in Oklahoma City with her cat, Punky, and her daughter, Lori. She teaches freelance writing, works full time as a registered nurse, has co-authored two medical textbooks, writes a monthly newspaper column and is currently writing a mystery.

Dorian Solot came of age as a volunteer at the Morris Animal Refuge in Philadelphia. She graduated from Brown University with a self-designed major in Animals and Human Culture, and is the co-author of *Unmarried to Each Other: The Essential Guide to Living Together as an Unmarried Couple*.

Sheila Sowder began writing fiction after retiring from an advertising career in Washington, D.C., and Indianapolis. She was awarded the 2002 Rose Voci Fellowship for Women Writers, has had several stories and essays published in literary journals, and is currently writing a mystery. Please e-mail her at *sksowder@aol.com.*

Carol Steiner received her Bachelor of Music and Master of Music degrees from Bowling Green State University in 1967 and 1971. She taught elementary, middle school and high school music for eighteen years. She enjoys swimming, exercise, playing piano, and working with children and animals. She and her husband Ray are active in Michigan Siamese Rescue.

Betsy Stowe is the author of *Calico Tales and Others* (Infinity, *www.buybooks ontheweb.com*), which has won five international awards, including the 2004 World's Best Cat Litter™-ary Award and a Muse Medallion™ from the Cat Writers' Association. The book is a loving collection of over fifty of her cat poems and photographs.

Natalie Suarez is a Registered Veterinary Technician with a Bachelor of Arts in International Relations. She currently lives in Texas and enjoys reading, photo booths and playing mah-jongg. Natalie is now working on her first mystery novel. Contact her at *chickiepants@gmail.com.*

Jennifer Gay Summers is a contributing writer for *Whole Life Times Magazine.* Her work has also appeared in *Orange County Family Magazine* and *Inland Empire Family Magazine.* She and her husband, Ron, have a menagerie that includes a dog, cat, fish and beloved daughter. Jennifer can be reached at *jgsummers@ verizon.net.*

Hoyt Tarola is retired from the daily rigors of the business world. He spends his winters on the coast in California surfing his favorite point breaks and his summers fly-fishing in southwestern Montana. His cat, Moki, is with him wherever he goes.

B. J. Taylor shares her home with three cats, one dog and a wonderful husband. She is working on a book titled *Find Your Dog a Job!* showing how a dog and its owner can make a difference in their community. B. J. has had numerous stories published in magazines and anthologies. She can be reached at *bjtaylor3@earthlink.net.*

Mike Twohy is the creator of the syndicated daily panel *That's Life,* and a regular contributor to *The New Yorker.* He lives in Berkley, California.

Barbara Vitale, retired after more than thirty-three years as a physical educator, now continues to work as a personal trainer specializing in water therapy and water aerobics, and substitute teaches in schools. She is the author of *An Amazing Woman, the Helene Hines Story, Living with MS and Enjoying Life,* co-author of *Physical Education Planners,* and several short stories.

It's all cartoons all the time as **Bob Votjko** makes a living poking fun at the human condition. You'll find Bob Votjko cartoons in newspapers, newsletters, magazines, books and on the internet. Vojtko lives in Strongsville, Ohio, with his wife, Susan, and their Boston terrier, Massie.

Daniela Wagstaff is president and co-founder of Companion Critters, Inc. (*www.critters.petfinder.org*), an all-volunteer, nonprofit animal-rescue group. Daniela and her son, Bryan, share their home in Rahway, New Jersey, with rescued dogs Shawnee and Dixie, rescued cats Claude, Abigail and Odessa, and a twenty-four-year-old cockatiel named Lola.

Beverly F. Walker enjoys writing, scrapbooking and being with her grandchildren. Beverly's other animal stories appear in *Loss Comfort and Healing from Animal Sightings: True Experiences of Animal Blessings* by Patricia Spork and *Angel Cats: Divine Messengers of Comfort* by Allen and Linda Anderson.

Sara Wye is a Licensed Mental Health Counselor in Rhode Island, her second career after twenty-one years as a broadcast and newspaper reporter. She received her master's degree from Lesley College in 1987. Sara also sings, writes, works on her 1920s house and enjoys her companion animals. Contact Sara at *sarap66@cox.net.*

Theresa Dwyre Young lives in Denver, Colorado, and contributes regularly to regional and national magazines. She has completed her first novel, *Don't Feed the Porch Cat,* and is looking for a publisher. Please contact her at *TheresaDYoung@aol.com.*